WORLds TO EXPLORE

Handbook for Brownie and Junior Girl Scouts

Illustrated

Girl Scouts of the U.S.A.
830 Third Avenue
New York, N.Y. 10022

Inquiries related to *Worlds to Explore: Handbook for Brownie and Junior Girl Scouts* should be addressed to the Program Department, Girl Scouts of the U.S.A., 830 Third Avenue, New York, N.Y. 10022.

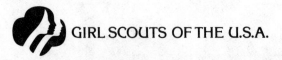 GIRL SCOUTS OF THE U.S.A.

Dr. Gloria D. Scott, *President*
Frances R. Hesselbein, *National Executive Director*

Authors/Contributors

Patricia Connally
Judy Cook
Nancy Garfield
Julie Gilligan
Carol Green
Mabel Hammersmith
Ely List
Edith Loe
Elizabeth Munz
Corinne Murphy
Lynn Obee
Roxanne Spillett

Art Director

Michael Chanwick

Art Studio

A Good Thing, Inc.

Credits

Illustrators

A.K.M. Studios, Inc. Pages 1, 4, 5, 85, 133, 173, 211, 287.

Ron Becker. Pages 116, 117, 290, 291, 294, 295, 298, 299, 300, 302, 303, 304, 306, 316.

Cary. Pages 14, 30, 90, 99, 111, 138, 139, 141, 142, 155, 158, 159, 160, 193, 207.

Bob Cassell. Pages 49, 51, 53, 54, 56, 57.

Renee Daily. Pages 9, 62, 63, 65.

Matt Delfino. Pages 3, 9, 34, 35, 64, 66, 67, 72, 76, 88, 94, 148, 201, 275, 288, 317.

Ric Del Rossi. Pages 41, 42, 44, 92, 180, 237, 238, 240, 241, 283, 292, 327, 329, 331, 349.

Len Ebert. Pages 32, 69, 87, 103, 109, 122, 163, 197, 209, 231, 266, 273, 324, 333, 335, 337, 369, 383.

Carolyn Fanelli. Pages 6, 39, 40, 58, 93, 95, 144, 159, 188, 213, 252, 264, 267, 269, 270, 278, 284, 293, 310, 321, 334, 340, 345, 353, 367.

John Johnson. Pages 10, 36, 37, 61, 86, 136, 149, 151, 204.

Uldis Klavins. Pages 2, 12, 16, 18, 38, 45, 46, 59, 98, 114, 145, 161, 169, 175, 177, 182, 242, 276, 297, 305, 307, 352.

Elsie McCorkell. Pages 96, 101, 105, 112, 118, 120, 121, 124, 131, 153, 157, 177, 178, 179, 185, 236, 246, 248, 249, 250, 254, 256, 257, 259, 263, 264, 265, 309, 313, 314, 323, 326, 327, 328, 329, 339, 342, 350, 351, 364, 366, 371, 373, 374, 375, 376, 380.

Yaroslava Mills. Pages 28, 33, 78, 150.

Charles Molina. Page 134.

The New Studio. Pages 47, 127, 128, 129, 130, 131, 150, 151, 164, 176, 187, 190, 191, 192, 195, 196, 199, 200, 202, 205, 243, 319, 320, 347, 360, 361, 362, 363.

Nancy Niles. Pages vii, 83.

Barbara Steadman. Pages v, 147, 154, 239, 260, 262.

Vantage Studios. Pages 73, 75, 79, 91, 107, 135, 137, 165, 168, 181.

Paul Williams. Pages viii, 84, 132, 172, 210, 286.

Photographs

A. Devaney, Inc. Page 218.

Ewing Galloway Stock Photo Agency. Page 226.

Girl Scout Library / Archives. Pages 21, 22, 24, 25, 28, 47, 296.

Eastman Kodak Company. Page 233.

Nigerian Girl Guides, courtesy World Bureau. Page 171.

Warsaw Photographic Studio. Pages 70, 213, 216, 217, 240, 241, 246.

Paintings/Sculpture

Page 213—Degas, Edgar. *Ballet Girl* (petite danseuse de quatorze ans). Bronze. The Metropolitan Museum of Art, bequest of Mrs. H. O. Havemeyer, 1929. The H. O. Havemeyer Collection.

Page 214—Primitive African (Cameroon) mask of wood and polychrome. The Metropolitan Museum of Art, Fletcher Fund, 1972.

Anonymous. Ukiyo-e School. *Acrobats.* Scroll, ink and watercolor on paper. The Metropolitan Museum of Art, gift of Mrs. Henry J. Bernheim, 1945.

Page 215—Flemish. Stained glass panel. The Metropolitan Museum of Art, bequest of George D. Pratt, 1935.

Pre-Columbian pendant, figure with headdress. Tairona style. (Colombia). Gold (tumbaga). The Metropolitan Museum of Art, gift of H. L. Bache Foundation, 1968.

Page 219—Whistler, J. A. McNeill. *The Music Room.* Etching. The Metropolitan Museum of Art, Harris Brisbane Dick Fund, 1917.

Page 220—Japanese. Stencil for textile. Paper. The Metropolitan Museum of Art, gift of Clarence McK. Lewis, 1953.

German Print Shop. Illustration in Jost Amman's *Book of Trades,* 1568, Frankfurt. The Metropolitan Museum of Art, Rogers Fund, 1913.

Page 221—Nevelson, Louise. *Sky Cathedral* (1958). Assemblage, 11 ft. 3½ in. x 10 ft. ¼ in. x 18 in., wood construction painted black. The Museum of Modern Art, New York, gift of Mr. and Mrs. Ben Mildwoff.

Page 223—Turner, Joseph Mallord William. *The Whale Ship.* Oil on canvas. The Metropolitan Museum of Art, Wolfe Fund, 1896.

Page 224—Cassatt, Mary. *Portrait of a Young Girl.* Oil on canvas. The Metropolitan

Museum of Art, anonymous gift, 1922.

Renoir, Pierre Auguste. *In the Meadow.* Oil on canvas. The Metropolitan Museum of Art, bequest of Samuel A. Lewisohn, 1951.

Monet, Claude. *Bridge over a Pool of Pond Lilies.* Oil on canvas. The Metropolitan Museum of Art, bequest of Mrs. H. O. Havemeyer, 1929. The H. O. Havemeyer Collection.

Degas, Edgar. *Woman with Chrysanthemums.* Detail: Woman's head with flowers to left of it. Oil on canvas. The Metropolitan Museum of Art, bequest of Mrs. H. O. Havemeyer, 1929, The H. O. Havemeyer Collection.

Page 247 and 250 (detail)—19th century American carpet, embroidered in colored yarns on twill weave woolen fabric. Zeruah H. G. Caswell. The Metropolitan Museum of Art, gift of Katherine Keyes, 1938, in memory of her father, Homer Eaton Keyes.

Page 285—Gorky, Arshile. *Water of the Flowery Mill.* Oil on canvas. The Metropolitan Museum of Art, George A. Hearn Fund, 1956.

Music

Page 33, "Make New Friends": *The Ditty Bag,* compiled by Janet E. Tobitt. New York, 1946.

Page 33, "Taps": The daylight version was approved by Lady Baden-Powell, World Chief Guide, and appeared first in the Guide magazine, April 11, 1952. Words used by permission of Pennsylvania Military College, now Widener College.

Page 37, "Whene'er You Make a Promise": From *Sing To-gether—A Girl Scout Song-book.*

Page 61, "Brownie Smile Song": Used by kind permission of Harriet F. Heywood.

Page 162, "San Sereni": *The Ditty Bag,* compiled by Janet E. Tobitt. New York, 1946.

Page 162, "Easter Trata": *Teaching Folk Dancing,* by Audrey Bramba and Muriel Webster. Theatre Arts Books, New York, 1946.

Page 268, "Allelujah": From *Sing Together—A Girl Scout Songbook.*

Page 268, "Music Shall Live": From *Girl Scout Pocket Songbook.*

Page 269, "Sweet Music Enchanting": *The Ditty Bag,* compiled by Janet E. Tobitt. New York, 1946.

Page 270, "Each Campfire Lights Anew": From *Sing To-gether—A Girl Scout Song-book.*

Page 271, "Early One Morning": From *Girl Scout Songs.*

Page 274, "Bow Belinda": From *Promenade All.*

Poetry/Prose

Page 36: Louise Driscoll. "Hold Fast Your Dreams." Used by permission of the author.

Page 39: Millay, Edna St. Vincent. "Afternoon on a Hill," *Collected Poems.* Copyright 1917, 1945, by Edna St. Vincent Millay. Published by Harper & Brothers, New York.

Pages 49-57: "Brownies and Other Stories," by Juliana Horatia Ewing, Children's Illustrated Classics, Inc., E. P. Dutton.

Page 86: Merriam, Eve. "Me, Myself and I," *There Is No Rhyme for Silver.* New York, 1962, by permission of Atheneum Publishers, Inc.

Page 133: Millay, Edna St. Vincent. "Renascence," *Collected Lyrics.* New York: Harper and Row, 1967.

Page 166: Smoki Corn Cakes. *Arizona Heritage Cookbook.* Arizona Cactus-Pine Girl Scout Council, Inc.

Page 206: *Who Says So?* This game is adapted from "Women's Work," *Daisy,* October 1976.

Page 279: Shannon, Monica. "Only My Opinion," *Goose Grass Rhymes,* copyright 1930.

Page 279: Baruch, Dorothy. "The Cat," *I Like Animals* by permission of the Bertha Ka-lusner International Literary Agency, Inc.

Page 280: Seuss, Dr. "If I Ran the Zoo," *If I Ran the Zoo,* copyright 1950 by Dr. Seuss. Reprinted by permission of Random House, Inc.

Page 288: LeGallienne, Richard. "I Meant to Do My Work Today," *The Lonely Dancer.* With permission of Dodd, Mead & Company.

Page 321: Teasdale, Sara. "Night," *Collected Poems.* Copyright 1920 by Macmillan Publishing Co., Inc., renewed 1948 by Mamie T. Wheless. Reprinted with permission of Macmillan Publishing Co., Inc.

Contents

GIRL SCOUTING IS...

Welcome to Girl Scouting!

Now that you are a Girl Scout, you belong to a "family" that has members in every part of the United States and nearly 100 other countries. In some countries, the members of this family are called Girl Guides. As a Girl Scout, you are a sister to every other Girl Scout and Girl Guide in the world.

Girl Scouts share—
• the Girl Scout Promise and Law
• Girl Scouting's special ways and days
• Girl Scout uniforms
• the Girl Scout pin
• meeting and working in a troop
• belonging to the World Association of Girl Guides and Girl Scouts

In the United States, girls who are 6 through 17 or in the first through the twelfth grade can be Girl Scouts. Girl Scouts are of all races and include all religious groups.

1

Girl Scouts wear different uniforms at different ages—Brownie, Junior, Cadette, or Senior. They meet together in troops to have fun and learn new things.

Many adults are Girl Scouts. Your leader is one. She is a grown-up friend who will help your troop do all the wonderful things that are possible in Girl Scouting.

Troop meetings can be held either indoors or outdoors—and no two meetings are ever exactly alike. These are some of the things you might do in troop meetings—

- singing
- playing games
- making handicrafts
- learning the Girl Scout Promise and Law
- making decisions and plans

- putting on skits
- practicing camping skills
- making new friends
- managing troop business
- working on patches or badges
- thinking up new ideas
- exploring the out-of-doors

Whatever goes on, it's because the girls, with the help of their leaders, planned it themselves.

But Girl Scouts do much more than just hold meetings. Some things they do are: helping out in their community • going on trips • working on special interests • hiking • camping • trying out new ideas • meeting, doing things, and having fun with other troops.

This opening chapter of your Brownie-Junior book will help you learn the things that every Girl Scout needs to know. It will also help you discover some things that are very special for Brownies and some that are special for Juniors. The rest of the book tells you about five exciting worlds that you can explore:

- **The World of Well-Being** will help you find out what's special about you and your home. It includes fun with food, quiet and active games, and ways to prepare for emergencies.

- **The World of People** will help you learn about others—your family and friends, your community, your country, and people all around the world. It includes songs, games, ceremonies, and handicrafts to help you do this.

- **The World of Today and Tomorrow** tells about some of the ways that people can change the world, why things work the way they do, and what the future holds for girls. You will read about things that you can do to make discoveries of your own.

• **The World of the Arts** will help you explore all the arts—including painting, sculpture, dancing, dramatics, puppetry, singing, and making musical instruments.

• **The World of the Out-of-Doors** will help you understand, appreciate, live in, and protect the natural world—whether you are at your troop meeting place, at home, in your community, or at camp.

All five worlds contain activities for both Brownies and Juniors. Some activities are harder than others. In each world, you start with things you think you can do. Then, after you have done these things, you move on to the ones you think are harder. By that time, they may not seem hard any more.

Suzy Safety

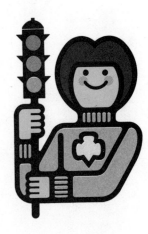

The little character shown here is Suzy Safety. Look for her in pictures all through your handbook. Whenever you see her, she will be reminding you to do something the safe way; so you should stop and ask yourself, "What do I need to think about to do this safely?" Suzy Safety will help you to take the safe road to adventures in Brownie and Junior Girl Scouting.

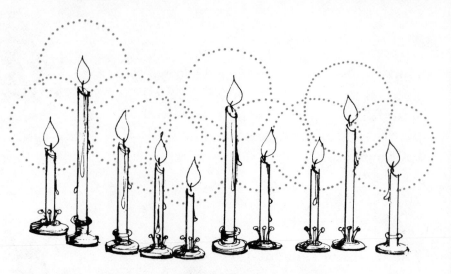

Becoming a Girl Scout

You become a Girl Scout for the first time at a special ceremony called an **investiture.** At this ceremony, you and the other girls who are being invested are welcomed into the Girl Scout family. As part of the ceremony, you make the Girl Scout Promise. You may wear your uniform for the first time there. If you are a Brownie, you get the Brownie Girl Scout pin. If you are a Junior, you get the Girl Scout pin.

Parents and friends are often invited to an investiture.

You might want to write down the date you became a Girl Scout:

I, _____, was invested as a

Brownie ( )   Junior ( ) Girl Scout on _____, 19___.

My troop number is _____

My troop leaders are _____

_____

The Girl Scout Promise and Law

The Promise that you make when you are invested is one of the most important parts of Girl Scouting. This is the Promise:

> **On my honor, I will try:**
> **To serve God,**
> **My country and mankind,**
> **and to live by the Girl Scout Law.**

Girl Scouts and Girl Guides all around the world make this kind of Promise. The words may be different, but the ideas are the same.

The Girl Scout Promise is a way of saying how Girl Scouts will try to act every day. Saying "on my honor" is a special way to let other people know you will do your very best to keep your Promise.

Let's take a closer look at what you have promised:

You will try to serve God. People serve God in many ways. People of different religions have different customs and ways of worship, but they are all showing their love for God.

In your troop, talk about—

• what serving God means to you.

• how people of many religions serve God.

• why it is important to respect the beliefs of people who differ from you.

You will try to serve your country and mankind. Serving your country means being a good citizen. It means learning about your country and obeying its laws. It means doing your best to help make your country a better place for everyone.

Serving mankind is helping people everywhere in any way you can. This could mean helping your family, your neighbors, or people in some other part of your country or the world. Some ways you help other people are by sharing what you have, cooperating with others, and always doing your part.

You will try to live by the Girl Scout Law. Laws help people to live and work together in groups. Girl Scouts have a special Law that helps them live and work happily with others. This is the Girl Scout Law:

I will do my best:
- **to be honest**
- **to be fair**
- **to help where I am needed**
- **to be cheerful**
- **to be friendly and considerate**
- **to be a sister to every Girl Scout**
- **to respect authority**
- **to use resources wisely**
- **to protect and improve the world around me**
- **to show respect for myself and others through my words and actions.**

The Girl Scout Law is something for you to try to live up to every day. It should become part of your life. If you want to understand the meaning of all of the Law, it is important to take some time to think about it.

Here is one way of explaining what the Girl Scout Law means. You will do your best...

To be honest: Be truthful in what you say and do.

To be fair: Treat others the way you want to be treated.

To help where you are needed: Find out what others need, and do what you can to show that you care.

To be cheerful: Look for the bright side, even when things don't go your way.

To be friendly and considerate: Be thoughtful of other people. Try to be the kind of friend you would want to have.

To be a sister to every Girl Scout: Think of Girl Scouts everywhere around the world—those you know and those you've never met—as friends.

To respect authority: Listen to people who are responsible for you and follow their directions.

To use resources wisely: Don't waste what you have. Make the most of your abilities; try to keep learning new things.

To protect and improve the world around you: Each of us can do something, even if it's something small, to make this world a better place. In your own way, help preserve the world of nature. Be a friend to animals, plants, and the earth.

To show respect for yourself and others: Do your very best in the way you treat others. Everyone is special in his or her own way. When you try to do the best you can, you usually think better of yourself.

Here are some things your troop can do to help all of you understand more about the Law.

- Everyone pick a part of the Law and draw a picture about what it means to you. Display the pictures and see if you can guess what they mean. Do you understand your friends' pictures? Do they understand yours?

- In patrols or small groups, make up and act out skits based on different parts of the Law.

- From magazines or newspapers, cut out pictures that can show something about the Girl Scout Law. You might use the pictures with new girls in your troop or with younger girls to help them understand the Law.

There are times when you are not sure what to do. Very often the Girl Scout Law can help you decide. Here is an example:

"I will try to protect and improve the world around me." Your troop has decided to do a basketry project, using natural materials. You find a spot where honeysuckle is in bloom. For the whole troop to make baskets, a lot of honeysuckle will be needed.

What would you do?

Talk it over in small groups or patrols, or with your troop, or with your family. Then see what you think about the ideas in the upside-down list.

What are some other times when the Girl Scout Law would help you decide what to do? Try to make up real-life situations for every part of the Law. Ask your leader to help you. Then try to decide what you would do in each situation.

Girl Scout Ways

Girl Scouts and Girl Guides all around the world have a special sign and a special handshake that are linked to the Girl Scout Promise.

The **Girl Scout sign** is made with three fingers, which stand for the three parts of the Promise. You give the sign whenever you say the Promise. You also give the sign when your leader invests you as a Girl Scout, and when you receive a patch or badge. You give the sign to other Girl Scouts and Girl Guides as a way of greeting them.

Would you take just a little and make smaller or fewer baskets?

Would you take all of it because you want to make sure you have enough?

Would you try to find out if it will grow back before you take any of it?

Would you decide not to take any of the honeysuckle?

Can you think of something else you would do?

The **Girl Scout handshake** is a more formal way of greeting other Girl Scouts and Girl Guides. You shake hands with the left hand and give the Girl Scout sign with your right hand.

Girl Scouts and Girl Guides also use a signal called the **quiet sign.** This is a very big help in meetings and other gatherings. When the person in charge raises her right hand high, other people stop talking and raise their own right hands. When everybody does this, there is quiet. Sometimes, in a meeting or around a campfire, Girl Scouts or Girl Guides form a **friendship circle.** Girls and leaders stand in a circle. Each one crosses her right arm over her left and clasps hands with her neighbors. Everyone is silent as a **friendship squeeze** is passed. When you are part of a friendship circle, you can feel its meaning. It stands for an unbroken chain of friendship with Girl Scouts and Girl Guides all around the world.

Two other things are shared by Girl Scouts and Girl Guides everywhere. They are the Girl Scout motto and slogan. In other countries, the girls say the motto and slogan in their own languages, but the meaning is the same.

The **Girl Scout motto** is "Be prepared." It means that Girl Scouts learn how to do things so they will be ready and able to help whenever they are needed.

This is what the motto looks like in some other languages. (The part in brackets will tell you how the words sound in English.)

Arabic	Stad-ee-doo (Sta dee do)	Stand ready
Danish and Norwegian	Vaer beredt (Vay uh bear ate)	Be prepared
French	Toujours prete (Too zhoor prêt)	Always ready
German	Allzeit bereit (Ahl site bear right)	Be prepared
Hebrew	Heye nachon (Hay yeh nu khown)	Be prepared
Hindi	Taiyyar (Tie are)	Be prepared
Korean	Joon-Bi (June bee)	Be prepared
Spanish	Siempre lista (See em pray lees tah)	Always ready
Swahili	Umwalola ukwafwako (Um wa lo lah uk wa fwa ko)	Be prepared

The **Girl Scout slogan** is "Do a good turn daily." It means that each Girl Scout will do something to help someone else every day.

Good turns do not have to be big. They do not have to take a lot of time. You do not have to do the same good turn every day. You do not receive a reward for doing a good turn, but you feel good inside. Can you think of some good turns that you could do every day?

A service project is a special kind of good turn that groups of Girl Scouts do. It takes more planning and more time. For example, your group could:

• Help plant flowers around a public building or statue in your community.

• Decorate the children's room in the public library.

• Offer to help at the local animal shelter, by feeding and loving abandoned animals.

• Plan a special afternoon for a neighbor's young children the week their mother brings a new baby home from the hospital. You might even bake a cake as a surprise for them.

Your leader will help you find out where you can give service. Watch and listen for things that need to be done, and talk them over in a troop meeting. When you do a good turn or work on a service project, you will be keeping your Girl Scout Promise to serve your country and mankind.

Your Uniform

Uniforms are worn by Girl Scouts and Girl Guides everywhere. These are some of the times and places you may wear your uniform: at troop meetings • at public ceremonies • at public events • in your church, temple, or synagogue on Girl Scout Sunday or Sabbath • when serving your community • when traveling as a Girl Scout.

Every Girl Scout wears two official pins on her uniform. Brownies wear the Brownie Girl Scout pin and the World Association pin. Juniors and all other Girl Scouts wear the Girl Scout pin and the World Association pin. You may wear your Brownie or Girl Scout pin and your World Association pin even when you are not wearing the uniform.

The Brownie pin and both of the Girl Scout pins have the shape of a **trefoil.** "Trefoil" means three leaves. These three leaves stand for the three parts of the Girl Scout Promise.

The World Association pin also shows a trefoil, because Girl Scouts and Girl Guides everywhere make a three-part Promise. The two stars stand for the Promise and the Law. The vein is the compass needle that points the way to go. The base stands for the flames of international friendship. The blue and gold colors stand for the blue sky and the sun that shines on children all over the world. (The same trefoil and the same colors appear on the World Association flag.)

Along with their pins, Brownie and Junior Girl Scouts wear official patches and stars. Juniors also wear badges. These pins, patches, stars, and badges are called **insignia.** They tell a great deal about the girl who is wearing them. The way you act when you wear your uniform shows that you really mean your Girl Scout Promise. You are proud of your uniform, so you keep it neat and clean. You may wear a watch, ring, religious medals, or small earrings for pierced ears with your uniform, but no other jewelry—not even Girl Scout jewelry.

If you are a Brownie Girl Scout, here's what your insignia tell about you:

Brownie Girl Scout pin shows that you are a Brownie Girl Scout.

Troop number shows what Brownie Girl Scout troop you belong to.

GIRL SCOUTS USA

Girl Scouts U.S.A. strip shows that you are part of the Girl Scout family in the United States of America.

World Association pin shows that you belong to a worldwide movement of Girl Guides and Girl Scouts.

Membership star and disc. Each star shows one year of membership in Girl Scouting. The green disc behind the star shows that you got the star as a Brownie.

Brownie B patch. You and your troop get one patch for each year that you work on Brownie B activities.

Bridging patch shows that you spent part of your last Brownie year doing things that will help you "cross the bridge" to Junior Girl Scouting. As one of your bridging activities, you might also earn a Dabbler badge (see page 68).

If you are a Junior Girl Scout, here's what your insignia tell about you:

Girl Scout pin shows that you are a Girl Scout.

Troop number and troop crest show what Girl Scout troop you belong to.

Council strip shows what council your troop is part of.

Girl Scouts U.S.A. strip shows that you are part of the Girl Scout family in the United States of America.

World Association pin shows that you belong to a world-wide movement of Girl Guides and Girl Scouts.

Brownie wings show that you were once a Brownie Girl Scout.

Brownie B patches and bridging patch. If you earned these patches as a Brownie, you may wear them on your Junior uniform.

Membership star and disc. Each star shows one year of membership in Girl Scouting. The yellow disc shows you got the star as a Junior.

Junior Aide Patch.

Sign of the Rainbow, Sign of the Sun, Sign of the Satellite.

Proficiency badges. You wear these if you have earned them.

Bridging patch shows that you spent part of your last Junior year doing things that will help you "cross the bridge" to Cadette Girl Scouting.

Patrol leader's cord shows that you are serving as leader of a patrol.

How Girl Scouting in the United States Began

Girl Scouting in the United States was started by a very unusual woman named Juliette Gordon Low. Juliette's nickname all her life was "Daisy." She was given this nickname shortly after her birth, when an uncle said, "I bet she's going to be a daisy!"

Daisy was born in Savannah, Georgia, on October 31, 1860. This was only a few months before the Civil War between the North and the South began. By the time the war ended, Daisy was almost four and a half years old.

Her first years were a confusing time for Daisy because her mother was from the North and her father was from the South. She had relatives fighting on both sides in the war. She and her mother spent some of the time in Chicago, with their northern relatives, because it wasn't safe for them to stay in Georgia during the war.

After the war, Daisy and her family returned to their home in Savannah. They spent their summers in the country.

Daisy enjoyed making up her own games, writing and acting in plays, drawing pictures, and playing with her pet animals.

Daisy and her brother and sisters had many projects. They sold a special drink called "peach gobble." They played "streetcar," riding down to the river in a goat cart or a donkey cart. They paid for their rides with paper money they made themselves.

Daisy put on plays and charged admission to raise money to help the Indians. Her grandfather up north had been an important friend to the Indians, and she had become their friend, too.

Daisy also started a magazine that lasted five years. It

"Daisy" Gordon, the founder of Girl Scouting, when she was six years old.

Daisy as she appeared in one of the plays she wrote as a girl.

Daisy with her brother Willy and one of her sisters, Nellie. There were six children in the Gordon family.

Daisy playing tennis with friends.

Daisy on her wedding day.

Daisy with her favorite parrot,
Polly Poons.

was special because only children could write and draw pictures for it. They all took the pen names of flowers, and, of course, Daisy used her own name.

She spent her winters at boarding school, where she was a good student and well-liked by the other girls. She had a special talent for art, and drawing was her favorite subject.

Daisy loved to form clubs. She once started a club called "Helping Hands." She decided to be the sewing teacher for the club, but she didn't know how to sew. The club members were nicknamed the "helpless hands" before they all finally learned to sew!

Daisy was a very active girl. She enjoyed sports and being out-of-doors. She loved to play tennis and was a very good horseback rider.

Daisy married Willie Low in 1886. She chose to be married on the same date as her parents because she hoped to have a happy family life like theirs. After that, she went to live in England and traveled a lot.

Two very sad things happened to Daisy. When she was a teenager, an ear infection left her partially deaf in one ear. Then, on her wedding day, a guest threw some rice at her for good luck, and some of the rice went into her other ear. When a doctor tried to remove it, Daisy became totally deaf in that ear.

Juliette Gordon Low was not one to be stopped by a handicap. Wherever she went, she was the life of the party. People loved to listen to her, and they enjoyed visiting her home because she was so friendly.

Daisy loved animals all her life and had many pets. Whenever she saw an animal that was sick or hurt, she tried to help. She was just as helpful when it came to people. Often she would slip away from her family to visit someone who was old or sick.

After her husband's death, she studied sculpture. In May, 1911, she went to a luncheon in England, where she met

Sir Robert (later Lord) Baden-Powell, the founder of Boy Scouting. Lord Baden-Powell, or "B.P." as he was called, had started Boy Scouting in 1908. At a rally in England, two years later, he found that girls, too, were interested in becoming Scouts.

At the rally, B.P. saw a group of girls wearing the shirts and the hats of the boys' uniforms with long skirts. The girls were marching behind the boys. When he asked them who they were, they replied, "We're the Girl Scouts." With so many girls becoming Scouts, B.P. decided the answer was an organization for girls. He asked his sister Agnes to help him start Scouting for girls that year. It was not easy for Agnes to start Scouting for girls. When she began in 1910, girls were not allowed to join in many of the activities that you do today. B.P. rewrote the handbook, *Scouting for Boys,* and called it *How Girls Can Help to Build Up the Empire.* The name was changed from "Scouts" to "Guides" for use by the girls' movement.

When Baden-Powell visited Daisy in Scotland in August, 1911, she heard about the Scouting movement for girls. She was so excited she began a Scottish Girl Guide troop. The seven girls in the troop visited her house on Saturday afternoons. Some of them walked as far as six miles to the meetings.

They had fun learning knots, flag history, the Girl Guide laws, knitting, cooking, first aid, map reading, and how to send messages by signals. Daisy tried to prepare the girls to earn a living. She helped them learn useful skills such as raising chickens and spinning. She started other Girl Guide troops in London before sailing to America to begin the first American Girl Guide troop.

When Daisy arrived in Savannah, she phoned her cousin, Nina Pape, and said, "Come right over! I've got something for the girls of Savannah, and all America, and all the world, and we're going to start it tonight!"

Daisy made this sculpture of her niece, Daisy Gordon Lawrence, who was the first American Girl Scout.

Daisy (right) with Robert, Lord Baden-Powell, and his wife Olave, Lady Baden-Powell.

Daisy with one of the early Girl Scout troops in Savannah, holding her own personal flag.

Daisy with girls at Camp Lowlands, the first Girl Scout camp.

Daisy talking with Girl Scouts and Girl Guides at Foxlease
World Camp in England in 1924.

After hearing the story of the British Girl Guides and how much they learned both indoors and out-of-doors, Nina was impressed. As a teacher, she thought that some of the girls at her school would be very interested in Scouting. So the word spread, and on March 12, 1912, 18 girls met at Daisy's house to form a Girl Scout troop.

The girls made their own uniforms without using patterns. Their long skirts and blouses of dark blue, with light blue ties, were copied from pictures of the British Girl Guide uniforms. Their badge patches were also handmade. The Savannah troop grew fast, and soon other troops were started in the Savannah area and in other parts of the United States.

Besides making their own uniforms, Juliette Low's first Girl Scout troop worked on Girl Guide requirements. They learned the Girl Guide law, played games, went on nature hikes, did bird watching, and kept bird books. With other troops in Savannah they started an inter-troop basketball league. They played on a court set up on a vacant lot across from Juliette's house.

Camp Lowlands, the first Girl Scout camp, was started that summer, and some of the girls in Daisy's troop went camping.

Daisy changed the name of the American Girl Guides to Girl Scouts in 1913. That same year, she decided to set up a national organization with headquarters in Washington, D.C. At that time, the girls decided to change the color of their uniforms from blue to khaki because khaki didn't show the dirt as much.

For the rest of her life, Daisy traveled and shared her ideas and dreams with millions of girls everywhere.

Daisy died in 1927. The Juliette Low World Friendship Fund was started a few months later to honor her and her vision of worldwide friendship. Every year, Girl Scouts all over the United States give money to this Fund—usually on

Juliette's birthday or on Thinking Day (see page 29). Part of the money is used to send Girl Scouts to other countries and to bring Girl Guides to the United States. The other part goes to the Thinking Day Fund set up by the World Association. It is used to help Girl Scouts and Girl Guides all around the world.

Few women have been honored as much by the United States Government as Juliette Low. During World War II, the government named a liberty ship after her. In 1948, there was a Juliette Low United States postage stamp. In 1974, Daisy was also honored by her own state of Georgia, with a bust of her in the Georgia Hall of Fame.

Juliette Low is remembered as a woman who worked for peace and good will. Her dream was to have young people make the world a friendly, peaceful place. She wanted young people to understand themselves and others. She wanted to give something special to the girls of the world, and that was Girl Scouting.

Follow In Daisy's Footsteps

Would you like to follow in Daisy's footsteps by doing some of the things she did as a girl? These are some things you could do:

- Start your own children's magazine, just as Daisy did.
- Make your own book about Daisy. Be both author and artist. (See page 282 for some pointers on bookbinding.)
- Try your hand at sculpture and painting. Donate your art work to a local center.

What are some other things you could do?

Girl Scouting's Special Days

Everybody likes to celebrate a birthday. Girl Scouts have three very special birthdays to celebrate:

October 31: Juliette Low's birthday (also known as Founder's Day).

February 22: Thinking Day, the birthday of both Lord Baden-Powell and Lady Baden-Powell, the World Chief Guide.

March 12: The birthday of Girl Scouting in the United States of America.

Juliette Low's Birthday

Girl Scouts honor Juliette Low on her birthday in many different ways. These are some things you might want to do:

• Put on a play, skit, or puppet show about Juliette's life for younger girls or another troop.

• Make a picture display of Juliette's life or the history of Girl Scouting.

• Learn some Girl Scout and Girl Guide songs, and sing them at a neighborhood gathering.

• Invite another troop to celebrate with you and have a party.

• Hold a Scouts' Own (see page 37) or a candlelight ceremony (see page 36).

• Give money to the Juliette Low World Friendship Fund.

Thinking Day: The Birthday of Lord and Lady Baden-Powell

The birthday of Lord and Lady Baden-Powell has become a day for Girl Scouts and Girl Guides everywhere to "think

about" each other. They also send greetings to each other. This shows the spirit of Girl Scouting and Girl Guiding that unites all members of the World Association in international friendship.

Here are some ideas for celebrating Thinking Day:

- Find someone from another country who is living or visiting in your community. Invite him or her to your troop meeting or a small Thinking Day celebration. Ask your guest to tell about the customs of his or her country, or to tell about Girl Guiding there.
- If there is someone from your community who has lived in another country, ask him or her to show your troop how to do one of that country's crafts.
- Invite a Girl Scout who has traveled outside the United States to share her experiences with you.
- Plant a garden to raise vegetables. You can share them with your family or with people in your town who need food.
- Send Thinking Day cards to greet Girl Scouts or Girl Guides you have met.
- Give money to the Juliette Low World Friendship Fund.
- Hold a Scouts' Own or a candlelight ceremony. Each Girl Scout could express how she feels about Thinking Day.

Girl Scout Birthday (Girl Scout Week)

Girl Scouts celebrate their own Girl Scout birthday for an entire week. The birthday is March 12, the date when the first Girl Scout meeting in the United States was held in 1912. The week in which March 12 falls is known as Girl Scout Week.

Some of the ways you might celebrate are by—

• wearing your Girl Scout uniform.
• holding a special ceremony with other troops in the neighboorhood.
• setting up a Girl Scout display at school or in the community. (This could tell about the history of Girl Scouting or what Girl Scouts do today.)
• participating in special services on Girl Scout Sunday or Sabbath.

Many Girl Scout councils plan a special theme for each day of Girl Scout Week. Ask your leader to find out if your council does this. If it does, you could plan something special for your troop meeting that would carry out your council's theme for that day.

Ceremonies for Girl Scouts

Girl Scouts hold ceremonies for many reasons. They plan each one so that it will really mean something.

Some troops start every meeting with a short ceremony. Others have one to end their meetings. Some troops have both an opening ceremony and a closing ceremony.

Many troops hold longer ceremonies for Girl Scouting's special days or on other important occasions. Ceremonies may also be part of a large get-together for many troops in

an area. Sometimes they are held just as a way of sharing as a group.

Ceremonies can be held anytime—morning, noon, or night. They can be held anywhere—indoors or out-of-doors.

Ceremonies can be formal or informal, with or without a guest. They can be held by large groups or small groups. The people in them can stand or sit in a circle or a horseshoe, in facing lines, or around a campfire.

A ceremony can be short or long. What it includes is up to the group planning it. Sometimes different groups will plan different parts of a large ceremony.

To start a troop meeting or begin a larger ceremony, you might want to say the Girl Scout Promise, hold a flag ceremony (see page 43), share thoughts for the day, or sing a song or two. (A fun round is "Make New Friends," page 33).

To close a ceremony, you could say "good-bye" in other languages, form a friendship circle (see page 12), or sing a "good night" or "good-bye" song. (A favorite closing is "Taps," page 33).

Make New Friends

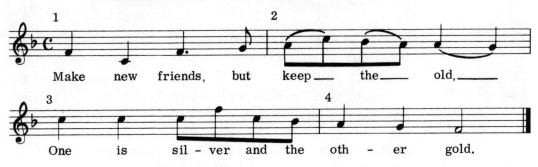

Make new friends, but keep the old,

One is sil - ver and the oth - er gold.

Taps

Slowly

Day is done, Gone the sun From the lake, From the hill From the
Thanks and praise For our days 'Neath the sun, 'Neath the stars, 'Neath the

sky, All is well, safe ly rest God is nigh.
sky. As we go, This we know God is nigh.*

The main part of the ceremony might include such things as poems, songs, dancing, choral readings, dramatics, candle lighting (see page 36), or perhaps a Scouts' Own (see page 37). Sometimes of course, the main part of the ceremony will be planned around a special theme or one of Girl Scouting's special days.

Girl Scouts have some ceremonies that are particularly important. They are investiture, fly-up, bridging, rededication, Court of Awards, Scouts' Own, candlelight, and flag ceremonies.

An **investiture ceremony** is held to welcome someone into Girl Scouting for the first time. You can read about this ceremony on page 6.

Fly-up Ceremony. Brownie Girl Scouts become Junior Girl Scouts in a fly-up ceremony. When you take part in this ceremony, you renew your Girl Scout Promise and get your Girl Scout pin. You also get Brownie Wings to show you have "flown up" from Brownies.

A **bridging ceremony** is held when you "cross the bridge" to the next age level in Girl Scouting.

A fly-up ceremony is a kind of bridging ceremony. If your Brownie troop completes special bridging activities, you will earn a bridging patch that you can wear on your Junior uniform. To find out how you can earn this patch, turn to page 67. You may get your bridging patch during a special ceremony or as part of your fly-up ceremony.

If you are a Junior, you will have a ceremony of your own when you become a Cadette. Any insignia that you earned as a Brownie or a Junior can be worn on your Cadette uniform. To find out more about bridging from Juniors to Cadettes, turn to page 82.

When you bridge from Brownies to Juniors or from Juniors to Cadettes, the troop you are leaving and the troop you are joining both take part in the ceremony. Parents and other guests are often invited.

A **rededication ceremony** is held at special times when Girl Scouts want to renew their Girl Scout Promise and review what the Girl Scout Law means to them. Troops often hold one at the beginning or the end of a troop year.

A **Court of Awards** can be held anytime during the year. It can be held by one troop or several troops. At this ceremony, girls receive badges and insignia they have earned. Often girls demonstrate, exhibit, or dramatize how they earned the awards they have received.

At a Court of Awards, tokens of appreciation are sometimes presented to adults who have helped the troop. Guests are often invited.

Candlelight Ceremony. Candle lighting can be part of many Girl Scout ceremonies. It is often used as part of a Scouts' Own and at investiture, fly-up, rededication, and Court of Awards ceremonies. (In areas where you are not allowed to burn candles because of fire laws, what could you use instead of candles?)

Three large candles and ten small candles in holders are arranged on a table. The troop stands around or near the table.

The three large candles are lighted as someone explains that they stand for the three parts of the Girl Scout Promise.

The ten smaller candles are lighted one at a time by different girls. Each girl says one of the ten parts of the Girl Scout Law as she lights her candle.

When all the candles are lit, the troop might sing a song or have one girl recite a poem. "Whene'er You Make A Promise" (page 37) is a good choice for a candlelight ceremony. You can look in one of the Girl Scout songbooks for other songs. A good poem to use might be "Hold Fast Your Dreams" by Louise Driscoll.

Hold Fast Your Dreams
Within your heart
Keep one still, secret spot
Where dreams may go,
And sheltered so,
May thrive and grow—
Where doubt and fear are not.
Oh, keep a place apart
Within your heart,
For little dreams to go.

Can you think of other poems to use?

Whene'er You Make a Promise

When e'er you make a promise Con-sid-er well its im-port-ance And when made, en-grave it up-on your heart.

Scouts' Own

A Scouts' Own is a quiet type of ceremony with a theme. It is called a Scouts' Own because girls and their leader plan it themselves. It is not a religious service and does not take the place of going to church, temple, or synagogue.

A Scouts' Own can be held at any time, indoors or outdoors. Your troop might have a Scouts' Own on a national holiday or one of Girl Scouting's special days.

It is a Girl Scout custom to walk quietly to the place where this ceremony is held and leave quietly after it is over.

If you are going to hold the Scouts' Own outdoors, choose a special place—one with a pretty view, or one you like for some other reason. Indoors, choose a symbol such as a flag or leaves that shows the theme of the ceremony.

A smaller group usually plans a Scouts' Own with the help of its leader.

First choose a theme. Then make a list of different ways you can tell or show the theme.

From your list choose one idea to open the Scouts' Own. Select the other ideas you want to include—one or two or half a dozen. Arrange them in an order you like. Decide how to end the Scouts' Own.

Decide who will perform or lead each part and who will lead the girls to the place for the ceremony and back again.

The spirit of a special day, such as Thanksgiving or the first day of spring, might be the theme for your Scouts' Own. Or the theme might be your country and your part as a citizen. Other possibilities include the life of Juliette Low, the beauty of nature, and friendship.

These are some ways to express your theme—

- songs for everyone to sing.
- shadow play scene.
- music played by one or two girls.
- poems or quotations.
- words a troop member writes for the Scouts' Own.
- choral reading.
- stories and legends.
- Girl Scout Promise.
- Pledge of Allegiance.
- thoughts about what the theme means to her spoken by each Girl Scout. If several troops are having a Scouts' Own together, each troop could contribute a thought.

If your theme is nature, you might want to include a poem such as this one by Edna St. Vincent Millay:

Afternoon on a Hill

I will be the gladdest thing
  Under the sun!
I will touch a hundred flowers
  And not pick one.
I will look at cliffs and clouds
  With quiet eyes,
Watch the wind bow down the grass
  And the grass rise.

There are many songs that have nature as a theme. You'll find some in the Girl Scout songbooks. Some examples are "Autumn" (*Our Songs*, page 22), "The Ash Grove" (*Sing Together*, page 124), and "Peace of the River" (*The Ditty Bag*, page 91).

Flag Ceremonies

Because the American flag is the symbol of our country, many ceremonies include a flag ceremony. This flag represents us in many different ways.

When American explorers became the first people ever to reach the North Pole in 1909, they set up a flag on a large peak of ice. At the first port they reached on their trip back home, they sent a telegram that was read all around the world: "We have nailed the Stars and Stripes to the Pole!"

Sixty years later, American astronauts were the first to land on the moon. They also set up an American flag to show that their country had made this dream come true.

The flag has stood for this country ever since the first one was made during the Revolutionary War. "The Star-Spangled Banner," America's national anthem, tells about the flag and the way people felt about it during the War of 1812. Maybe you already know the first verse:

The Star-Spangled Banner

Oh, say, can you see, by the dawn's early light,
What so proudly we hailed at the twilight's last
    gleaming?
Whose broad stripes and bright stars, through the
    perilous fight,
O'er the ramparts we watched were so gallantly
    streaming.
And the rockets' red glare, the bombs bursting in air,
Gave proof through the night that our flag was still there.
Oh, say, does that star-spangled banner yet wave
O'er the land of the free and home of the brave?

Music for "The Star-Spangled Banner" is in *Sing Together* (page 26).

The importance of the flag as a symbol of the nation is also shown by the **Pledge of Allegiance,** which Americans make to it:

I pledge allegiance to the flag of the United States of America and to the Republic for which it stands, one nation under God, indivisible, with liberty and justice for all.

We show our respect for our country's flag in many ways. These have been gathered together in a Public Law that tells how everyone should treat the flag.

The most important thing to remember is that when you fly the American flag in the United States, you always give it the position of honor. You put it either to the *right* of other flags, *in front* of other flags, or *higher* than other flags.

Right means "the flag's own right." Imagine that you are holding the flag in front of you. Stand so you are facing the people who will see it. With the flag in that position, your right is "the flag's own right." The American flag should be to the right of your troop flag. If it is flown with the flag of other countries, it always goes on the right. All the flags should be the same size and the flagpoles should be the same height.

In front can mean "ahead" or "first". Suppose the color guard is holding two or more other flags in a ceremony. The American flag can be in the center as long as it is a little *ahead* of the others. If several flags are being carried in a parade, the American flag is always the *first* one.

If you fly the American flag along with state flags or the flags of other organizations, you fly it *higher* than the others. The American flag may be larger than the others or it can be on a taller pole or a little platform. In the United

States, no flag is ever larger or flown higher than the American flag.

Just keep the key words in mind: right, front, higher. That way you will always be able to figure out where to put the American flag.

How to Salute

Girl Scouts use the citizen's salute whether they are in uniform or not. You place your right hand over your heart.

When to Salute

You stand at attention and salute: when the flag is being raised or lowered • when the flag passes you in a parade • when "The Star-Spangled Banner" is played.

Sometimes "The Star-Spangled Banner" is played when there is no flag present. When that happens, turn to the direction of the music, stand at attention, and salute.

People salute only the flag of their own country. If you are ever someplace where people from another country are saluting their flag, you should just stand at attention.

Other Tips

Here are some other things that Brownies and Juniors should know about how to treat the flag:

• Fly the flag only from sunrise until sunset. (Exception: It can be flown at night if a spotlight is on it.) Do not fly it in bad weather unless it is an all-weather flag.

• When you hang the flag on a wall or in a window where people will see it from the street, make sure the blue part is at the top and to the flag's own right.

• Do not ever use the flag as a drapery or cover. Do not place anything on top of it. Do not ever allow it to touch the floor or ground.

• Keep the flag clean. Wash it or have it dry cleaned when it is soiled.

• When a flag gets old and is too worn and torn to use, do not throw it in the trash. Instead, it should be destroyed. The best way is to burn it.

When to Hold a Flag Ceremony

These are some times when your troop might have a flag ceremony: at investiture, rededication, fly-up, and Court of Awards ceremonies • as part of the program at a ceremony on one of Girl Scouting's special days • as an opening or closing at troop meetings or camp days • at community ceremonies or celebrations.

At the flag ceremony you say the Pledge of Allegiance. You might also sing a patriotic song and repeat the Girl Scout Promise and Law.

The American flag and your troop flag are used in the ceremony. Sometimes the flag of the World Association of Girl Guides and Girl Scouts is also used. At an international ceremony, there might be flags from many countries of the world.

Every flag ceremony has a color guard. This is a team that carries and guards the flag. It is called a color guard because the American flag is sometimes called "the colors." The girls who carry the flags are called "flag bearers." The girls who stand beside the flags are called "guards." There is also a Girl Scout-in-charge. Her job is to announce each part of the ceremony.

These are the steps in a flag ceremony you might use in your troop:

1. The girls stand in a horseshoe. The Girl Scout-in-charge says, "Color guard, fall out." The color guard goes to where the flags are.

2. The color guard salutes the flags and picks them up. The American flag is always lifted first. (If the flags are in stands, the American flag is taken out first.) The girls carrying the flags stand side by side. The guards stand on either side of the girls.

3. The Girl Scout-in-charge says, "Color guard, advance." The color guard marches to the open end of the horseshoe. Everyone stands at attention.

4. Members of the color guard stand silently throughout the ceremony because their job is to guard the flag. All the other Girl Scouts salute the flag.

5. The Girl Scout-in-charge leads the Pledge of Allegiance. She says, "Girl Scouts, the flag of your country, pledge allegiance."

6. The Girl Scout-in-charge says, "Color guard, retreat." The color guard leaves the horseshoe and carries the flags back to their stands or to the place where they are stored.

7. If the flags are placed in stands, the guards help the flag bearers. The American flag is the last one placed. The color guard salutes the flag and returns to the troop.

The ceremony ends when the color guard is out of sight of the troop or when it puts the flags away.

This is the way to fold the flag. The grommets for fastening on ropes are on the outside. Then the flag will be ready to use the next time.

National Centers

Girl Scouts from everywhere in the United States can meet other Girl Scouts at three special places, called national centers. They are: Juliette Low's birthplace, Macy, and National Center West.

The Juliette Gordon Low Girl Scout National Center is the beautiful home in Savannah, Georgia, where Daisy was born and where she lived before her marriage. Edith Macy Conference Center is near New York City. Girl Scout National Center West covers 15,000 acres of land in Wyoming. Your leader can tell you how to get more information about these centers.

International Friendship Centers

There are four special centers where older Girl Guides and Girl Scouts from all over the world can meet: Our Cabanā, in Mexico • Our Chalet, in Switzerland • Olave House, in London, England • Sangam, in India.

Each of them belongs to all Girl Guides and Girl Scouts. Perhaps you may visit one of them some day.

The things you learn as a Brownie or a Junior Girl Scout can help you be prepared for such a visit. When you learn songs, games, dances, and crafts, you are learning things to share with girls from other countries. Sometimes the events at the world centers are carried out in another language. The languages you study in school will help you understand your new friends.

Get Ready, Get Set, Go!

Up until now, you have been reading about things that all Girl Scouts need to know, no matter how young or how old they are.

But there are many things in Girl Scouting that are special for Brownies and many others that are special for Juniors. You will find them here in "Girl Scouting Is..."

If you are a Brownie, turn to the next page. It is the beginning of a whole section about Girl Scouting for girls your age. You will discover the secret of the Brownie name. You will find out how Brownies run their troop. And you will learn to do many things that only Brownie Girl Scouts do. Turn the page and find your way into Brownieland!

If you are a Junior, you can skip the part about Brownies and turn to page 69. There you will find the beginning of a section about Girl Scouting for Juniors. You will discover how troop government is carried out by Junior Girl Scouts. You will find out about activities that are just for Juniors. You will learn about awards that only Juniors can earn. Turn to that section and start your journey down the fun-filled path of Junior Girl Scouting!

Brownie Beings—
Being Brownies

How did the Brownie Girl Scouts get their name?

When Scouting was started for older boys and girls by Baden-Powell, it wasn't long before younger girls wanted to be Scouts, too. Baden-Powell wanted to give them something special all their own. He remembered a story called "The Brownies." He thought, "Brownies will be a good name for girls who like to be helpful as well as to play."

Here is the story. See if you agree.

The Brownie Story

Once upon a time, a little girl and boy named Mary and Tommy lived in a village in the North Country of old England, where the great meadows are called "moors." They lived with their father and their grandmother. Their father

was a poor tailor who worked very hard all day. Then, at night, he did the best he could to clean the house. He swept the stone floor and washed the dishes. He brought in wood and made the fire.

The grandmother was too old to do housework. She tried to help the tailor by making rugs out of the pieces of cloth left over from his work. But Mary and Tommy just played all day.

"Bairns are a burden," said the tailor one day as he sat at work. By "bairns" he meant children, as everyone in the North Country knows.

"Bairns are a blessing!" said the grandmother.

"Ah, not my bairns," said the tailor. "What they take out to play with, they lose. What they bring in to play with, I have to clean up. And not a bit do they do to help me."

"There's Mary," murmured the old lady. "She has a face like an apple."

"And is about as helpful," said the tailor.

Just then the door flew open. Mary and Tommy ran in. Their arms were full of sticks and moss, which they threw on the floor.

"Take that rubbish outside," said the tailor. "I've swept this floor once today, and I will not do it again."

Mary said, "Tommy, you take it out," and sat down near the grandmother. Tommy kicked some of the moss across the room and out of the door, making the floor look worse than ever. The sticks were left on the floor.

"And those sticks, too!" the tailor said as he walked out.

"You pick them up, Tommy," said Mary. "What makes Father so cross, Granny?"

"He is wearied, my dear, and you two do not help him."

"What could we do, Granny?"

"Many little things, if you tried. Ah, what this house needs is a brownie or two. The luck of our house left when the brownie left us."

"What was the brownie, Granny?"

"A very helpful little person, my dear."

"What did she do?"

"She came in before the family was up. She swept up the hearth and set out the breakfast. She tidied the room and did all sorts of housework. She always ran off before anyone could see her. But they could hear her laughing and playing about the house sometimes."

"What a darling! Did they pay her, Granny?"

"No, my dear. The brownies always help for love. But the family left a pancheon of clear water for her at night. And now and then, they left her a bowl of bread and milk or cream. She liked that, for she was very dainty. Sometimes she weeded the garden. She saved endless trouble, both to men and maids."

"Oh, Granny! Where is she now?"

"Only the Wise Old Owl knows, my dear; I don't."

"Who is the Wise Old Owl, Granny?"

"I don't exactly know, my dear. It's what Mother used to say when she could not answer our questions."

"Tell us more about the brownies, please," said Mary. "Did they ever live with anybody else?"

"There are plenty of brownies," said the old lady, "or used to be in my mother's younger days. Some houses had several."

"Oh, I wish ours would come back!" cried both the children in chorus. "She'd —"

"—tidy the room," said Mary.

"—wash the dishes," said Tommy.

"—bring in wood for the fire," said Mary.

"—sweep the floor," said Tommy.

"—and do everything!

"Oh, I wish she hadn't gone away! May we put out some bread and milk for her? Maybe she will come back if we do," said Mary.

"Well, well," said the grandmother. "She's welcome, if she chooses to come. There's plenty of work for her to do here."

Mary and Tommy put out a pan and filled it with bread and milk. Then they went off to bed.

That night Mary could hardly sleep. She kept thinking about the brownie. "There's an owl living in the old shed by the pond," she thought. "It might be the Wise Old Owl herself. If it is, she can tell me where to find a brownie. When Father's gone to bed and the moon rises, I'll go look for the Wise Old Owl."

The moon rose like gold and went up into the sky like silver. Mary crept softly through the kitchen. There was the pan of bread and milk, but no brownie had touched it. Mary went out onto the moor.

It was a glorious night, though everything but the wind and Mary seemed asleep. Mary hurried to the pond in the woods. All was still, so still that Mary could hear her heart beating.

Then suddenly, "Hoot! Hoot!" said a voice behind her.

"It's an owl!" said Mary. "Maybe it's the one I'm looking for." The owl flew by her and sailed into the shed by the pond.

"Come up! Come up!" said the owl.

The owl could talk! Then it must be the Wise Old Owl! The Old Owl sat on a beam that ran across the shed. Mary had often climbed up there for fun. She climbed up now, and sat face to face with the Owl.

"Now, what do you want?" said the Owl.

"Please," said Mary, "where can I find a brownie to come and live with us?"

"Oohoo!" said the Owl. "That's it, is it? I know of two brownies."

"Hurrah!" said Mary. "Where do they live?"

"In your house," said the Owl.

"In our house! Then why don't they help us?"

"Perhaps they don't know what has to be done," said the Owl.

"Just tell me where to find those brownies," said Mary. "I can show them what has to be done."

"Can you?" said the Owl. "Oohoo!" Mary was not sure whether the Owl was hooting or laughing.

"Of course I can," she said. "There is plenty to do at our house!"

"Well, Mary, I can tell you how to find one of the brownies. Go to the north side of the pond in the wood when the moon is shining. Turn yourself around three times while you say this charm:

'Twist me and turn me and show me the elf,
I looked in the water and saw ———'

"Then look into the pond to see the brownie. At the very same time that you see the brownie, you will think of a word that ends the magic rhyme."

Off went Mary, and in no time she reached the edge of the still, dark pond. The moon shone upon it, making it look like a mirror. Mary stood at the north side. Then, slowly, she turned herself round three times while she said the rhyme:

"Twist me and turn me and show me the elf,
I looked in the water and saw ———"

Then she stopped and looked into the pond. There she saw — only her own face.

"How stupid," said Mary. "I must have done it wrong." She looked in again. "There's no word to rhyme with elf, anyway. Belf! Helf! Jelf! Melf! What nonsense! And then to look for a brownie and see nothing but myself! Myself? Myself? But that does rhyme with elf. And it's just what I did, too. How very odd! Something must be wrong. I'll go back and ask the Old Owl about it."

So back Mary went to the shed and scrambled up beside the Old Owl.

"Whoooo," said the Owl, "and what did you see in the pond?"

"I saw nothing but myself," said Mary.

"And what did you expect to see?" asked the Owl.

"A brownie," said Mary. "You told me so."

"And what are brownies like?" inquired the Owl.

"Granny says brownies are very helpful little persons."

"Ah!" said the Owl, "and the one you saw was not? Are you sure you did not see a brownie?"

"Yes," said Mary. "I saw no one but myself. I'm not a brownie."

"Are you quite sure?" asked the Owl again. "All children can be brownies. Couldn't you sweep the floor, set the table, fetch the wood and water, tidy the room, and pick up your own things?"

"I don't think I should like it," Mary said. "I'd rather have a brownie do it for me."

"And what would you be doing meanwhile?" asked the Owl. "Being idle and lazy, I suppose—someone who never helps—who makes work instead of doing it!"

"Oh, no!" cried Mary. "I don't want to be like that. I'll go home and tell Tommy and we'll both try to be brownies."

"That's the way to talk!" said the Owl. "Now lean against me and I'll take you home."

The Owl's soft warm feathers seemed to be all around Mary; there was a singing of wind, and before she knew it

she was in her own little bed above the tailor's shop.

Mary could hardly wait for daylight to come. She waked Tommy and told him what had happened. Then together they crept downstairs. Before their father was awake, they did every bit of work they could find to do. They even found the tailor's measure that had been lost for a week. Then they crept, laughing, back to bed.

When the poor tailor came wearily downstairs, he looked around and rubbed his eyes. He looked round again and rubbed them harder. The table was set. The floor was clean. The room was bright and shiny as a new penny.

For a while the tailor could not say a word. Then he ran to the foot of the stairs, shouting: "Mother! Mary! Tommy! Our brownie has come back! And look," he said as he sat down at the table, "she has even found my measure! This is as good as a day's work to me."

Day after day went by and still the brownies stuck to it and did their work. They were the joy of the tailor's life. Every day they seemed to find more and more helpful things to do for him and for their grandmother.

One morning, the tailor woke up very early. He heard laughter coming through the floor from the kitchen below. "It must be the brownie," he thought. He put on his clothes and crept downstairs. When he opened the door to the kitchen, he saw Mary and Tommy dancing around the room.

"What's this?" he asked, when he could find his breath.

"It's the brownies," sang the children.

"The brownies? Where are they?" cried the tailor.

"Here! Here! We are the brownies!"

"But who did all the work? Where are the real brownies?"

"Here!" said Mary and Tommy as they ran into their father's arms.

When Granny heard all the noise, she came downstairs, too. The tailor told her about how he had found the brownies.

"What do you think of it all, Mother?" asked the tailor. "Bairns are a blessing," said the old grandmother. "I told you so."

Turning into a Brownie

Do you want to turn into a real Brownie, as helpful as the Brownies of olden times? To become a Brownie Girl Scout, you must:

• Be six, seven, or eight years old, or be in the first, second, or third grade.
• Come to Brownie troop meetings and find out what Brownies do.
• Pay national membership dues.
• Make the Girl Scout Promise.

Everyone Helps in the Troop

Your Brownie troop is your troop. Your leaders help you all the time, but it takes every one of you to make it a good troop.

Every Brownie helps make the rules, not just one person. Every Brownie has a turn doing the jobs that must be done at each meeting.

And, most important, all of you together decide what you are going to do at your troop meetings.

Brownie Ring

At a troop meeting, Brownies make decisions and plan what they will do in a special way. It is called the **Brownie Ring**. All the girls sit in a circle. This makes it easy to see each other.

Round and round and round about,
Take the hand of a Brownie Scout.
Here we are in Brownie Ring,
Ready for most anything!

There are many things to talk about in the Brownie Ring. You will all have lots of ideas. But, of course, not everyone can talk at once!

When you have something to say, you make the **talking sign**. Then you wait until your troop leader or the girl who is leading the Brownie Ring calls your name. That will mean it is your turn to talk. In this way, each Brownie gets the chance to say what she thinks. You tell what you like to do. You listen to the other Brownies tell what they like to do. There will be times when even good friends will not agree on the same plan for a troop. It is at these times that Brownies vote on what will be best for the group.

Often Brownies vote by just raising their hands. But sometimes you might want to have a secret vote. One way to do this is for each girl to cover her eyes with one hand or arm and raise the other hand. Then your troop leader or the girl who is leading the Brownie Ring counts the votes.

If your troop does not vote for your ideas this time, you

may want to put these good ideas in a dream box. When your troop needs ideas again, you'll have a whole boxful.

Troop Dues

Some of the best ideas your troop will think of will not cost anything. For others, you need some money. This money comes from troop dues. You pay these dues every week.

The dues are up to you. You talk about dues in your Brownie Ring. Then you decide, with your leader, how much your dues should be.

Committees

Suppose your troop decides to do something special, like going on a hike or giving a party. There will be many important jobs to do.

Will everybody do all of the jobs? You would never get done. Instead, a few of you take one job, and a few of you take another. Then the work gets done on time.

The girls working together on a job are called a committee. You are responsible for your part of your committee's work. Do you know what being responsible means? It means that you will do what you say you will do. You will do it as well as you can. Responsible is a good word for Brownies to learn and a good thing for Brownies to be.

Officers

As you work together on committees, you learn more and more about doing your share. You become more responsible and are able to do bigger jobs. You may then take turns being officers. In a Brownie troop, officers are changed often, so that everyone learns how to be one.

When all of you have taken turns being officers, your troop may be ready to elect officers. Your leader will let you know when you are ready.

When you elect an officer, vote for the girl who can do the job best. Suppose you want your best friend to be treasurer. But she is not very good at arithmetic. Would you vote for her for this job? Your friend will understand that you are being fair if you vote for another girl.

If you are elected an officer, do the best job you can. But you do not have to be an officer to help run your troop. Everyone's ideas are heard in the Brownie Ring.

Brownie Smile Song

1. I've some-thing in my pock-et. It be-longs a-cross my face, And I keep it ver-y close at hand in a most con-ven-ient place.

2. I'm sure you couldn't guess it
   If you guessed a long, long while.
   So I'll take it out and put it on--
   It's a great big Brownie Smile!

The "Brownie Smile Song"

Sometimes you do things in your Brownie Ring just for fun—like singing. On page 61 you will find a special song you might like to sing. It is called the "Brownie Smile Song."

The Brownie B's

The Brownie B's stand for things you can be because you are a Brownie Girl Scout, with a troop and grown-up leaders to help you. Brownie Girl Scouts join together to:

- Be Discoverers.
- Be Ready Helpers.
- Be Friend-Makers.

A **discoverer** finds out about things. You will find out things to make and do for yourself, your family, and your friends. You will find out about your own home. You will find out about the out-of-doors. Sometimes you will know what you want to discover. Other times you will just happen to discover things by surprise.

A **ready helper** is someone who helps cheerfully. She seems to get as much fun out of helping as out of playing. She has learned to do many things well enough to be of real help. One of your biggest Brownie discoveries will be finding out how to be a ready helper.

As a Brownie **friend-maker,** you will do much more than just be friendly. Being a friend-maker means going out of your way to make friends. It means learning about people. You find out what are the friendly things to do. You learn to understand the feelings of other girls, and this helps you get along with them. It helps you to make new friends.

There is a national patch plan based on the Brownie B's. Here's the way it goes: Your whole troop works together to be discoverers, ready helpers, and friend-makers. Then, each member of the troop will receive a patch. The patches will have different colors—yellow for the first year, red for the second year, and blue for the third year. Look at page 17 for pictures of these patches.

There are discoverer, ready helper, and friend-maker activities for every chapter in this book. To get a Brownie B patch, you and your troop will need to do twelve of these activities during the year.

Here are some examples of things you might do. Your leader will know about others that are suggested in her leader's guide.

Be a Discoverer in Girl Scouting. Find out what the World Association pin stands for. Find out what Thinking Day is. Help plan a special ceremony for Thinking Day and receive your World Association pin.

Be a Discoverer in the World of Well-Being. Draw or list what men do to take care of a home and family. Draw or list what women do. Can men and women do things that are on each other's list? Can *you* do some of the same things? Find pictures that show women doing work that men usually do and men doing work that women usually do.

Be a Discoverer in the World of People. Discover what is special about each girl and her family. Look at likenesses and differences in family activities, food you especially enjoy, customs you observe, and holidays you celebrate. Draw pictures or make posters from magazine pictures to show what is special about each family.

Be a Discoverer in the World of Today and Tomorrow. Build a model plane and fly it, or put together a model train or car so it will run. Or build a model airport, put together a train track, or make your own highway system. Then make safety signs for the things you've built.

Be a Discoverer in the World of the Arts. Paint or crayon a picture to show the different seasons, using only colors and shapes. Tell each other how different colors make you feel—warm, cool, happy, sad. Make up a poem or song about colors or invent a color game.

Be a Discoverer in the World of the Out-of-Doors. Discover what is underneath where you walk: animal burrows, mole holes, underground water, sewer pipes, or subways. Make drawings of what you think that unseen, underground world looks like.

Be a Ready Helper in Girl Scouting. Make booklets about what Brownies do, or about Juliette Low, or about how Girl Scouting began. Donate them to a school or local library. (Ask them to display the books during Girl Scout Week.)

Be a Ready Helper in the World of Well-Being. Learn about bicycle safety, rules of the road, what signs to obey, and hand signals. Make posters about safe biking and put them in public places. Show and tell the other girls about bicycle safety.

Be a Ready Helper in the World of People. Make up a guidebook, with pictures, for people who have just moved into your community. Tell them where the different important buildings are located. Give information about the places where children and families like to shop or play. Perhaps the Welcome Wagon organization would like to have your book to give to new families.

Be a Ready Helper in the World of Today and Tomorrow. Make a time capsule for a future Brownie troop. Fill it with discoverer ideas and ways to be ready helpers and friend-makers. Arrange with your council to store the time capsule and have it opened in two or three years.

Be a Ready Helper in the World of the Arts. Make calendars with cheerful pictures. Give them to the visiting nurse service so the nurses can leave them with sick people they visit at home.

Be a Ready Helper in the World of the Out-of-Doors. Visit an animal shelter, a zoo, a flower shop, a botanical garden, or a nature center. Find out how you can care for plants and animals.

Be a Friend-Maker in Girl Scouting. Bring friends who are not Brownies to a Brownie meeting. Show them your uniform and this book. Teach them a song your troop likes, play a game, or make something at the troop meeting. Tell them how they can become Brownies, too.

Be a Friend-Maker in the World of Well-Being. Invite another troop to a party (perhaps the Junior troop older Brownies are to fly up to). Plan, shop for, prepare, and serve a snack as part of the planning. Look on page 117 for suggestions.

Be a Friend-Maker in the World of People. Have an exchange visit with a Brownie troop in a nearby community or across the city.

Be a Friend-Maker in the World of Today and Tomorrow. Tape-record stories or songs for people who would especially enjoy them. These people might be senior citizens or younger children. They could be handicapped people or people in the hospital.

Be a Friend-Maker in the World of the Arts. Have a few buddy sing-along meetings. Pairs of girls learn a song ahead of time to teach everyone else. Tell something about each song—its background, the country it came from, its composer, or the kind of song it is. (See *Brownies' Own Songbook* and *Sing Together.*)

Be a Friend-Maker in the World of the Out-of-Doors. Make a bird feeder or wildlife feeding station for a windowsill, a backyard, a city park, the troop's favorite spot, or some property your council owns. Make plans to keep this feeding area supplied all winter, until the animals can find natural food again.

Bridge to Juniors Patch

In your final year as a Brownie, you can take part in bridging activities. Bridging activities are things that help you get ready to "cross the bridge" to Junior Girl Scouting. You do these things with other Brownies who are also getting ready to be Juniors. Together, you are called a bridging group.

If your group does four bridging activities, each of you will receive a Bridge to Juniors patch.

Here are some examples of bridging activities you might take part in. Your leader will be able to tell you about some others.

- With your bridging group, look on pages 71-74 of this book for information about the patrol system. Together, plan an activity using the patrol system to share with the younger Brownies in your troop or another Brownie troop.
- Go on one overnight camping trip with your bridging group and a Junior troop.
- Visit a Junior troop meeting. Find out something you didn't know about Juniors. Talk in your bridging group afterwards about all the things you learned.
- Look at the dabbler badges in the *Girl Scout Badges and Signs* book. You may earn one of these badges.

Looking Back and Looking Ahead

Your last months as a Brownie Girl Scout will be busy ones. At the same time that you are looking forward to becoming a Junior, you will be looking back at all the things you have done as a Brownie. You know that many of these things will help you be a good Junior Girl Scout. Your bridging activities will be especially helpful.

When you become a Junior, there may be some girls in your troop who never were Brownies. You will be able to help them learn some of the things you have learned. That will help them to be good Juniors, too.

And now, on to Junior Girl Scouting!

The Path of Junior Girl Scouting

Every step along the path of Junior Girl Scouting is filled with adventure.

You'll hike in the sun, in the snow, in the rain. You'll explore on foot, take a bus or a train. Sit under a tree. Learn to fix a scratched knee.

Indoors, too, there's plenty to do. You'll cook and sew, tell stories you know. Put on a play, make figures of clay, make bracelets and rings—all kinds of things.

To become a Junior Girl Scout, you must:

- Be nine, ten, or eleven years old, or be in the fourth, fifth, or sixth grade.
- Attend troop meetings.
- Pay annual membership dues.
- Make the Girl Scout Promise.

You and your Junior Girl Scout troop will decide what things you want to do. Some of them are things you do with all the girls in your troop. Others you do with a small group. Some you may even do with girls from other troops or with girls at a Girl Scout camp.

Junior Badges, Patches, and Signs

As soon as you become a Junior Girl Scout, you can work on a variety of badges. There are 76 of them for you to choose from. What if you and the other members of your troop have an interest that is not included in any of these badges? You can develop a special "Our Own Troop's" badge on that subject.

There is also a Junior Aide patch you can earn by helping Brownies get ready to bridge to your troop.

And there are three signs you can work on, the Sign of the Rainbow, the Sign of the Sun, and the Sign of the Satellite.

Finally, there is a Bridge to Cadettes patch you can earn during part of your last Junior year.

The badges, patches, and signs are insignia that you wear on your uniform. If you'll look in the *Girl Scout Badges and Signs* book, you'll find out how you can earn them.

Troop Government

In a way, your Girl Scout troop is like a country. It belongs to all members. The troop members are the citizens.

A country needs some plan of government to help it run smoothly, and so does a troop. With the help of your leaders, you and the other girls in the troop can set up your own troop government. Good government will make it easier to make decisions and set up troop rules.

A Girl Scout troop is a democracy. In a democracy each person can say what she wants the government to do and can vote for what she wants. Then, when a decision has been made, she does her part to carry it out. This is the way citizens in a democracy help to run their country. This is the way Girl Scouts help to run their troop.

There are different types of troop government. Discuss them in your troop and decide which type might be best for you.

Patrol System

The most widely-used form of troop government is the patrol system. To start this system, your troop divides into small groups. You might have anywhere from five to eight girls in each group. These small groups are called patrols.

Suppose your troop has 30 girls. You might have five patrols with six girls in each. Suppose your troop has only 20 girls. Then you might have two patrols with seven girls in each and one with six. Or you might have four patrols with five girls in each. Your leader will help you decide how many girls should be in each patrol.

Next, decide which girls will be in each patrol. Here are four ways to decide—

- **by numbers.** Suppose you decide to have six patrols with five girls in each one. Give each patrol a number. Write each number on five slips of paper and have each girl pick one out of a hat. The number each girl picks is the patrol she will belong to.

- **by interests.** All of you list your interests. Pick out the ones that are shared by the largest numbers of girls. Form patrols around these interests, with each girl volunteering to join the one that appeals to her most. For example:

Art	Music	Sports	Cooking
Corinne	Mavi	Vicky	Betsy
Juana	Pat	Lynn	Julie
Debbie	Mariko	Elaine	Thea
Mabel	Carol	Bianca	Nancy
Angie	Ely	Betty	Carlotta
Michele	Maura	Roxanne	Lillian

• **by goals.** All of you together decide what you want your troop to accomplish by the end of the year. You might come out with some goals like these:

Goal 1   To work with other people.

Goal 2   To learn camping skills.

Goal 3   To find out how Girl Guides in other countries live.

Goal 4   To learn about nature.

Each girl then chooses the goal she wants to work toward. Everyone who chooses the same goal will be in the same patrol.

• **by buddies.** Pair off into buddies. Each two buddies write their names on one piece of paper. Shuffle the papers and deal them, like cards, into patrols.

Can you think of some other ways to form patrols?

Patrols

Making new friends is part of the fun of Girl Scouting. If the girls in your troop are from different schools or are in different grades, it may be a good idea to mix them in the patrols.

Shooting Star Patrol

Each patrol will want to choose a name for itself. For example, the name could be the Shooting Star patrol, the Horseshoe patrol, the Daisy patrol. Sometimes patrols invent an emblem that they use on a patrol flag or on their patrol equipment.

Horseshoe Patrol

After you have set up patrols, you choose a patrol leader and an assistant patrol leader for each patrol. How do you think patrol leaders and assistant leaders should be chosen? How long should they serve? Switching leaders occasionally gives more girls a chance to hold office.

Daisy Patrol

Patrol leaders and assistant patrol leaders often stay in office until the whole troop decides to elect new ones or to make new patrols. The patrol leader's job is to: organize the patrol to get a job done • help new members • keep a record of dues and attendance for the girls in the patrol • lead discussions • represent her patrol at Court of Honor meetings. The assistant patrol leader's job is to help the patrol leader at patrol meetings. She does the patrol leader's job when the patrol leader is absent.

A patrol leader wears a cord on her left shoulder as a sign of her office. The cord has two gold circles. The larger one stands for the whole troop; the smaller one stands for the patrol. When new patrol leaders are elected, they receive their patrol leader cords at an installation ceremony held by the entire troop.

Court of Honor

Patrol members make plans and decisions for their patrol. The Court of Honor makes plans and decisions for the whole troop. The patrol leaders and the troop leader are all members of the Court of Honor.

Two other troop members, the troop scribe and the troop treasurer, are also members of the Court of Honor. They are elected to do special jobs. The troop scribe writes letters for the troop. She also takes notes at the Court of Honor meetings. The troop treasurer collects the weekly dues from the patrol leaders and works with the troop leader to keep a record of the dues collected and how the troop spends them.

The Court of Honor is a system of representative democracy. It is like the system the United States government uses. Every person in the country can't go to Washington, D.C., to run the government. That's why we elect people to represent us. The Court of Honor represents all the members of the troop.

The Court of Honor usually meets briefly before or after regular meetings. It may also hold some open meetings where all troop members can watch how it works.

These are the things the Court of Honor does:
- It suggests plans for patrols to discuss and to vote on.
- It asks for ideas and suggestions from patrols.
- It makes decisions for the whole troop.
- It sets up a kaper chart (job chart) with the troop jobs each patrol will do.

Patrol	Sept. 7	Sept. 14	Sept. 21
(shooting star)	Opening Song or Game	Closing Ceremony	Clean Up Meeting Room
(horseshoe)	Closing Ceremony	Clean Up Meeting Room	Opening Song or Game
(flower)	Clean Up Meeting Room	Opening Song or Game	Closing Ceremony

Steering Committee System

Like the patrol system, the steering committee system is a form of representative government. In this system, the whole troop votes for a group of girls to speak for them. This elected group is called a steering committee.

A steering committee can have a president, a vice president, a secretary, and a treasurer. It can also have other officers. This depends on how many girls are in the troop, how many activities and projects the troop discusses and carries out, and what the troop feels the steering committee members should do.

The steering committee may hold its meetings by itself. Or it might have an open meeting in front of the other troop members. It makes plans based on the feelings and ideas of everyone in the troop.

Town Meeting System

In the town meeting system of troop government, the troop is not divided into smaller groups. The total troop helps make decisions.

Everyone listens to everyone else's ideas, opinions, suggestions, and feelings. Everyone takes part in decision-making and leadership.

With this system, you need "guiders" to guide group discussions. You and the other troop members will decide how to choose discussion guiders. Will a guider be elected by the whole troop for a specific period of time? Will she be a girl whose name is drawn from a hat? Will a different girl serve as guider for each discussion?

Making Plans

You and your troop will be planning what you want to do. Here are four steps you will use: getting ideas, making decisions, carrying out the activities, and rating what you did.

Getting Ideas. Each girl has ideas about what she would like to do in Girl Scouting. Look at all the ideas the troop has. Here are some fun ways to share ideas and get all of you dreaming:

- Each girl brings to the meeting a picture, drawing, sample, or description of an activity she would like. She tells why she thinks the whole troop might also like it.

- During a meeting, each girl gets a large piece of newsprint and crayons and draws an activity she would really like to do with the troop. The pictures are displayed around the room for all to see and talk about.

- Each girl writes down five things she would like improved in the neighborhood or town. Put all the ideas on a blackboard. Talk about how Girl Scouts could help make these improvements.

- Have a brainstorming session. Everyone says what she would like to do, no matter how silly or impossible it sounds. Nobody makes any comments about the ideas when they are given. Just write them all down. Afterwards, go through the list and pick the ones everybody likes best.

- Keep a dream box to put ideas in. Whenever someone says "I wish we could————," jot down her idea and put it in the box. Next time you are looking for ideas, you'll have a boxful.

Making Decisions. There are usually more good ideas than you can use. The troop will need to vote on which ones to carry out.

If the vote is close, maybe you can have different activities for different groups. Sometimes patrols are formed around these interest groups (see page 72).

In some meetings you will have two activities going on at the same time. One group might do needlework while another does leathercraft.

When the whole troop does one project or takes a trip, it is important to have everyone agree on the plans. Perhaps you will have to work out some compromises before everyone is happy about the final decisions.

Once you decide what things you want to do, you will need to make a calendar that shows when you will do them.

Pretend these are some of your troop's plans.

You are going on a camping trip in October. (The reservations were made last spring.) You also plan to go to a councilwide Juliette Low birthday celebration on the first Saturday in November. You have agreed to do the flag ceremony at this event.

At your first meeting in the fall, you had a brainstorming session to think up ideas for meetings. Below is a list of activities you agreed you would like to do in the next four months. The list also shows how much time the activities will take.

Activity	Time Needed
Prepare for camping weekend.	2 meetings
Practice flag ceremony for Juliette Low birthday celebration.	1 meeting
Make international toys for children's home for the holidays. (Will you deliver the toys on troop meeting day or on another day?)	3 meetings (2 to make toys, 1 to deliver them)
Learn folk dances to teach children at the children's home when delivering toys.	1 meeting
Practice trail marking in park.	1 meeting
Have ice skating party.	1 meeting
Visit museum of art to see collection of Indian beaded necklaces.	1 meeting
Make beaded necklaces.	1 meeting
Put on a play for parents and friends. (This means rehearsals, making scenery, costumes, invitations, etc.)	6 meetings (at least)
Hold a Thanksgiving party at a senior citizens' center and sing songs.	2 meetings (1 to plan the party and practice songs, 1 to have the party)

As you can see, there are more ideas than meeting days. Decide which ones you would include on your calendar for the first four months of the troop year and which ones you would save for later.

After you have tried to make a calendar for these imaginary activities, make one for your troop's real plans. Start with dates you have chosen for special events, like a camping trip or a Juliette Low birthday party.

Also, remember to figure out how long things will take. Not everything takes a whole meeting to do. Some activities will take more than one meeting. You might need one or more meetings for planning and one meeting for doing.

If you have more good ideas than meetings, save some ideas for another time.

Carrying out the Activities. When you have finished planning, the action begins. Make sure you do your part to make the activities fun. Doing your part means things like sharing, taking turns, listening to others, and helping to clean up.

Rating What You Did. After each activity is over, see how you would rate it. In your troop, talk about how everyone felt about the activity. Did you have fun? Did you learn something interesting? Would you like to do this, or something like it, again? What changes would you make another time?

Troop Dues

Girl Scout troops need money for many things. Some of these are project supplies, trips, games, books, and troop equipment. Most troops have found that a good way to pay for these things is to collect weekly troop dues from each member. It's like having a troop bank account. Each week, troop members "deposit" their dues in the account. When the troop needs money for a project it has planned, money is "withdrawn" or taken out of the account.

Before you decide how much the dues should be, the troop will need to talk about—

• what you'd like to do at your meetings.
• how much money you will need to do what you've planned.
• what supplies or equipment the troop will need.
• how much these supplies will cost.
• how much the troop members feel they can afford.

Set dues at an amount everyone in the troop feels is fair. Later on you can always have a troop discussion if the dues are too low or too high. Perhaps you'll decide to change the dues.

Sometimes, your troop may find that its plans are bigger than its pocketbook. You may need to skip an activity or two. Or you may need to change your plans a bit to save money. For example, you could:

• Go roller skating, but not have refreshments afterwards.
• Go to camp, but find volunteers to drive you instead of renting a bus.
• Donate toys to the children's home, but make the toys yourself instead of buying them.
• Do leathercraft, but borrow the tools from another troop instead of buying them. (In exchange, you could do something for the other troop, like teaching them knotcraft.)

Sometimes troop dues aren't enough for all of the activities planned and supplies needed. Your troop might then plan a special project to earn the money you need. Talk to your Girl Scout leader about the types of projects Girl Scouts in your area are allowed to take part in.

Trim your plans to fit your budget. If you don't want to cut your dream plans to pocketbook size, you have to build up your pocketbook to dream size.

On to Cadette Girl Scouting

You are a Junior Girl Scout, eleven years old or in the sixth grade, and you have come to a bend in the path of Girl Scouting. What comes next? Cadette Girl Scouting. During your last few months as a Junior, you can do "bridging" activities that will help you get ready to join a Cadette troop. At the same time, you will be earning the Bridge to Cadettes patch. Details are in *Girl Scout Badges and Signs*.

As a Junior Girl Scout you have learned many things. As a Cadette you will learn even more and do much more on your own. You can explore careers in more depth than you did as a Junior. You can move from badges to interest projects to develop your skills in expanded ways. There are Challenges to meet, volunteer service projects to do, leadership insignia to strive for — all leading up to the Girl Scout Silver Award.

When you become a Cadette, you will be entitled to wear a new uniform with a new Cadette/Senior sash. Insignia that you earn as a Cadette and later as a Senior will go on the front of this sash. If you have received Brownie Wings and/or the Bridge to Cadettes patch, you may wear them on the front of your new sash, too. Other insignia earned as a Brownie or Junior may be worn on the back of the sash.

Your experience as a member of a Junior troop will help you become a good member of a Cadette troop. Sometimes several Cadette troops get together for a special event. Ask a

Cadette to visit your troop and tell you about Cadette Girl Scouting.

When you become a Cadette, there may be some girls in your troop who have not been Juniors. You will be able to tell them about the things you have learned. That will help them to be good Cadette Girl Scouts, too.

THE WORLD OF WELL-BEING

What is it that makes people happy and healthy? You can't catch it with a butterfly net, and you can't keep it in a shoe box. What is it?

Well-being is many kinds of things. It is—

- being loved and loving others.
- feeling special to yourself and to those who are special to you.
- knowing what you can do well.
- knowing and sharing your feelings.
- being part of different groups.
- sharing good times with family and friends.
- taking care of your body.
- using your mind and your muscles.
- working, playing, and relaxing.
- using your talents to grow and help others.
- doing your part at home and in the community.
- living in a safe and healthy place.
- being prepared to help others in emergencies.

In this world there are many activities for you and your troop to try. You'll discover how to stay happy and healthy and help others stay that way too.

You're Special

Isn't it strange
That however I change,
I still keep on being me?

Though my clothes get worn out,
Though my toys are outgrown,
I never grow out of me.

—EVE MERRIAM

Everyone is special in her own way. Find out what's special about yourself and others.

With your troop or family, talk about what each person: does well • doesn't enjoy doing • would like to do better • would like to do next week, month, or year • dreams of becoming in the future.

In what ways are you like others? not like them?

Everyone is important to herself and to others. And others are important to her. What people are special to you?

Find the help wanted section in a newspaper and read some ads to see how they are written. Write a "friend wanted" advertisement. It should tell what you like in a friend. Read the ads written by troop members out loud. What things does everyone like in a friend? Did you ask for something no one else did? Are you the kind of friend to others you'd like for yourself?

Here's something to try when you don't all know each other yet. Make name tags. Then walk around, find, and write down—

- the youngest girl.
- the girl who has the most sisters.
- the girls who have lived in the same place their entire lives.
- the girls who have moved the most.
- the favorite ice cream flavor of the most girls.
- the girls whose mothers, grandmothers, sisters, or cousins were Girl Scouts.
- the girls who are not in your class at school.

Add your own ideas.

When you've found out all this, you are on your way to getting to know each other.

Make a collage, draw pictures, or collect photographs of activities your family likes. Show them to others in your troop. What do many families like to do? Try out other families' ideas for fun with your family or with your troop.

You're a girl, a Girl Scout, and a student. You might also be a sister, a pet caretaker, or a ball player. What else are you? Play a troop or patrol guessing game. Take turns acting out and guessing different things girls can be.

How many different things did the group come up with? How many are *you*?

How Do You Feel Today?

Every day you *feel*. Feelings are very real. Everyone has them. They are not always the same. Your feelings are part of what makes you special. The way you feel about yourself affects the way you act and the way others act, too.

How do you feel today? happy   sad   or so-so?

Talk about what makes people feel happy. How do you act when you feel happy? How do you treat other people?

Try sharing your good feelings with people you like. When you tell them about how you feel, they might feel that way, too!

Pick a girl in your troop who has made you feel really good. Write her a "thank you" note telling her what she did to make you feel this way.

Talk about what makes people feel unhappy or angry.

Some people yell or hit others, kick things, take it out on a pet, eat too much, or break things that belong to others. Do you think these ways of acting make people feel better?

Letting your feelings show can help make you feel better. Here are some ways to let feelings out that won't hurt you or anyone else.

- Tell someone you like how you feel (they've probably felt the same way sometimes).
- Cry if you want to.
- Kick an empty cardboard box.
- Punch some clay or pillows really hard.
- Write about how you're feeling.
- Bounce a ball or run as fast as you can.
- Draw a really ugly picture.

How do you act when you feel unhappy or angry? How do you treat others?

With crayons or paints, draw a picture or design to tell how you feel. Talk about your pictures with others.

Save your picture. Some other time, when you know you are feeling different, try another picture. Compare them. How are they alike or different?

Make a "me" puppet or mask. (See pages 256 to 258 for ideas for making puppets.) Then use it to act out situations like these—

- how you treat your pet when you're disappointed that you can't go to the circus.

- how you act during troop meeting clean-up time if you received a good grade that day. a poor grade.

- how you act if it's raining and your troop had planned a picnic.

Your Body Is a Complicated Machine

Anger, worry, jealousy can make you feel terrible. So can hunger, fever, or a bad cold.

Love, friendship, belonging can make you feel good. So can eating the right foods, getting enough rest, and having the doctor check you and say you're in great shape.

Keeping your body healthy is an important part of feeling good. Your body is like a very complicated machine. It does thousands of jobs that you don't even know about. And just a few simple things are all you need to do to keep your body healthy. Your family and other people in the community might help you with some of them.

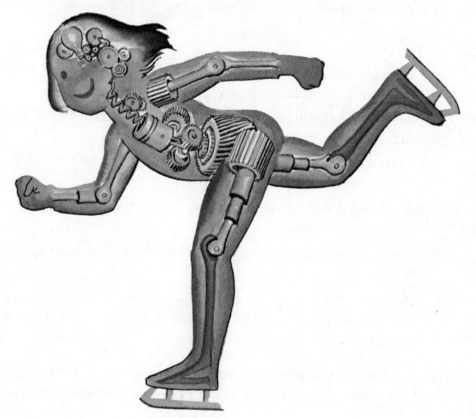

Do you do these daily?

• Wash yourself and brush your hair and teeth.

• Eat a variety of good foods.

• Get enough sleep.

• Relax during the day.

• Get fresh air and plenty of exercise.

• Do things safely.

• Dress correctly for the weather.

Do you do these when needed?

• See the doctor and dentist for checkups.

• Get the shots you need to protect you from disease.

• Follow the doctor's instructions when you are ill.

Things to try:

• Try some of the games on pages 97 to 101. Some are good for exercising and some are good for relaxing.

• Talk about the foods that are good to eat. See pages 114 to 118 for some more things to try.

• Visit a doctor or dentist (or both), and ask them to explain what they do during a checkup.

• Find out what shots babies and children get to protect them from diseases.

• Go on a hazard hunt by yourself or with others. See page 95.

• Put on a "Dressing for the Weather" fashion show. You model the right clothes to wear for different kinds of weather.

Make a chart to keep track of everything you do for several days. (Don't forget that a day is 24 hours!) For each day add up the time you spent sleeping, relaxing or doing quiet things, exercising or doing active things. Here are some hints.

- Relaxing or doing quiet things: reading, watching TV, eating, resting, painting, homework, class work, indoor chores like washing dishes, riding in a car or bus, personal care, meetings, quiet games.

- Exercising or doing active things: active games, running, walking, riding bikes, chores like shoveling snow, mowing the lawn, or sweeping floors.

Compare your own charts. Are your charts for a weekday and a day on the weekend the same? If they are different, what are the differences?

Which days did you feel best? Why do you think you did? Look at the charts kept by other troop members.

Using your "me" puppet or mask (see page 90), act out how you feel and act when:

- You don't sleep enough.
- You don't play outside because you've been watching TV all day.
- You were so busy you didn't relax all day.
- You eat too much or too little.
- You have a toothache.

How Is Your Safety Sense?

Ouch! Thud! Bang! Crash! What do these sounds mean to you? Could they mean that someone is not using safety sense? Having safety sense means using your senses—sight, smell, touch, and hearing—to think and act safely. It helps keep accidents from happening.

Try out your safety sense by trying to pick out trouble spots in this picture.

Using your safety sense, go on a hazard hunt: in your troop meeting place • in your kitchen • in a backyard or play area.

Talk about or act out the safety rules for: crossing the street • driving your bike • riding in a car, bus, or train • having a fire drill • talking to strangers.

Fitness Is Fun

Keeping fit is an important part of feeling your best. Every day your body needs activity that makes the muscles work hard. It's easy and fun to keep fit with friends. Dancing, swimming, tossing a Frisbee or ball, flying kites, biking, hiking around the neighborhood or at camp, skating, playing games, and taking part in sports are just some ways to help your body work its best. What ways to keep fit do girls in your troop like?

Make a circle out of heavy cardboard. Label it with the exercises shown in the picture, or exercises everyone knows. Make a hole in the center of the circle and fasten it to a larger piece of cardboard with a paper fastener. Draw an arrow on the bottom of the larger piece.

Any time the troop wants to take a break, spin the wheel and do whatever is written in the space that stops nearest the arrow. Do it for one minute, or as long as you like. Spin again as many times as you like.

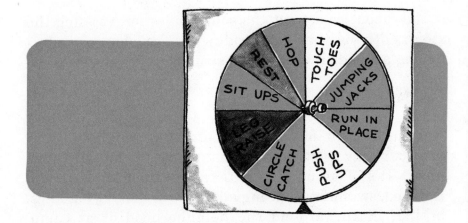

Other things to try:

Start and stop a record player or radio (this is like playing Musical Chairs) while using the Wheel of Fitness. When the music stops, spin the wheel again. Start the music and do the activity above the arrow until the music stops again.

Put the name of each activity or exercise on a card. Put the cards in a box or bag. Draw them from the box instead of using a wheel.

Be a Good Sport

A good sport is someone who plays fair and always tries her best. Playing games and sports is more fun when you play with good sports. If you play alone or on a team, there are often game rules to follow. You will play a game better if you practice game skills. But win or lose, it's how you play the game that counts!

What kind of sport do you think you are?

With troop members, talk about how following the Girl Scout Law and being a good sport are alike.

Many games can be played in a group with everybody ending up a winner. Here are a few suggestions. On your own, try making up some games which a group can play and all can win.

Mechanical Match Game. Put the names of different machines on pieces of paper. Make two or three for each machine. Each girl picks a paper from a hat. Everyone tries to find her match before the rest of the group by acting out her machine using sounds, but no words.

Catch the Caterpillar's Tail. Form a line and walk like a caterpillar (see page 100). The last girl in the line hangs a bandana (the tail) from her back pocket. Team tries to catch its own tail. First girl in the line has to catch the bandana. Try also with more than one team catching each other's tail.

Time to Stretch

Here are some activities and games to enjoy when everyone feels like stretching and moving around.

Have one person beat out different rhythms on a cardboard box or tabletop or play music while the group

dances to the beat. Try to move as many ways as you can—bend, leap, hop, stretch, walk. Dance alone or with a partner. Another time, jump rope or bounce a ball while moving to the beat.

Take turns being the leader and calling out the names of things for everyone else to move like.

Objects to try: different machines, animals, or vehicles.

Also fun: different colors or words like excitement, gentle, hurry.

Sometimes the game leader can say "freeze," and each girl will have to stop moving and stay in the position she's in until "melt" is called. Then everyone can start moving again.

See "The World of the Arts," page 272 and "The World of People," page 161, for dances that are also fun to try.

Walk like an Animal

Try moving like these animals. Do them just for fun or divide into teams and use one for an animal relay race. Another time, pick a different animal for the relay.

Kangaroo: Jump forward, land on both feet squatting.

Bear: Walk on hands and feet, keep legs stiff.

Ostrich: Hold ankles, walk forward, keeping legs stiff and head high.

Crab: Sit on floor, lift up with hands and feet, walk on all fours.

Seal: Walk forward on hands, dragging legs behind you.

Lame Fox: Walk forward on hands and one foot, hold other foot up behind you.

Butting Goat: Crawl forward, pushing a large ball with the top of your head.

Caterpillar (for a team): Everyone in line holds ankles of person in front of her; team moves forward together.

Add some you make up on your own.

Other ideas for relays—
- knot-tying relay.
- rolling old automobile tires.
- jump rope: pick a style and a number of jumps.
- obstacle relay: set out things for each team.
- wheelbarrow race: one girl walks forward on her hands while another holds her ankles.

Dash and Dodge Ball

Here's a game that will keep everyone moving so she doesn't get sent to the North Pole.

What you'll need: two teams, an open area with a dividing line in the middle; beach ball, or volley ball.

What you do: Teams spread out on each side of a dividing line. They takes turns getting the ball first. The ball is thrown over the line at girls on the other team. It must hit a girl below her waist, and it must bounce first. If a girl is hit, she must "go to the North Pole" on the other side (see picture). If a ball is caught on the fly, the girl who threw it goes to the North Pole. If girls in the North Pole catch the

North Pole can be:

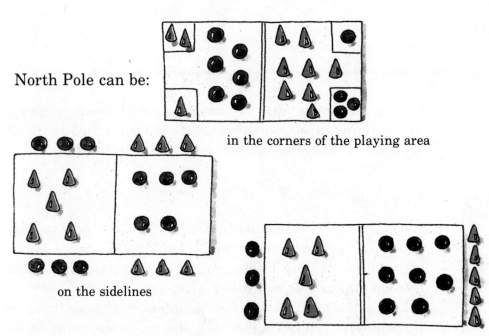

in the corners of the playing area

on the sidelines

on the end lines

ball, they can try to hit girls on the other team. If they hit someone, they can get away from the North Pole and go back to their team's side. A team wins by having the most players when time is up or by sending all the other team members to the North Pole.

Other ways to play:

Use two, three, or four balls at the same time.

Do something before throwing the ball at a girl on the other team. You might try hopping twice or bouncing the ball three times before throwing.

Set up the same number of milk cartons or plastic bottles on each side. Each team guards its cartons from being knocked over by the ball thrown by the other team. A team wins when the other team's cartons are all knocked over.

See "The World of the Out-of-Doors" for other outdoor games.

Fitness Favorites

Biking, swimming, and ice skating, as well as jumping rope and running, are favorite ways for children and adults to keep fit. Here are some safety tips to keep in mind.

Bicycling

Keep your bicycle in good condition. Find out how to keep your bike in good condition and make simple repairs. Someone who works in a bike shop might help you with this. Have a troop bike inspection using what you learn.

Learn how to drive your bicycle safely. With your troop set up a bicycle safety course. Ask the police department for help. Invite others in your community to join as you practice signaling, stopping, and accurate driving around a marked course. If you have judges, a time limit, and a point system for each activity on the course, it becomes a game.

Find out and follow local laws about bicycling. Invite a policewoman or policeman to a troop meeting to talk about the bicycling rules in your area. Share what you learn with other bikers.

Swimming

If you have not yet learned to swim well, stay where you can easily touch bottom, reach the edge of the pool or wade to shore. Know how deep the water is and whether there is anything under the surface—logs and rocks, for instance—before diving.

Always swim with a buddy. Enter and leave the swimming area together. You are each other's special guards.

Always swim where there is a lifeguard and rescue equipment—a ring buoy or boats. Follow the rules where you are swimming. Do not shove or push other swimmers.

Call for help only when you need help. When someone calls for help, get a lifeguard immediately.

Leave the water before you become tired or cold. Wait a while after a meal before you go into the water.

Ice Skating

Skate only on ice that has been tested. Keep candy and gum wrappers off the ice because they can make skaters fall. Always skate with a buddy.

Before you start to skate, collect a pole, a plank, or a board tied to a rope that you could use to help if a skater should fall through the ice. Put it where you can reach it.

If a skater does fall through the ice, keep away from the thin ice or you may fall in, too. Slide your rescue equipment out to the skater, and tell her to hang on to it and wriggle onto solid ice. Then you can pull her toward you. If *you* fall through, kick your feet and wriggle onto solid ice.

Games for Quiet Times

Here are some games to play when everyone would like to relax for awhile.

My Name Is. Everyone sits in a circle, clapping her hands against her knees. The first person says, "My name is_____" while doing a hand action. The second person says, "Her name is_____," repeating the name and hand action of the first person. Then she says, "My name is_____," and makes up a different action for her name. Each girl repeats "Her name is _____" and the hand actions for *all* the girls before her, and adds her own name. Repeat this until everyone has a turn. Remember to keep clapping.

Shape Game. Two girls sit back to back so that neither can see what the other is doing. Both girls are given the same colored shapes. They can be blocks or paper cutouts. One girl makes a design with these shapes and tells the other girl where she is putting each piece. The other girl listens and tries to make the same design. When the designs are done, see if they came out the same.

Kim's Game. Divide into teams. Give each team paper and pencil. Place 10 to 20 objects on a table. Allow team members to study objects for two minutes. Cover up the objects. Teams make a list of all the objects they remember. The team with the longest correct list wins. (This game came from the story "Kim" written by Rudyard Kipling. In the story, Kipling has the game used as an observation exercise for secret service agents in India. Kim's Game is a favorite of Girl Scouts and Girl Guides all over the world. Each time you play it, different objects can be used.)

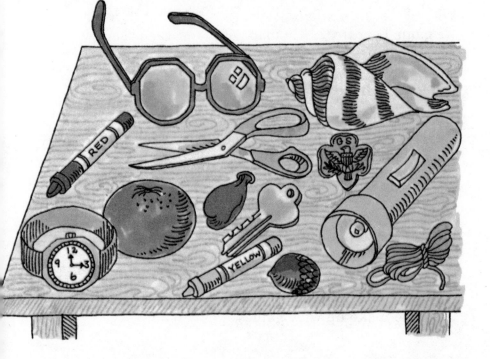

Invent-a-Game

Would you like to invent a game? It's fun to make up games and play them with others.

Figure out who will play:

- individuals
- buddies
- threesomes
- teams
- whole group

Decide how game is played:

- what is done—guess, answer questions, use new skills, figure out a code.
- how game starts
- how game ends—time limit, first done, most points.
- what are the rules—boundary lines, scoring.

Gather what you will need:

- questions
- balls
- paper and pencils
- clues
- rope
- markers
- game board
- map
- compass
- music
- blindfold

Decide where to play:

- indoors
- out-of-doors
- large or small area
- sitting in a car or bus without distracting the driver

Try to invent a game: for buddies to play out-of-doors using a 3-meter length of rope and a blindfold • for the whole troop to play indoors, which tests camping skills and doesn't use any equipment • for teams to play in a bus using music and a compass.

See "The World of the Out-of-Doors," page 332 to find out how to make up wide games.

Hobbies to Enjoy

A hobby can be almost anything you really enjoy doing to relax, have fun, and use your talents. Here are just a few of the many types of hobbies: collecting objects, sports and games, singing or playing musical instruments, traveling, arts and crafts, camping, biking, photography, sewing, writing stories and poems, cooking, and woodworking.

Do you have something you really like to do? What do others in your troop, your class at school, or your family enjoy doing?

A talent scout looks for or "scouts" for people who are talented in sports, music, dramatics, or in other ways. You can be a talent scout. Find out the talents or hobbies of people you know by asking what they really enjoy doing. You can also ask people whom you meet while exploring your community. (See "The World of People," page 140.)

- Keep a list of interesting or unusual hobbies and the person who knows about them in a troop idea book.

- Have a hobby or talent roundup. Show or teach each other your specialties.

- Invite someone from the community to demonstrate, talk about, or teach a specialty to the troop.

- Learn more about your hobby by reading and visiting museums or exhibits.

- Get together with other girls who enjoy the same things to share ideas, and learn more about your hobby.

- Use your talents and hobbies to make others happy or to serve the community. Read aloud a poem you wrote; teach songs; play an instrument; make toys; display collections for others to enjoy; create craft objects to give as gifts.

See "The World of the Arts," "The World of the Out-of-Doors," and "The World of Today and Tomorrow" for other hobby ideas.

Home Is a Special Place

Your home is more than the rooms that you live in. It's your family. It's a place to share love and happy times. It's a place where you work, eat, play, and learn to get along with others. Your home is where you start making discoveries about the world around you.

All families are alike in many ways. No two families are exactly the same. Some families are large and some are small. Some have several adults, some have two, and others have one. Each family has its own special ways to make a happy, healthy home. Each member of the family is important and can help do the jobs that need to be done.

How many ways to help where you are needed can you add to those in the picture? How many ways can you use the Girl Scout Law to help make a home happy, healthy, and safe? Talk about it with others in your troop.

A home filled with happiness is a nice place to live and to visit. It makes people feel good. Here are some ways you can help fill your home with smiles. How many can you do? What other ways can you think of?

- Plan a surprise for a special occasion.
- Fix up or decorate a special spot.
- Help prepare for and entertain guests.
- Spend time with your family telling stories, singing, or playing games.

- Invite friends to meet your family.
- Share things you like with family members.
- Take care of plants, or a garden, or arrange flowers.
- Do something special with a younger brother or sister.
- Keep your own belongings neat.
- Help keep your home clean.
- Help fix or repair something worn.
- Teach something you know to your family—a grace, a song, a craft.
- Do an extra chore without being asked.
- Make something beautiful for others to enjoy.
- Help prepare or serve meals.
- Help take care of someone sick.

Parents and Others at Home

Parents or other people who take care of you help make a happy, healthy home in many special ways. Someday you might be a parent, and you will have your own special ways, too. Some adults spend their day working at home. Others work away from home full-time or part-time. Some do volunteer work. Many parents are students. Sometimes children spend their day in these same ways, too!

Pretend you are a news reporter for a newspaper, radio, or television. Observe what parents or other family members do during the day, at home and away from home. Ask them what they think are the five most important things they do to keep the family happy and healthy. Draw, tell, or act out your news "story" at a troop meeting.

With your troop, try to think of the jobs done by men and women at home: shopping, making repairs, cleaning, paint-

ing, taking care of young children, and others. Write each one on a slip of paper and put them in a hat. Take turns picking a job, acting it out, and having others guess what job it is. Talk about whether or not you feel all the jobs can be done by both men and women.

Everyone Was Little Once

You have probably forgotten what it was like to be very small. Find out what you were like by asking a parent, grandparent, older brother or sister, or an older friend. Collect pictures of yourself at different ages. Look at drawings you made. Ask about things you liked to eat, toys and books you enjoyed, when you started to crawl, to walk, and to talk. Try to find out some of these same things about your parents or aunts and uncles when they were little. Talk to your grandparents about them and look through family picture albums.

Playing with and helping to take care of younger children and babies is a useful and enjoyable way to help at home. You'll be a better helper if you learn as much as you can about younger children. Here is a way you can find out about them and how to help with their care.

Watch a baby or a younger child several times. Write your discoveries in a diary. See if you can discover—

• what she can do for herself.
• what she needs others to do for her.
• what she likes to play with.
• things *you* never knew before.
• things that surprised *you*.

If other girls in your troop keep a discovery diary, get together and talk about what each girl has discovered. All

babies are different. You will learn more about them by sharing diaries with each other.

Discovering Your Home

Are there mysteries for you to solve in your home? Look around your home carefully. Find five objects that are a mystery to you. You can name them but you can't explain them, like a sewing machine, an antique kitchen gadget, the toilet tank, anything. Ask someone to explain or show you how to use at least one of your mystery objects. Check books if you need to. Tell others in your troop about your mystery and the solution.

In small groups, think up what you would put into clue capsules that would help people 100 or even 1000 years from now know what homes were like in your lifetime. If you can, actually put the things or clues you pick into a box. Trade boxes with another group. See if each group can figure out why the other group included the things it did.

At a meeting or at home, try to think of items found at home that: come from another country • were not there when your grandparents were your age • start with each letter of the alphabet.

Each time you play, try thinking of something different. Add your own group of items.

Be a Clever Consumer

Did you know that you are a consumer? Everyone who uses goods such as food or art supplies, and services such as dry cleaning or transportation, is a consumer. Whether it's your own money, your family's, or your troop's, money will stretch farther when it is spent wisely. If you compare goods and services to find the best buy and make smart choices, your money will buy more.

Pretend your troop wants to take ice skating or roller skating lessons (a service). Discuss and decide which would be the best buy:

You could take lessons at Rink A:
- Rink A charges each girl 50¢ per lesson and 25¢ for skates.
- Rink A charges each girl 50¢ per lesson, but if you wait two months and come during the slow season they won't charge for skates.

Or you could take lessons at Rink B:
- Rink B charges each girl 40¢ per lesson and nothing for skates. Rink B is crosstown. The bus ride costs 15¢ each way.
- Rink B charges $10.00 per lesson for a whole troop. If only a few girls come, the troop must still pay $10.00.

Or you could take lessons from Senior Girl Scouts:
- A group of Senior Girl Scouts will teach you for free at Rink A which charges each girl 25¢ to skate (without lessons) and 25¢ for skate rental.
- The Seniors can't give lessons on your regular troop meeting day.

Think about:
- How many girls are in your troop?
- What are the troop's other plans?
- Could the troop meet on another day?
- Could the troop have extra meetings for a while?

There is no right answer. If you buy something that isn't what you want just because it's cheap, it isn't a good buy. You decide what's the best and safest.

How do you make decisions? Talk with others in your troop about times when: adults help you decide ⋄ friends help you decide ⋄ you decide for yourself. Learning how to make wise choices will help you throughout your life.

How does your troop make decisions? Are activities planned so that everyone gets a chance to do what she wants to sometimes? Look at the different ways troops can make decisions in "Girl Scouting Is...," pages 78 to 80.

Recipe for Health and Happiness

Mealtime is a good time to relax and enjoy talking to others. Food that tastes and looks good and is served with care can perk people up. Learning how to prepare and serve foods can be fun. Some people even think of cooking as their hobby.

What we eat depends on many things. Look at the people above. How would what they eat be different?

Start learning about foods and how to prepare and serve them. You could do this alone or with others in your troop. Then you will be ready to help fix meals at home for yourself and others and to fix meals out-of-doors on Girl Scout outings. Cookbooks for beginners often have pictures that teach you how to cook.

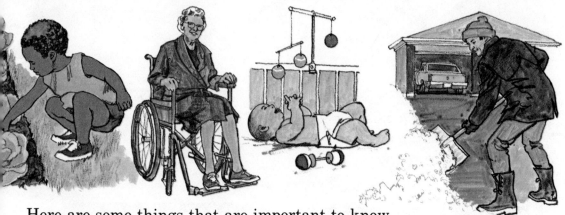

Here are some things that are important to know—

- how to follow package directions and recipes.
- how to set an attractive table.
- how to measure liquid and dry ingredients.
- how to make simple dishes you and your family like.
- how to use the stove safely.
- how to shop for the best buy.
- how to clean up as you work.
- how to plan the amount of food you'll need.
- how to plan meals using the four food groups.

Make plans to visit a restaurant and ask the cook to show or tell you about the foods on the menu. Plan to make something you learned about, after your trip. Supermarkets, school cafeterias, bakeries, and all sorts of food markets are also fun to visit.

Within your troop, swap and try recipes for family favorites. Try fixing someone else's favorite for your family.

The Four Food Groups

Foods help your body grow and run smoothly. They give you the energy to work and play. No food has everything your body needs to do its many jobs. Eating many kinds of foods each day is the best way to make sure your body gets what it needs.

Most foods belong to four food groups. You can use the four food groups to check whether you are eating correctly and to plan meals at home and for camping trips. An easy rule to follow is: Eat a food from each of the four food groups at every meal.

Have a troop tasting party. Try to serve "tastes" of foods that most of the girls have never tried before. Each girl can suggest something she has eaten that might be new to the others. Taste something from each of the four food groups. Try food from other places, or fixed in a new way, if you can.

Smart Snacking

Well-chosen snacks can help to keep you healthy. What kinds of snacks do you choose? soft drinks and candy? These foods are not in the four food groups because your body does not need sweet foods to stay healthy, and they are not good for your teeth.

Here are some snacks that are good for you and taste good, too. Add other snacks you can think of from the four food groups. Plan to try them when the troop has refreshments for special occasions.

Fruit and Vegetable Group:
banana, plum, orange, melon,
raisins, dates, figs, carrot,
radish, cucumber,
fruit and vegetable juices.

Meat Group: cooked meat
and poultry,
peanut butter, eggs, nuts.

Milk Group: cheese, ice cream,
milk, cocoa, yogurt, eggnog,
cheese pizza,
puddings made with milk.

Bread and Cereal Group:
crackers, biscuit, muffin, toast,
granola, grits, waffle, rice pudding,
bread pudding, noodle salad.

Others: soup, popcorn, sunflower
and pumpkin seeds.

Make 50 playing-size cards out of cardboard or heavy paper. Pick 25 different snacks from the list. Include some you added. Draw a picture of each snack on two blank cards. Now you have a deck of 25 snack pairs. Make up your own card games, or play Snack Hunt, which is played like Go Fish, and Poor Snack, which is played like Old Maid. (You'll need to make a wild card with a picture of a poor snack like candy or soda to play Poor Snack.)

How Are You Eating?

For a few days, see if you eat a food from each of the four food groups at least three times a day. Include any snacks you eat. Keep track on a chart like this one.

					TOTAL FOR MEAL
BREAKFAST	✓	✓	✓	✓	4
LUNCH	✓	✓	✓	✓	4
SUPPER	✓	✓	✓	✓	4
SNACKS	✓			✓	2

Get Ready to Sew

A needle is one of the oldest tools in your home. Needles were made out of animal bones and wood long before they were made of metal. With them, you can make and repair a number of articles for yourself and your home. You can also do service projects.

Get Ready. It is a good idea to have a sewing kit of your own. Include a few needles with large eyes, scissors, pins and pincushion or pin box, thread, a thimble that fits your finger, and a tape measure. Keep your sewing supplies in a box or metal container. Decorate it if you like.

Get Set. Now you have the supplies you need to begin. Before you sew, ask someone to show you how to:
• Thread a needle.
• Tie a knot at the end of the thread.
• Make a running and basting stitch.
• Make an overcast stitch.
• Use a thimble to push the needle.
• End a row of stitching so that it won't pull out.
• Sew on buttons, snaps, and hooks and eyes.

With an adult's help, you might also learn to thread a sewing machine and stitch backwards and forwards in a straight line.

Sew. Now you are ready to make and repair things for yourself and others. Here are just a few ideas on what you can make. For more ideas, look in "The World of the Out-of-Doors," page 348.

A sit-upon is easy to make and handy, too. Its funny name tells what it is.

You'll need: newspaper, two squares of heavy plastic or oilcloth a little larger than the newspaper. (You might use an old plastic tablecloth.)

What you do:

1. Put a cushion of newspaper between the squares of plastic.

2. Stitch the edges of the plastic using a running stitch or overcast stitch.

3. Sew a piece of cord on two corners so that you can tie your sit-upon around your waist when you are not using it.

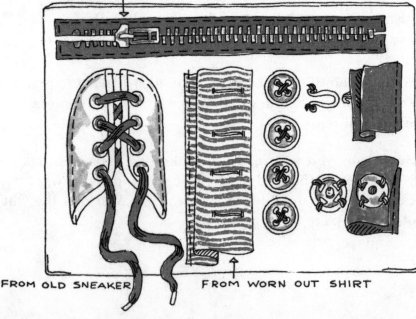

Dressing cards are a great way to practice your new sewing skills. When they are done, give them to young children who are just learning to dress themselves. Then they can practice their new skills.

You'll need: a piece of heavy fabric, a piece of cardboard, assorted odds and ends (see picture).

FROM WORN OUT SKIRT OR PANTS

FROM OLD SNEAKER   FROM WORN OUT SHIRT

What you do:

1. Sew as many things as you can find to the fabric.

2. Staple or glue the fabric to cardboard.

A sunshine poncho is something you'll have fun making and be proud to wear. Make yours from an old blanket, or sew together scraps of fabric cut from clothing that is worn out or too small.

You'll need: a square piece of fabric about 1 meter wide.

What you do:

1. Spread square out flat.

2. Find center of square.

3. Carefully cut slit large enough for your head.

4. Fold neck edge towards inside about 1 cm and stitch down.

5. Hem entire edge of poncho.

6. Stitch each side in one spot as shown in picture.

7. Trim poncho the way you like.

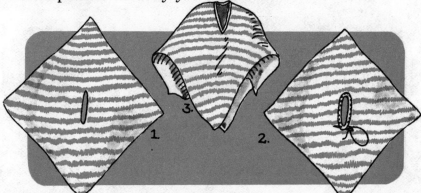

A rain poncho is handy for rainy days at camp or around your own neighborhood. You can make one out of heavy plastic or an old shower curtain. All you do is follow steps one, two, and three for the sunshine poncho, using plastic instead of fabric.

121

Community Health and Safety Helpers

Many people in the community are your health and safety helpers. Do you know who they are?

- Who keeps the parks and playgrounds clean?
- Who gives you health checkups and vaccinations?
- Who cleans the streets and collects garbage and trash?
- Who keeps stray animals from running around loose?
- Who makes sure that people obey traffic rules?
- Who checks to see that your teeth and gums are healthy?
- Who puts out fires?
- Who checks for air and water pollution?
- Who checks to see that food is safe to sell?

Talk about what it would be like if one or more of these jobs weren't done. How would it make things less healthy and safe?

With your troop, find out more about community helpers by visiting them where they work. Or ask them to visit you at a troop meeting. Ask them—what they do at their jobs • what they like about their jobs • how you and others can help them do a good job.

See "The World of People" for more ideas on how to discover your own community.

Emergency Who's Who

Look up the telephone numbers on this list in the phone book. Then make a list to keep by the phone at home.

- Mom at work_____

- Dad at work_____

- Poison Control Center_____

- Doctor _____

- Police_____

- Ambulance_____

- Fire Department_____

- Hospital Emergency Room _____

- Health Department_____

- Air Pollution Control _____

- Dentist _____

Talk in your troop about what you'd have to tell someone if you made an emergency phone call—your name, and where and what the emergency is.

Pretend to make different kinds of emergency phone calls at a troop meeting. Take turns making the phone calls and being the person who answers.

Fire Safety

With your troop and your family, talk about and practice what to do in case of fire. It's good to plan the way to get out from different rooms ahead of time.

If your clothes catch on fire:

1. Drop to the ground. Never run! If you run, you give the fire more oxygen and the fire burns faster.
2. Cover your face with your hands.
3. Wrap a coat or blanket around you to smother the flames, or roll over slowly to shut out the oxygen.

If another person's clothes catch on fire:

1. Get the person to the ground. Roll her over.
2. Wrap a coat or blanket around the person to smother the flames, or roll her over slowly.
3. Be careful that your own clothing does not catch fire.

If fire breaks out in your home:

1. Get yourself and other people out of the house.
2. Go to the nearest telephone or alarm box and call the fire department. Give your name and address. If you call from an alarm box, stay there to direct the fire truck when it arrives.

If smoke comes into the room and the door is closed:

1. Do not open the door.
2. Feel the door. If it is cool, open it a little and brace it with your foot. Do not stick your head out until you feel the air with your hand. If the air is not hot, walk out of the house immediately.

3. If the door is hot, block the crack under the door with a rug. Go to the window and call for help. Stay by the window.

See "The World of the Out-of-Doors," page 363, for fire safety outdoors.

First Aid

First aid is the help you can give someone who is hurt. It's the "first" aid the injured person gets. When a person is badly hurt, a doctor should be called to take care of the person. First aid can make the person as comfortable as possible until the doctor comes. A good first aider should remember she's not a substitute for a doctor. She's just a *helper* who was there *first*.

You can be prepared for and prevent accidents if you know first aid and safety rules. Making first aid kits to be used at home, in the car, and at all troop meetings and outings is another way to be prepared.

First Aid Checklist

- first aid book
- soap
- safety pins
- scissors
- calamine lotion in unbreakable container
- tweezer
- needle
- matches
- adhesive tape and sterile dressings
- rubbing alcohol in unbreakable bottle
- triangular bandage or clean cloth
- emergency telephone numbers: doctor, ambulance, police, fire, poison control center
- change for phone calls

Girl Scout's Quick Guide to First Aid

	Helpful To Know:	What To Do:
Any Emergency	Always call an adult when an accident happens Always call a doctor if the injury is serious. Take first aid kit on troop outings and keep one at meeting place.	Wash your hands before giving first aid. Do not touch the wound with anything unclean, or breathe or cough directly over it. Touch sterile dressing by corners only. Don't touch the part that will cover the wound.
Bites, Stings		For animal bites, call a doctor. Put calamine lotion on insect bites and stings. (Use cool water or a wet cloth if you have no lotion.)
Bleeding	Rapid bleeding needs to be stopped quickly. Loss of blood may make a person faint or even go into shock.	Place dressing over wound. (Use your bare hand if you have no dressing.) Place hand over dressing and press **firmly. Do not** take your hand away until you're sure bleeding has stopped. Raise wound above level of person's heart if possible.

	Helpful To Know:	What To Do:
Bleeding		Treat for shock. (See page 130.) Call a doctor if bleeding is severe.
Blisters		Do **not** break the blister. Wash area with soap and water. Cover with sterile dressing.
Burns	First aid can be given for burns that make the skin turn red, or red and blistered. But, if the skin is charred, the burn is too bad for you to take care of. **Call a doctor right away.**	Do **not** wash the burn. Do **not** break the blisters. Do **not** use ointment or petroleum jelly. Run cool water over a minor burn. Cover burned area with sterile cloth.
Bruises	Skin changes color because small blood vessels under the skin have broken after being banged.	Put cold, wet cloth on bruised spot right away.

	Helpful To Know:	**What To Do:**
Cuts, Skinned Knees and Elbows, Scratches		Wash area with soap and water. Cover with sterile dressing.
Fainting	A person may faint when she's hungry, tired, afraid, or in a crowded area; when she sees blood, or is in pain. Her skin will feel cold, and she may look pale. Her eyes will close, and she'll fall or slump.	If someone feels faint: –help her to lie down or sit with her head between her legs. If someone faints: –leave her lying down. –loosen tight clothing. –wipe her face with cool cloths. (Do not pour water on her face.) –call a doctor if she does not open her eyes quickly.
Frostbite	Frostbite happens when part of the body starts to freeze in cold weather. The skin turns white or greyish yellow and feels very cold and numb.	Quickly put the frostbitten area in **lukewarm** water. Dry gently when warmed up. **Don't rub.**
Plant Poisoning	When a poisonous plant has been touched, the skin may get red and itch. Learn to recognize poison ivy, poison oak, and poison sumac. They all have three-leaf clusters.	Wash area that has touched plant with soap and water. Put rubbing alcohol on area. If rash appears: –put calamine lotion on mild rash. –see a doctor for bad rash.

	Helpful To Know:	**What To Do:**
Shock	A person often goes into shock when an accident happens. The skin will feel cold. Breathing will be fast. Person may sweat and feel weak and nauseous.	Treat all bad accidents for shock by: –keeping person lying flat with her head lower than her chest. –loosening tight clothing. –keeping person warm and comfortable.
Something in the Eye	When something gets in your eye, it must be removed very carefully so that your eye's surface is not scratched.	Do not rub. Have an adult help you remove it. She will know if a doctor is needed.
Splinters	A splinter is something, usually wood, that gets stuck under the skin.	Sterilize a needle by putting its tip through the flame of a match. Wipe the needle with a sterile dressing. Use the needle to lift the skin over the splinter. Slide the splinter out, using needle or tweezer. Cover the area with a sterile dressing.

	Helpful To Know:	**What To Do:**
Sprains, Fractures, and Broken Bones	A sprain is an injury to the soft tissue around the joints. Fractures and broken bones are cracks and breaks in the bone.	**Don't move** the person. Call a doctor. Treat for shock. (See page 130.)
Sunburn	The sun can burn and cause painful reddening and sometimes blistering. People can even get a bad sunburn on a **cloudy** day.	To prevent: –wear protective clothing. –stay out for short periods of time. –stay in the shade. –use a sun protection lotion. –protect your eyes by wearing a hat with a brim, or dark glasses. To treat: –bathe the sunburned area in cold water. –see a doctor if sunburn is very painful.

THE WORLD of PEOPLE

Our world, everybody's world, is a world of people. A baby's world is often just the family. Little children have a world that is a bit larger, the world of their neighborhood. By the time you go to school, you know your world is much bigger. Soon you find out it goes all the way around the earth and includes a lot more people.

There are many ways that you and your troop can explore the world of people: in your family, through your community, and around the world. As you explore, think about how you are seeing others and how they are seeing you. Do you understand more about people and how they live? Do you see more of the ways other people contribute to your world?

> The world stands out on either side
> No wider than the heart is wide.
> —EDNA ST. VINCENT MILLAY

Everyone wants a better world. As you and others care more and more about the people in our world, it will improve.

Your Heritage

Families come in all sizes and shapes. Some children live with two parents, some with one; or a child may be loved and cared for by people who are not her parents.

Grandparents, aunts, uncles, and cousins are part of everybody's family. Yours may live far away, but they still belong to you.

Each family has a heritage, its own special background of events, people, places, and stories. Find out about your heritage by asking older friends and members of the family.

Family Names

My full name _____.
How did your parents pick your first and middle names?

Most people don't know how they got their last name (family name), but it's fun to guess. Do you have a *son, uez,* or *vitch* on the end of your name, like David*son*? Those letters mean *son of,* so Davidson is the son of David. The father's name years ago must have been David.

Names like *Fields* or *Wall* show where the family lived long ago. *Carpenter* or *Fisher* tells the kind of work the father did. Then there are names that show how other people felt about them, like *Goodrich* or *Swift*. (Would you like to have a race with Mr. Swift?)

Have you ever named a pet? How did you decide on a name? by a mark on the animal, the way it acted, or where it came from?

Does your family have a car or boat you have given a special name? Why did it get that name?

How much do you know about your family? What are the names of your parents and your grandparents?

My parents' names _____

_____

My grandparents' names _____

_____

Do you know what kind of work each of them did or does? Try to find out from your family.

Do you know where each of them was born? Mark on a map or make a list of places your parents and grandparents have lived that your family knows about. Are all of the places on a map of the United States or do you need a world map?

With your troop, make a map showing the birthplaces of parents and grandparents of all the girls in your troop. Do you need a world map or just a map of the United States for your troop? How many different states do the girls' parents and grandparents come from? How many countries?

What Was It like when Your Parents Were Children?

Ask your parents to tell about: funny or scary things that happened when they were children? the first day of school? a favorite toy? something they won or did well? their best friend? a teacher they liked? jobs they had to do at home? Girl Scouts or Boy Scouts? How was it different from being a girl or boy nowadays?

Try a troop display to tell what it was like when your parents were children. Hunt for "early junk" in attics, basements, and storerooms. Old comics, newspapers, magazines, catalogs will give you lots of ideas from the

135

pictures, headlines, and news items of those days. Can you find report cards, ribbons, trophies, diaries, autograph books, postcards, stamps, record jackets, ads of popular products, stuffed animals, or toys to add to your display?

Perhaps your local library, bank, or historical society would like to add to your troop's collection. They may even have a place to display it. Or using some of the things you have collected, you can make a memory box, or scrapbook. Have you found "early, early junk" that would show what was happening when your grandparents were children?

What did you find out about being a girl in your mother's or grandmother's time? Would you have liked growing up then? Did you find something from those days you would like to do or try? What was it?

Your Community

You and your family are part of a community. You may think of this community as your neighborhood, city block, town, village, farming area, or even your city. Your family makes an important contribution to that community by living there, paying taxes, playing there, going to school, having jobs or a business, joining clubs, shopping there, attending local events and meetings, going to church, temple, or synagogue, and by helping to make your community a better place to live.

Getting to know your community is an important part of living in it. Helping to make the community better is an important part of being a Girl Scout. Here are some activities to try.

How Did Your Community Get Some of Its Names?

Look at your street, town, city, county, local areas. How did they get their names? from other towns people came from, an American Indian chief, an early settler, a local builder? What about your school, community buildings, or parks?

Make a note of all the streets you pass from your house to your school, your troop meeting place, a friend's house, or a favorite spot in your community. Try to locate several names that are unusual.

You probably will find some names like Main Street and Broad Street that almost every town has. Try to find out how the streets got their names. (Is Main Street really the main street in your town? Was it the most important street when the town was new?) See if you can find out whether any of them were once American Indian trails, cow paths, mail or stagecoach routes, wagon trails, railroad beds, or trailer truck routes.

If you can't find interesting street names, try buildings, areas of your town or city, or names of nearby towns or villages.

One way to find out how places got their names is to ask people who have lived on the street or in the area for a long time, teachers, librarians, the historical society, or the town or city clerk.

With your troop or patrol, make a large map of your area showing some of the streets, buildings, neighborhoods, or towns and villages that have interesting names.

In looking for names, did you find signs that were damaged or removed? Your troop may want to paint signs or restore them for your community. You can also make new signs for streets, buildings, or areas that don't have them.

What Did It Look Like?

If you were a large bird flying over your neighborhood, town, or city 200 years ago, what would you see? trees, houses, cabins, farms, buffalo, boats? Suppose you flew over the area 50 years ago. Then what would it look like? Would it differ from a view today? Imagine flying over it 50 or 100 years from now! Would the buildings look like greenhouses or thermos bottles or be all underground?

With your troop, make an exhibit of changes that have occurred in your community in the past and of those that may come in the future. You could do this with old and recent photographs, or with drawings borrowed from the town or city hall, library, or historical society. Or you could make your own drawings or 3-D models of paper, papier mâché, or natural materials. You might put your models in boxes with the tops cut off, so that you could look down on them—like a bird flying over.

Who Lives in a Ghost Town?

What is a ghost town? Have you ever been to one or seen one on television? They may have everything a community has—buildings, roads, places to work and play—but they don't have _____.

No people! What kind of community is that? Could you have a community without parks? streets? buildings? Sure you could. The Plains Indians and the desert Bedouins have had communities, but without parks, streets, and buildings. The most important part of a community is the people in it. Find out about the people in your community. Try exploring your community.

Go to the hospital, firehouse, police station, community center, town or city hall, jail, farmers' market, and other places to find the answers to the questions below. Before you go, think about what else you might find at each of the places. Look for ways your community helps you and ways you and your troop can help the community. Most important of all, find out about the people in your community. If you know the answer to a question below without visiting a place, go anyway and try to learn something new about it.

- Which door of the nearest hospital do you go through if you are in a hurry to get into the hospital?
- Where can you take old cans or newspapers?
- How close to the largest door on the nearest firehouse is the alarm bell?
- Where do the police keep and train police dogs and horses in your community or in a nearby one?
- Do you see minority people working as doctors, nurses, firemen, and police officers in the places you visit?
- How many businesses, stores, or farms are run by women in your area?

- If you want to buy or give away used books, toys, or clothes, where can you go?
- How often are the largest streets in your area cleaned?
- Where could families go in your area if their houses were destroyed in a storm or fire?
- Where can you get licenses for dogs? bicycles?
- What individuals or clubs are responsible for planning your community's largest yearly celebrations?
- What is the best spot in your area to see at least two kinds of transportation at the same time?
- How many stores and shops in your community have been there since 1900? less than a year?
- Does the nearest jail really have bars?
- When is the nearest farmers' market open?

Before you go, look at the hints in "The World of the Out-of-Doors," page 322, for traveling around your community.

Your Dream Community

Would you like to live where you could go swimming or walk in the woods every day? Would you like to live where you could have all the animals you wanted? Would you like to live high up in the city, but be able to play in a big park and ride your bicycle anywhere? Do you wish big stores or a little store were closer to you? Would you like a long ride to school or a short walk?

With your patrol or troop, plan a community you would like to live in and make a model of it. Styrofoam or boxes make good building materials.

Before you start building, think about these questions together:

- How large an area will the community cover?
- How many people can you have in the area without hurting the land?
- What kind of land and water do you want near it?
- Will it be a rural or village area, town, suburban area, city?
- What kinds and sizes of houses or apartments will you allow in your community? How close together can they be?
- What types of transportation do you want? Will you have some streets where only bicycles and pedestrians are allowed?
- What buildings and stores will you need?
- Will there be places to work?
- Where will children play and everyone go to have fun?

Friendship Ideas

People living in a community need lots of things, but most of all they need friends. A friend can chase away loneliness, make you laugh instead of cry, and make you feel good about yourself.

How can you be a friend and show you care about people? How can you be a real friend to people you know?

You can make people feel important by smiling, remembering their names, listening, or saying something nice to them. Showing your interest in things someone else enjoys and caring about the other person's problems is being a friend. It is also one of the best ways to live by the Girl Scout Law: to be cheerful, friendly, and considerate, to be a sister to every Girl Scout, and to show you are respecting yourself and others by what you say and do.

How about people you have never met? You can start right now! Why not right near your own home? Sharing is a good way to show you care. What things can you share? What ways can you share?

Look at the friendship ideas below. Each one tells about a way in which Girl Scouts showed they *really cared* and were friends to people who needed what Girl Scouts had and wanted to share. Choose some friendship ideas to do and add some of your own.

• Paint furniture at a day care center.
• Make toys, and give a birthday or holiday party at a children's home.
• Collect canned cat and dog food and newspapers for a humane society.
• Collect used clothing; repair and label it for disaster victims.
• Plant and care for flowers around a nursing home or in a neighborhood playground.

- Give up ice cream and snacks and send the money saved to help feed hungry children in this and other countries.

- Adopt grandparents and remember them with cards, gifts, and visits.

- Invite handicapped girls to join the troop and help them to be part of troop activities.

- Make "What Girl Scouts Do" scrapbooks for Welcome Wagon to give new families in the community.

The Wider World of People

Do you know what is in the base of the Statue of Liberty? The American Museum of Immigration has been there since 1972. This museum shows what people of many races and religions, from all parts of the world, have contributed to our country.

You can see some of these contributions in your home community, too. Start by discovering the rich family heritage of each Girl Scout in your troop. Then you can learn about the names, foods, skills, crafts, and customs that other families have brought to the community. You can also learn about people around the world. A good way to do this is to find out about the beautiful objects or music they make and the special celebrations they have.

The American Indians came here before anyone else. One of their special contributions, which all of us can enjoy, is art and design. Beadwork is just one of the crafts that American Indians used to make jewelry or to decorate clothing and other things. Some of their beaded designs look like flowers; others are geometric. Different tribes used different colors and designs. Beads made out of clam shells and woven together in a design were called wampum. Because it was hard to make, wampum became valuable and was used for money.

Beadwork is a lot of fun to try. You can make a necklace, cross-over ring, or bracelet using the two-thread technique. See figures A, B, C for using this method for beadwork. Be sure to use strong thread, like nylon.

You can also sew the beads directly onto cloth or leather. Use waxed button or carpet thread. An embroidery hoop will help hold the material in place while you work. Sew each bead on individually if the item will get much wear (figure D). For decorating, string four or six beads at a time, lay them in place on the article, push the needle through to the back, and fasten the thread. (figure E).

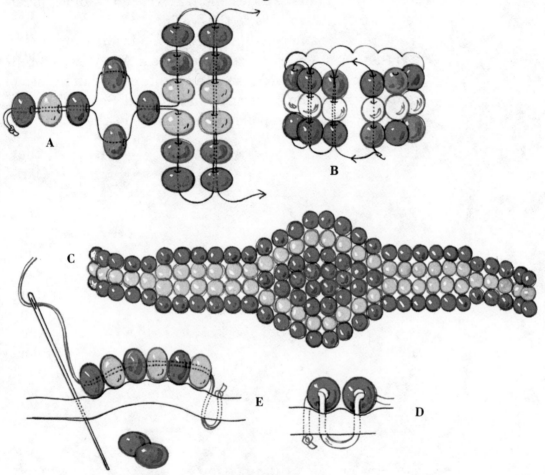

How can you find out more? Go to a museum to look at beadwork designs and other examples of American Indian artwork. Ask an art teacher, or someone else in your community, to show you how to do other kinds of beadwork or American Indian crafts. Look in library books on beadwork for more ideas.

Black American Music

One of many contributions to our country by black Americans has been music. Blues and jazz written by black musicians are a gift from us to the world.

Before blues and jazz, black people made folk songs to say how they felt. A spiritual such as "Steal Away" was a religious song, but it could also be a secret invitation to escape from slavery by the Underground Railroad. Some of the folk songs were more outspoken. Here is one of them.

Oh Freedom

Oh free-dom, oh free-dom, Oh free-dom o-ver me. And be-fore I'd be a slave, I'd lie bur-ied in my grave, and go home to my Lord and be free.

No more moaning, no more moaning,
No more moaning over me;
And before I'd be a slave,
I'd lie buried in my grave,
And go home to my Lord,
  and be free.

No more weeping, no more weeping,
No more weeping over me;
And before I'd be a slave,
I'd lie buried in my grave,
And go home to my Lord,
  and be free.

Oh, what singing, oh, what singing,
Oh, what singing over me;
And before I'd be a slave,
I'd lie buried in my grave,
And go home to my Lord,
  and be free.

Oh, freedom! Oh, freedom!
Oh, freedom over me;
And before I'd be a slave,
I'd lie buried in my grave,
And go home to my Lord,
  and be free.

How can you find out more? Look in Girl Scout songbooks, and read the pages on music and dance in "The World of the Arts." Listen to records of blues and jazz music. Ask a music teacher or someone else in your community to tell you about the story of American jazz. Look in library books on American music for more ideas.

How Do We Celebrate?

Have you ever seen the Chinese New Year celebration with the large, colorful dragon winding its way through one of our big city streets?

Have you ever seen the beautifully decorated Easter eggs made by people from Eastern Europe who now live in our country?

Have you ever seen the lovely lighted Menorah for Chanukah that Jewish people use in December?

Have you ever seen the Spanish "luminarias" lining the roofs of the houses and nearby sidewalks on Christmas Eve?

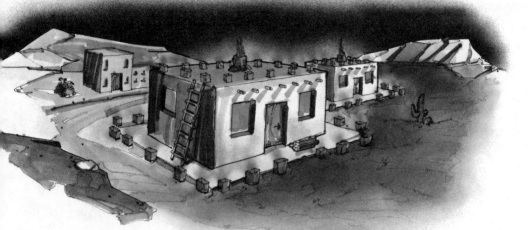

The heritage and different backgrounds of many people in this country add beauty and fun to our holidays and festivals. Many Americans have brought their way of celebrating from other countries.

The Japanese Girls' Festival (Hina Matsuri) is a national holiday in Japan. This holiday, March 3, is known also as the Doll or Peach Festival and is celebrated by some Japanese-American families. They display dolls and peach blossoms in their homes on this day. Many Japanese children make their own dolls and toys.

151

You can make a paper Japanese lady. First try making her with any lightweight paper. When you can do it easily, you might make one from pretty wrapping paper or leftover wallpaper. Start with a piece of paper 6 cm wide and 9 cm long.

1. Fold the top down ½ cm and then fold the paper in thirds. Open it up to look like this.

2. Glue a piece of thread at least 30 cm long in the middle of the paper and fold corner A over like this. (The thread can be used for hanging the doll later.)

3. Cut a piece of paper 11 cm long and 1 cm wide. Fold it in half lengthwise.

4. Then fold it in the three steps shown here.

5. Slip this piece under fold A and glue the end down to the center of the paper and to fold A.

6. Fold over corner B as shown.

7. Turn in right side on fold.

8. Turn in left side on fold.

9. Cut a piece of paper 1 cm wide and 4 cm long for a belt to fold around her middle. Glue the ends down in the back.

10. Cut a piece of paper 7 cm wide and 8 cm long with rounded corners for sleeves. Snip in 2 cm twice on the top and bottom about 2 cm apart.

11. Cut away half of the top and bottom flaps.

12. Glue one tab of the sleeves to the back of the lady at her waist.

13. Fold the sleeves down.

14. Cut a piece of paper 1 cm wide and 6 cm long and fold it in half lengthwise for the bow.

15. Then fold the bow in the three steps shown here.

16. Glue the bow to the tab on the sleeves.

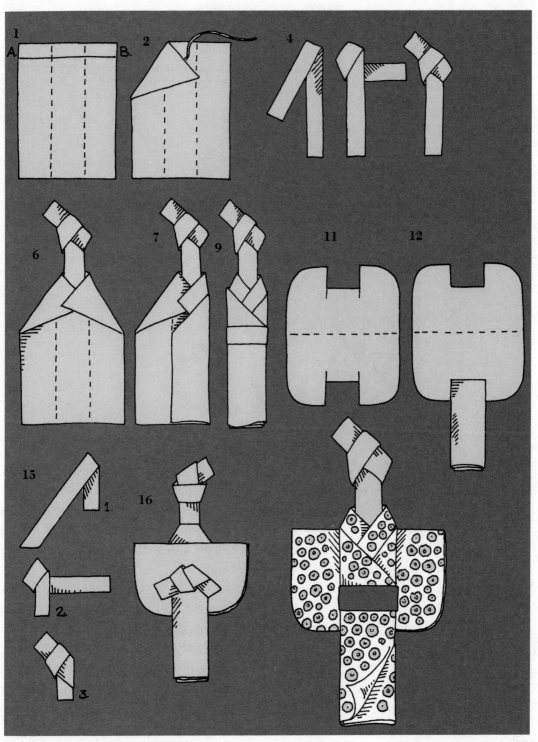

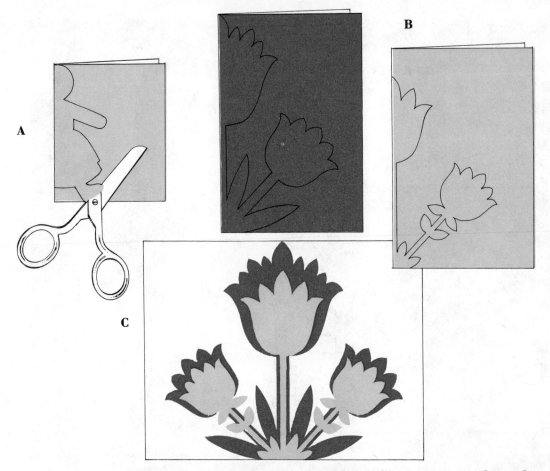

Wycinanki designs are used for Christmas cards and tree decorations in Polish-American homes. These are paper cutouts that are used for decorations at other times of the year, too—especially Easter. Because these designs came from the farm homes in Poland, they often show a rooster, flowers, or scenes from a farm village.

First make a simple cutout with paper. Fold the paper in half and cut your design (figure A). You can sketch your designs first on the wrong side, but free cuts are best.

Then make a Wycinanki with plain-colored wrapping paper (figure B). When your design is cut out, you can paste it on heavier paper or cardboard or hang it up by a string (figure C). You may add colored paper cutouts to your design.

154

One of the highlights of Christmastime in Mexico is the breaking of the piñata. Piñatas are part of the Christmas Eve festivities in some Mexican-American homes today. A piñata is an animal or other shape made of papier mâché or earthenware and filled with candy, nuts, fruits, or presents. Decorated with colored paper, it hangs from the ceiling or a tree outside. The children are blindfolded, twirled around three times, and then given three tries to break the piñata with a long stick.

Your International Family

As a member of Girl Scouts of the U.S.A., you have a Girl Scout/Girl Guide family around the world. Girls in nearly 100 countries do some of the same things you do, celebrate holidays, play games, sing, and dance.

Celebrations and festivities in all countries are colorful, happy occasions. Lights are used for holidays in many parts of the world. They add much beauty to the celebration. On what holidays do you use lights or candles?

If you were a Girl Guide or Bluebird (Brownie) in Thailand, you could celebrate the Festival of Lights, Loy Krathong. On festival days in October and November, you could float your krathong, a little cup of banana leaves, down a nearby river or waterway. In the krathong you would put a lighted candle, a coin, and some incense.

Some people say this ceremony will quiet the spirits who live in the rivers. Rivers and klongs (canals) are very important to the Thai people for travel and for food. As a Girl Guide in Thailand, you might live right on a klong and do your shopping there, on the market boats.

Try making your own krathong out of paper. Start with a rectangular sheet of paper.

1. Fold paper in half crosswise.
2. Fold this in half.
3. Open and fold corners.
4. Fold up one side of bottom flap.
5. Turn over, fold up the other side.
6. Fold in corners.
7. Holding the two corners, push them together to look like this.
8. Fold up bottom point to top.
9. Turn over and fold up other point.
10. Holding two corners, push together again.
11. Take two points at top, a and b, and pull out. Lo and behold—your boat!
12. Push point of boat in about 4 cm with eraser end of pencil.
13. Melt a few drops of wax into it. Then set a birthday candle into the wax. Light candle. Set afloat.

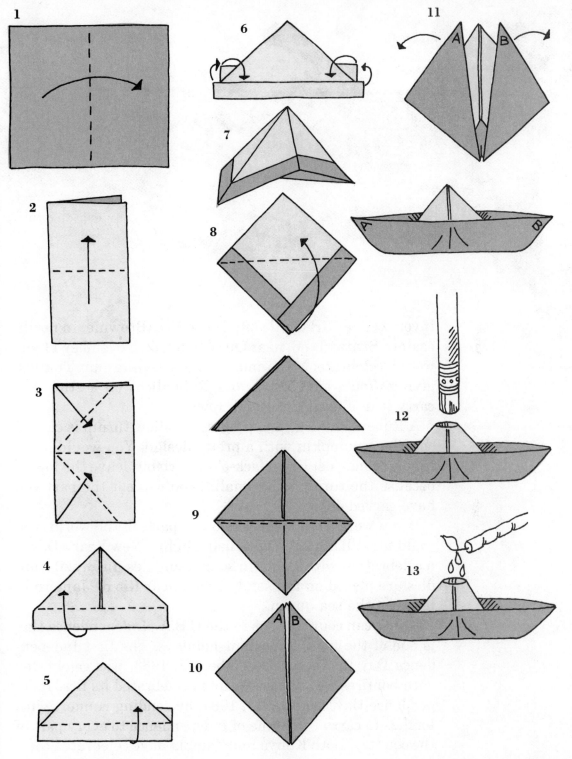

If you were a Girl Guide or a Little Bee (Brownie) in north-eastern Switzerland, near Our Chalet, on November 11 you would celebrate Martinmas, which is like our Thanksgiving. You would hang your Rübenlicht on a stick and carry it in a parade through town.

A Rübenlicht is a turnip light. A yellow turnip is carved out like a pumpkin with a pretty design. You would put a candle inside just like a jack-o'-lantern but leave the top off because the turnip is so small. (You can eat the part you have carved out.)

If you were a Girl Guide in other parts of the world, you could see still more festivals using lights. New Year's Day is a celebration with lights in some countries. In Brazil, candles are placed on the sandy beach near Rio de Janeiro in honor of the sea queen.

In African countries, as in the U.S.A., Independence Day is one of the most important holidays. The first Independence Day in Kenya, December 12, 1963, was celebrated with bonfires and dances. Zambia celebrated its first Independence Day, October 24, 1964, by sending runners with torches to carry the flame of independence to every part of the country. Both Kenya and Zambia have celebrated their

Independence Days since the first one with parades and dances. Kenya still has bonfires like the ones in 1963.

In Moslem countries of Asia and Africa, you would see many lanterns and lights decorating the mosques for the Fast of Ramadan, in the fall.

Which of these ceremonies remind you of ones held in Girl Scout meetings and camps?

Celebrations around the world often include games, songs, or dances. Here are some for you and your troop to try.

If your troop would like to celebrate the Japanese Girls' Festival, you can play **Me Kakushi** (Hiding Eyes). This game is played on March 3 in Japan. One player is blindfolded and stands in the center of the circle, holding one arm out with her hand turned up. Everyone else walks around in the circle until someone stops to touch the hand of the blindfolded girl. When she is touched, the girl tries to grab the one who tapped her. Catching even a finger counts. The one caught is blindfolded, too, and they both stand blindfolded. The blindfolded players may call out directions like, "Clap hands and say your name" or "Watch out, creep about." Whatever the directions, the players should still keep moving around in a circle and tapping the hands of the blindfolded. The game ends when everyone is blindfolded.

Games and dances are an important part of celebrations in Africa. Here's a fun game from Gambia in West Africa, where there are Girl Guides and Brownies. It's called **Capture the Crocodile.** There are two different villages who want the crocodile. You will need three teams with the same number on each team and a long strong rope. Two of the teams represent the villages; one is the crocodile. Use a large grassy area without rocks to play this game.

In the middle of the field, have the crocodile team stretch out their arms to measure the width of the river. Mark both "banks" of the river with chalk or a string. Two meters from each "bank" mark the edge of the villages.

The rope should stretch from village to village. Each village wants the crocodile and tries to pull her out of the water. To get the crocodile, the villages must pull all of her out of the river. If any villager falls in the water, the crocodile gets her for her team. This way the crocodile can win, too! Play the game a set time or until one village or the crocodile wins.

Children in Puerto Rico love to play **San Sereni,** a singing game named after the children's saint. Words and music are on the next page. The words mean "San Sereni of the good life, the shoemakers go thus and so it pleases me."

Action: The players hold hands and skip to the left around one player chosen to be in the center. The player in the center pantomimes the motions of a shoemaker. After the word "zapateros" (shoemakers), the others stand still and copy the actions of the center player on the words "así, así, así, así."

When you sing the song again, other players go to the center, in turn, and in any order perform the motions of different occupations: los carpinteros (carpenters), las lavanderas (washerwomen), las planchadoras (ironers), los campaneros (bellringers), las costureras (dressmakers), los jardineros (gardeners), los barqueros (boatmen), etc.

San Sereni

Puerto Rico Singing Game

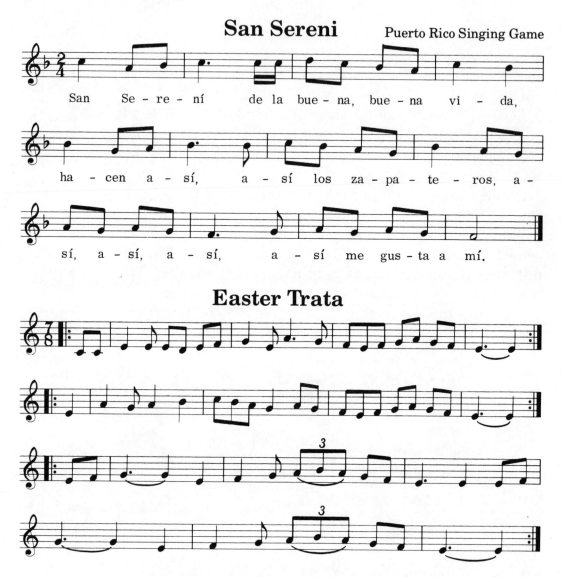

San Se - re - ní de la bue - na, bue - na vi - da,

ha - cen a - sí, a - sí los za - pa - te - ros, a-

sí, a - sí, a - sí, a - sí me gus - ta a mí.

Easter Trata

If you were a Greek Girl Guide or Brownie and lived in the town of Megara near Athens, you would see this dance just once a year. The **Trata** is danced on Easter Tuesday by the women of the town. They wear their best outfits: blue or purple velvet jackets with gold embroidery, dark pleated skirts, bright-colored silk petticoats, gold jewelry around their necks, thin silk veils, and caps of silver coins.

The women cross arms and hold hands as they stand in line to begin the dance. The women sing the song as they dance.

1. Step on right foot forward and to the right.

2. Step on left foot a little forward of your right foot.

3. Bring right foot up with left foot.

4. Step back to the right on left foot.

5. Step back on right foot behind left.

6. Bring left foot back next to the right. You should be a few steps to the right of where you started. Now do the same steps over until the song is finished, moving further and further to the right each time.

African Beadwork

Another way to find out about how other people live is to make some of the articles that are popular in their country. Beaded jewelry is very popular in many nations in Africa. Patterns and bead colors and their meaning change from place to place on the continent. The beads are made of ivory, stone, wood shells, dried berries, wood, and glass. Berry juice and natural coloring are used for dyes.

Have you tried the American Indian beadwork on page 146? If you did, you can use those directions for making African beaded jewelry. The method of stringing and sewing on beads is the same, but the designs and uses change.

Beaded necklaces in Africa vary from two strands with different colored beads to more than 25 strands. Earrings, pendants, and bangles are popular. You might try making some of the ones shown on this page. Beads are used also to decorate articles like fans, fly whisks, and walking sticks. (Why would someone in Africa need each one of these?)

Dolls, doilies, and aprons are made of beads, too. Of course, some of the special ceremonial clothes would be decorated with beads. There is a well-known artist in Nigeria, Jimoh Buraimoh, who uses beads in his oil paintings.

Breads of the World

Have you ever noticed the many kinds of bread in a grocery store, supermarket, or bakery? They are made with flour from grains, like wheat or rye. These grains grow in different climates in many countries.

People in almost every country and in different areas of the United States have a favorite bread. What kinds of bread do you like? How many kinds do you know? What are they made from?

Can you find out where these breads come from? Look in "Scrambled Words" below for each country.

1. Nan: a cracker-like bread.
2. Limpa: a sweet rye bread.
3. Ddeg: a bread that may have dates, chestnuts, cinnamon, honey, sesame oil, radishes, the inner bark of the pine tree, and leaves of rare plants in it.
4. Chambique: a raisin bread.
5. Colisa: a small, square three-layered bread with seeds on the top.
6. Lavash: a thin flat bread.
7. Chapati: a very thin, flat, round bread made of wheat or corn flour.
8. Sourdough bread: a crisply-crusted white bread.
9. Oatcakes and barley bannocks: small, round breads that are fried.

Scrambled Words

1. Rain
2. Deewsn
3. Rakoe
4. Mebilug
5. Rupe
6. Nemiraa
7. Aidin
8. Miaacren Tswe
9. Doncalts

You might try baking some bread yourself. See if someone in your family or neighborhood knows how to bake a bread popular in another country or another part of the United States.

Girls in a troop in Arizona found this bread-like recipe when working on the Indian Lore badge. It comes from an old American recipe for corn cakes. You will find they look like pancakes.

American Indian Corn Cakes

2½ cups corn meal	2½ cups milk
¾ cup flour	2 eggs
4 teaspoons baking powder	3 tablespoons vegetable oil
1 teaspoon salt	

Mix all ingredients until thoroughly blended. Batter will be thin. Use about two tablespoons of batter for each cake. Fry on greased griddles or skillets. Serve with powdered sugar or syrup. Makes about 30 cakes.

The Needs of People

As you find out more and more about people in your community, our country, or around the world, you see how people do many of the same things. People everywhere have many of the same needs—
• enough food to stay healthy
• clothes to wear
• a place to live
• work to do
• others to love and care about them
• the help of people in other places

But we eat different foods, wear different clothes, and live in different kinds of houses. Why is that? Mostly because of the climate and land around us.

There are good reasons for what we eat, what we wear, and what kinds of houses we have. Who would want to live in a house in Alaska that was built for the jungle? Would you eat fish if you lived somewhere in the desert? How about wearing a ski jacket in Africa?

You know from watching television that some children have more than other children. There are people who have almost everything they need or want. Other people can afford what they need to live with and have a little left over for extras that make their lives more pleasant and comfortable. But in many places people do not even have the things they need to live.

Is there anything you can do to help? First, look back at the friendship ideas on page 143 for suggestions. Then, think about the things you need and those you could do without. Fill in the columns below: *Things I Need* (those you couldn't live without) and *Things I Could Do Without* (those you like but don't really need). Add more lines if you can use them.

Things I Need	**Things I Could Do Without**
_____	_____
_____	_____
_____	_____
_____	_____
_____	_____

Where Do Things We Need Come From?

Look at your list of needs on page 167. Think of how many different materials it takes to make a house, or even a meal for your family. Are there any of these that come just from your family or your community? Do you know which ones are made or grown in your state? in the United States? Are there many items that come wholly or partly from other countries? The answers may surprise you.

Think of the foods that you eat or you have seen in the store. Fill in as many of the blanks as you can. The first letter is given for you. In the second column, write down where it comes from—your state, another part of the United States, another country.

Food	Where it comes from
Grapefruit	
I	
R	
L	
S	
C	
O	
U	
T	

World Food Game

One of the most important human needs is enough food to stay healthy. Yet in many parts of the world, including our own country, there are people who do not have enough food. Try this activity with your Girl Scout troop to see how the world's food supply is divided.

To play you will need: 15 to 20 girls, one small box of raisins (1½ oz.–42.5 grams), and one large box of raisins. First, give one girl the small box of raisins, about 100 raisins. Then, five girls may have 25 raisins each from the large box. Everyone else receives four raisins each.

Your troop represents the peoples of the world. The raisins show the amount of the world's food most people in different areas of the world have to eat. The girl who has the small box of 100 raisins has a share like that of most people in the United States, Canada, or Western Europe. The girls with

25 raisins have a share like people in the Soviet Union or countries in Eastern Europe. Everyone else represents the areas of Africa, Asia, and Latin America where there are many people, and many of them don't have very much to eat.

After you have divided the raisins, be sure to think and talk about how this made you feel. Try to answer some of these questions together.

Were the raisins divided fairly? How did you feel about the number you received? Why shouldn't every girl be given the same number of raisins? Do you think everyone should have the same number? Is it possible for everyone to have 100 raisins with the number of raisins you have? What way would you divide the raisins? What does this tell you about being a child in different parts of the world?

This may not make you feel very good inside, but it may help you to understand what it is like to be a child in some parts of the world. It may help you to think about the things you need and those you can do without (see page 167). It may encourage you to try some of the friendship ideas on page 143.

Juliette Low thought about people in other countries, too. That is why the Juliette Low World Friendship Fund (JLWFF) was started. The fund makes it possible for older girls from many countries to visit each other and learn more about how children live in different countries. The JLWFF also helps Girl Guides and Girl Scouts in many parts of the world (page 27). Part of the money goes to countries in Africa, Asia, and Latin America, where Girl Guides and Girl Scouts are doing something so that people have more food. They make gardens, share the food, and show people in the villages how to have good gardens of their own.

Girl Guides and Girl Scouts around the world believe that

people are important, whether they are in their own community or country or in another part of the world. They are finding out, just as you are, about the people of the world, the way they live, and the ways they have fun. Most important, Girl Guides and Girl Scouts everywhere are finding ways to show they really care about people.

THE WORLD OF TODAY AND TOMORROW

The world you live in is always changing. In a few years, the world will be very different.

- What would happen if...?
- How can we find out...?
- How can we be sure that...?
- Where can we find out about...?
- What ways can we use to...?
- What was it like without...?
- What will it be like when...?

Since time began, people have asked questions about the things they didn't understand. People try to answer these questions by experimenting and exploring. Their discoveries might be brand-new ideas. People have always been interested in making their lives better. Sometimes they use their new ideas to invent ways to make their lives more comfortable. Each time this happens the world changes in some way.

- Those who lived near the sea found ways to help them catch more fish.
- Those who lived on farm lands invented things to help them grow more food.

In your world railroads, bridges, computers, televisions, airplanes, highways, and tape recorders are all things people invented—new ways to make their lives better.

Find out more about your world. Do your own exploring and discovering. Ask your Girl Scout friends to join you. Your questions, discoveries, and good ideas can help make the world of today an even better world of tomorrow.

Exploring Objects

One way people find out about the world is through exploring. When you explore something, you are seeing what you can find out about it. Simple, everyday objects can be explored by doing different things with them. Some objects you could try are:

- pebbles
- cookies
- leaves
- apples
- balls
- feathers

Some things you could do are:

- Put it in liquid.
- Roll it.
- Set it in the sun.
- Cut it up.
- Cook it.
- Chop it up.
- Mix it with something.
- Freeze it.
- Measure it.
- Drop it.
- Spin it.
- Pour it.

What happened to the objects?

- Did they change in size?
- Did they change in shape?
- Did they change in color?
- Did they change in smell?
- Did they break?
- Did they stay the same?

174

Try writing down what happened.

Talk over with some members of your troop other interesting objects to explore.

Think about: what you will do ◆ what materials you will need to do it.

Find out: what happened ◆ why it happened.

Would You Like to Experiment?

Another way you can find out is by experimenting. The first step is deciding what your question is and what you want to find out. Then you decide on a plan for doing the experiment and gather the materials that you will need.

Try some of these experiments alone or with your troop or patrol. Watch everything carefully to see what happens. Then, plan some experiments of your own.

Measuring

To do most experiments, you will need to measure. Measurement is a way to tell how much there is. It can tell how much length, how much weight, how much heat, or how much volume.

In this country, we usually measure objects with a 12-inch ruler or a yardstick. But long ago people measured length by the size of their own feet.

Not everyone measures things in the same way. Most of the rest of the world uses another system of measurement, called the **metric system.** It is the way people in our country will be measuring very soon.

In the metric system, length is measured by meters. A centimeter (cm) is one hundredth of a meter (m).

The ruler on this page is ten centimeters long. How long is it in inches?

Practice measuring in meters and centimeters, so that you will be ready for a change to the metric system. You can copy the ten-centimeter ruler on a short stick or piece of cardboard. Then you can make a meter ruler that is ten times the length of the small one.

Use the small ruler to measure your

height _____cm   waist _____cm

shoe _____cm   pencil _____cm

With the stick that is one meter long, you could measure a table, a room, a tent, a bus, an elephant.

Have you heard the weather report when the temperature is 75° Fahrenheit and 24° Celsius? Celsius is from the metric system. Thermometers are marked either in degrees Fahrenheit (°F) or in degrees Celsius (°C). Some thermometers have both Fahrenheit and Celsius.

Your body temperature is 37°C. A comfortable room temperature is about 20°C. Water boils at 100°C and freezes at 0°C.

Using thermometers that show Fahrenheit and Celsius, or listening to a weather report that gives temperatures both ways, keep a record of both readings for a week. Would you wear a coat if it was 4°C? 30°C? Would you wear a sweater if it was 20°C? 40°C?

Someday you will be asking for a liter of lemonade, milk, or cider at the store. A liter is just a little more than a quart.

See for yourself exactly how much a liter is. Make a box of cardboard that is ten centimeters on each side. You will need to measure five squares the length of your small ruler. Cut them out, and then tape them together. Leave the top of the box open. Put a plastic lining inside your box. You have just made a liter container. Count the cups of water needed to fill it.

Grams are used in the metric system to measure weight—how heavy something is. Your druggist uses grams to measure the amounts mixed in a prescription. Look at cans and boxes in the supermarket, and you will see that many of them are now showing weights in grams and kilograms as well as in ounces and pounds. You will also see that it is not usually possible to change the number of grams into an even number of ounces.

A kilogram is one thousand grams. You probably weigh between 27 and 50 kilograms.

No one is sure how long it will be before most people in the United States of America are using the metric system for all kinds of measuring. Experts say that kitchen weights and measures will probably be the last to change.

In this book, measures of length are in meters. Measures of liquid and of weight are in old-fashioned cups and quarts, ounces and pounds. Temperature readings are given in both Fahrenheit and Celsius.

Water

You know water is used for bathing, drinking, and watering plants. See what else you can find out about water by experimenting.

Does water freeze the same way as other liquids? Make frozen pops, and see.

You need: measuring cups, paper cups, circles of cardboard to cover the paper cups, Popsicle sticks, a pencil, 2 cups of clear fruit juice, and water.

Try: Put plain fruit juice in the first cup. In the second cup, put ½ water and ½ fruit juice. In the third cup, put ¾ water and ¼ fruit juice. In the fourth cup, put water. Mark the cups with the pencil: juice, ½, ¼, water. Cover the cups with cardboard circles. Put a Popsicle stick through each circle. Set all cups, sticks up, in the freezer. After 40 minutes, check each one by jiggling. Then check every 20 minutes. Which cup freezes first? Which freezes last? When all are frozen solid, tear off the cups and enjoy the pops.

Find out: Some things mixed in water lower the temperature at which water freezes. Would salt water freeze as

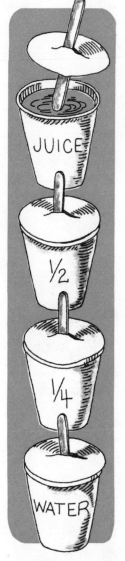

quickly as plain water? Did you ever think about why we put salt on sidewalks in the winter when there is ice?

What happens to water when you heat it?

You need: fruit juice, 2 clear glasses, hot water, and cold water.

Try: Fill one glass with hot water and the other with cold water. Into each glass drop the same amount of fruit juice. In which glass does the juice spread out faster?

Find out: Water is made up of tiny, invisible parts called molecules. When the molecules are packed very tightly together, they form a solid block of ice. When a solid is heated, the molecules move around and spread farther apart. The block of ice melts into liquid water. When the liquid is heated, the molecules move even faster. The molecules of hot water mix with fruit juice faster than those of cold water. Would this have anything to do with the reason why soap works better with hot water than with cold?

Does anything else happen to water when you heat it more?

You need: masking tape, 3 glasses of the same size, and water.

Try: Use the tape to mark a spot in the same place on all three glasses. Fill each glass to the bottom of the tape. Place one glass in the refrigerator, one in a sunny window and one anywhere else in the room. Every day or two, check the amount of water in each glass. In which one does the water go below the mark first?

Find out: When water is heated, some molecules move so fast they jump right out and turn into water vapor, a gas in the air. We call this evaporation. The water evaporated in the warm place faster than in the cooler places. What happens to the water if you leave a teakettle on the fire too long?

179

Space Travel

In the world of tomorrow, you may have the choice of living on a station out in space, with a space shuttle to carry people back and forth from earth. Rockets have already made it possible for us to get started with space travel.

What pushes a rocket ship into space? You can make a balloon on a string move the same way a spaceship does.

You need: a large balloon, masking tape, 1 plastic soda straw, 2 meters of string, 2 chairs.

Try: Thread the piece of string through the straw. Tie each end of the string to the top of the chairs. Move the chairs as far apart as possible. Blow up the balloon and hold it shut. Tape the balloon to the straw. Release the balloon and see what happens.

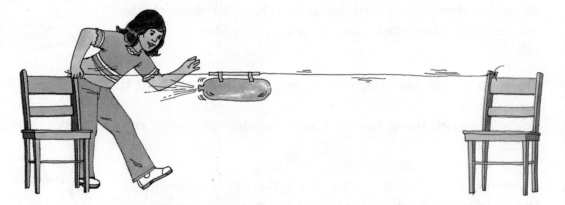

Find out: As air rushes backward out of the balloon, it pushes the balloon forward. The Law of Action and Reaction tells us that, for every action in one direction, there is an equal action in the opposite direction. If you have seen a space launch on TV, you know that the rocket ship goes up in a burst of flame. Hot gases rushing out of the bottom of the rocket push the rocket upward and send the astronauts off into space.

Sound

Every day you hear lots of sounds. People, animals, and machines make some of them. The whole purpose of a musical instrument is to make certain sounds.

How does a stringed instrument work? You can make one with a milk carton and rubber bands. It may not be very musical, but it will show you something about sound.

You need: a half-gallon milk carton, 3 identical rubber bands, 1 teaspoon salt (or sand).

Try: Cut a hole in the side of the carton, leaving a 2.5 cm border all around the hole. Stretch the three rubber bands over the ends of the carton. Make sure the rubber bands are sitting over the hole. Pluck the rubber bands as if you were playing a guitar. Now turn your "guitar" on one side. Sprinkle the salt on the upper side. Pluck the rubber bands and see what happens.

Find out: Sounds are caused by vibrations. Vibrations made the salt move.

Try using different-sized rubber bands. Which make the lowest sounds? Which make the highest sounds? Now look at a real guitar. Some strings are heavier than others. Which make the lower sounds?

You can experiment with other ways of making sounds. Blow across bottles that have different amounts of water in them. Then try making the marimba in "The World of the Arts" (page 265).

Food

If you have spent any time around a kitchen, you have seen that many foods change shape or color, get harder or softer, and even smell different as they are prepared. Did you ever wonder why?

What makes dough rise? Here is an experiment that ends with making pretzels you can eat.

You need: sugar, salt, ¼ ounce active dry yeast, 3 spoons, measuring cup, 3 glasses, a large pot, 4 ½ cups flour, egg yolk beaten with 1 tablespoon of water, coarse (kosher) salt.

Try: Dissolve the yeast in one cup of lukewarm water. Divide the yeast mixture into three glasses. Add one teaspoon of sugar to the first glass, one teaspoon of salt to the second, and nothing to the third.

Stir each glass with a different spoon. Make a warm water bath by filling a pot with an inch of hot water from the faucet and setting the glasses into the pot.

Watch for fermentation, which shows as bubbles in the yeast solution. Check after 10 minutes to see which glass shows the most bubbles.

Empty the glasses into a large bowl. Add the flour and mix to form a stiff dough. Add just enough water to form a

ball. Knead the dough on a floured surface for 8 minutes. Kneading means to punch the dough down hard, pushing away with the heel of your hand; then pull the far edge of the dough back toward you, and punch again.

Grease a large bowl, put in the kneaded dough, and turn so that each surface becomes slightly greased. Cover the dough with a clean, damp towel and let it rise in a warm place to twice the size, 45 minutes to an hour.

Grease two cookie sheets. Pinch off about 24 small balls of dough. Roll each ball on the counter until it looks like a long stick. Shape sticks into pretzels and place on cookie sheets. With a pastry brush, paint each pretzel with the egg yolk and water mixture. Sprinkle with salt. Let the pretzels rise again. Ask an adult to help you light the oven and preheat it to 475°F (232°C). Bake for 10-15 minutes or until the pretzels are golden and firm.

Find out: The dry yeast is made up of tiny plants, so small you cannot see what one of them looks like. The plants give off carbon dioxide, a gas that makes bubbles in the water. Carbon dioxide bubbles make your dough light and puffy.

Yeast plants, like other living things, need food to grow. They are particularly fond of sugar; so the glass of yeast and sugar probably showed the most action. The sugar was quickly broken down by the yeast into carbon dioxide gas.

How is milk made into yogurt? You can watch it happen in your own kitchen.

You need: 1 quart skimmed milk and 1 cup of plain yogurt to get the first batch started.

Try: Heat the milk slowly until a "skin" forms on top of it. Cool milk until it is lukewarm. Stir in yogurt. Put in a glass container, cover, and wrap container in a towel. Leave out at room temperature. After 8 to 12 hours, tilt the container. If the mixture moves away from the sides in one piece, it's ready. If not, wait awhile longer.

Refrigerate your yogurt until time to eat. You can use one cup of it and another quart of skimmed milk to make the next batch!

Tasty to add to yogurt: fruits, maple syrup, honey, jelly, or preserves.

Find out: Yogurt contains tiny living things, even smaller than yeast plants, which are called *microorganisms.* Micro means too small to see with your eyes. Organism means a living thing. The only way you see a microorganism is with a microscope.

The microorganisms in yogurt work on milk to make it get thicker and change taste. The milk becomes yogurt, too. Some microorganisms are harmful. They can cause sickness and disease. Many others are helpful, and we use them to make different foods and drugs. Did you know that you have microorganisms in your own body? They help to digest meals and keep your body healthy.

Magnets

Magnets have many uses. They are handy to hold up notes in the kitchen because they stick to steel surfaces like a refrigerator door. Sometimes they are built into the refrigerator door to hold it closed. Did you know that magnets are also used in electrical motors? Some magnets are strong enough to pick up a car; junkyards use them on cranes.

Where does a magnet get its power? You can make an ordinary sewing needle into a magnet. Then you can use the needle to make a compass like the ones that sailors used hundreds of years ago.

You need: a cork, a large sewing needle, a paper clip, a bowl (any kind except metal), a magnet, 5 small pieces of masking or Scotch tape, 4 small pieces of paper with one of the following letters on each: N, S, E, W.

Try: Rub the point of the needle against the magnet. Move in one direction only, over and over; do not move the needle back and forth on the magnet. After about 25 strokes, hold the needle point near a paper clip. If the paper clip does not move toward the needle and stick to it, rub the needle on the magnet some more. When the needle can move the paper clip, you will know that the needle has become a magnet. (If this does not work after 100 strokes or so, your magnet is probably not strong enough. Try to find a heavier one.)

Fill the bowl with water. Balance the needle on the cork. Tape it there, and float the cork in the bowl. Be sure there is no metal anywhere near.

Watch the cork and needle turn. When it stops moving, the point of the needle will be toward the north. Test this by carefully turning the bowl halfway around. The needle should move around to north again.

Stick the N piece of paper on the rim of the bowl in front of where the needle points. Stick the S piece of paper in front of the needle's eye. Put the E and W pieces of paper halfway between the N and S on the rim of the bowl. Can you figure out which side each one goes on, without looking at the picture?

Find out: A plain piece of steel can pick up part of a magnet's power. Then the steel will, like any other magnet, try to turn toward the north. By floating the needle in water

185

you leave it free to do this. But if another piece of steel (or iron) gets in the way, the needle will turn toward it instead of toward the north.

You will find more about compasses on pages 326 to 327 in "The World of the Out-of-Doors."

Light

We get light from the sun, the moon, and electricity. What else? You can make many discoveries about light. Here are some of them.

How does light travel? Surprisingly, a rainbow can give you the answer.

You need: A shallow bowl of water with a pocket mirror or crystal perfume bottle in it, paints and brushes, 2 flashlights, paper.

Try: Set the bowl of water on a table in a completely darkened room. Shine a flashlight on a mirror or crystal bottle leaning against the edge of the bowl. Different colors will appear on the wall. Look at all the colors of the rainbow.

Each person in the troop should pick a color. Turn the light back on in the room, and try to make an exact copy of your color from memory. Using paints and paper, try mixing different colored paints to get the right color. Then turn the

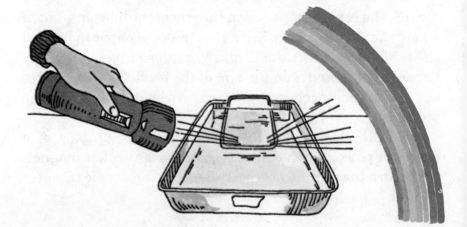

lights off, make a rainbow again, and hold each painting in the flashlight beam near the rainbow. How many painted colors match the rainbow colors?

Find out: Regular light is made up of all the colors of the rainbow. The colors combine to make a light that seems to have no color. We can think of light as traveling in waves, like water. Some waves are shorter than others. Each different-sized wave is a single different color. A mirror in water helps to separate the different waves so that you can see their colors.

The rainbow in the sky, after it rains, comes from sunlight passing through water droplets in the air.

Some light waves are too long or too short for our eyes to see. People have discovered ways to use them for X ray, TV and radio signals, and laser beams.

You have just seen how a mirror can separate light into waves. **What else can a mirror do with light?**

You need: 2 pocket mirrors about the same size, 2 books or blocks of wood, and a quarter.

Try: Stand the mirrors on edge, with short ends touching. Prop them up with the wood or books. Now change the distance between the faces of the mirrors. Do you see more quarters? How many quarters can you make? Too bad they can't all be spent!

Find out: Light can be reflected. A mirror bends the light rays that come to it and causes the reflection of an image, like a picture of what is facing the mirror. (Look carefully. Is there something different about your quarter in its mirror image?)

The multiplied quarters were a reflection of a reflection. The image of one quarter bounced back and forth between the mirrors, making it look like more quarters. Did you ever look in a kaleidoscope? Now you can imagine how it is made.

Is the sky really blue? In this experiment, you make a slice of blue sky in a jar.

You need: soap, scissors, 1 quart jar, water, spoon, aluminum foil, nail, flashlight, and a rubber band.

Try: Cut a piece of soap the size of a pea. Fill the jar with water and dissolve the soap in it. Wait until the water looks clear again. Wrap aluminum foil around the front of a flashlight and hold it in place with a rubber band. Use a nail to make a small, clean hole through the foil. In a completely darkened room, shine light through this hole into the jar. It will look blue.

Find out: Soap particles in water scatter blue light better than other colors. The light bounces off these particles and looks blue. Sunlight reflected from water droplets in the air makes the sky look blue on a clear day.

Make a Pinhole Camera

Pictures on film are made by light. Even a tiny ray through a pinhole can do this. You can make a pinhole camera using a size 126 film cartridge with materials you can probably find around your house. The camera will take real pictures that your photo dealer can develop for you.

To make a cartridge pinhole camera, you will need:
- 1 cartridge of film, size 126.
- 1 piece of thin cardboard, painted black, 3.2 x 14.6 cm.
- 1 piece of stiff cardboard, painted black, 3.8 x 7.0 cm, with a 1.3 cm square cut in the center.
- 1 piece of heavy aluminum foil, 2.5 cm square.
- 1 piece of black construction paper, 2.5 cm square.
- 2 strong rubber bands.
- 1 No. 10 sewing needle.
- black tape.
- a nickel or a dime.

You are going to make a small box to fit between the round parts of the cartridge. The box must be black inside, and put together without a single crack where light can get through. Light entering from any place besides the pinhole will partly destroy the image reaching the film.

How to Put the Camera Together

1. Measure and mark the large piece of cardboard into four equal parts.
2. Place the cardboard, marked side up, on something hard and flat. Use a sharp knife to cut along the lines you have marked, but just through the top layer of

cardboard. This will make it easier to fold the cardboard. Don't cut yourself.

3. Fold the cardboard into a box with open ends, and tape the edges together with black tape.

4. Place the square of aluminum foil on something hard and flat. Using only the point of the sewing needle, make a very tiny pinhole in the center of the aluminum foil.

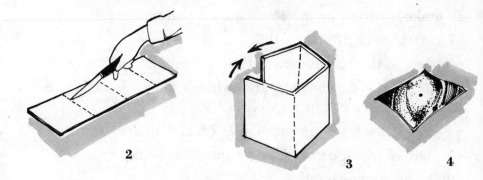

2   3   4

5. Place the aluminum foil over the square opening in your second piece of cardboard. The pinhole should be in the exact center of the square opening. Tape the foil to the cardboard on all four edges.

6. Put the small piece of black paper over the pinhole, and tape it along the top edge. This will be your shutter. You will lift the flap when you want to expose the film by

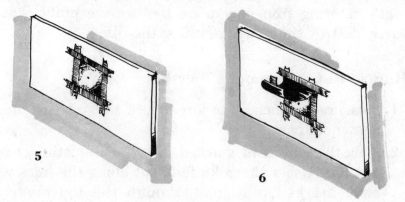

5   6

letting light through the pinhole. Use a small piece of tape at the bottom of the black paper to hold it down between exposures.

7. Tape the separate piece of cardboard to one end of the box. Use plenty of tape, and make sure all the edges are taped together so that no light can get into the camera box.

8. Fit the open end of the camera box into the flat place between spools of the cartridge. It should be a tight fit so that no light can get into the camera.

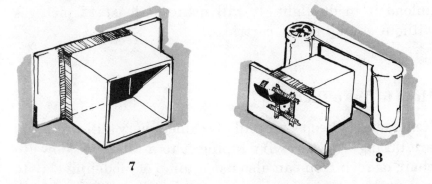

9. Use the two strong rubber bands to hold the box in place on the cartridge.

10. Now you are ready to wind the film. Put the edge of a nickel or dime in the round opening on top of the film cartridge.

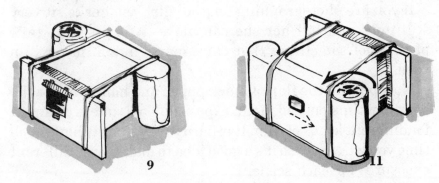

11. To make the film move ahead in the cartridge, turn the coin counterclockwise (opposite the way a clock's hands move). Watch the yellow paper that you can see in the small window on the label side of the film cartridge. As it moves, you will see borders and numbers printed on it. Keep turning until the third and fourth numbers in the first series show through the window. Then stop and take your picture. You do this again for each picture until the roll is finished.

This camera is very easy to use because you can load and unload it in daylight. It will make at least 12 pictures without changing the cartridge.

How to Take Pictures

Remember to keep your pinhole camera very still while you are taking a picture. Try taping it to a table, windowsill, chair, or rock. You can also use a lump of modeling clay to mount the camera firmly on something like a kitchen stool. Look over the top of the box to make sure the camera is aimed at whatever (or whomever) you want to photograph.

Don't worry about the focus. A pinhole camera will keep things that are close and things that are far away in the same focus.

If you are photographing another girl, ask her to sit very still until you tell her she can move. It is easier to take pictures of something that can't move, like a flower in a vase.

Now pull up the flap of black paper, and hold it up for the length of time needed for an exposure. This time is different for different kinds of film. It is hard to say exactly how much time you will need; so it's a good idea to make three different exposures for each scene.

This chart tells you about how long it will take for each kind of film:

	Bright Sun	Cloudy Bright
color film (ASA 80)	3 seconds	12 to 15 seconds
regular black-and-white film (ASA 125)	2 seconds	8 seconds
fast (extra sensitive) black-and-white film (ASA 400)	½ to 1 second	2 to 4 seconds

If you take one picture at the recommended exposure time, one at twice the recommended time, and one at half the recommended time, you should be fairly sure of getting a good picture.

Building It Yourself...
An Introduction to Carpentry

Have you ever tried to build something with wood?

Do you know how to use tools?

You can make many useful items from wood, or you could make a wooden wall plaque, or a sculpture for decoration.

The first step is to get to know the tools and to practice using them. See if you can match the picture of the tool to the description of it.

What Tool Am I?

I am used to pound nails into wood. I can also remove nails from a piece of wood.

I have a handle like an egg beater and can make holes in wood.

I am used to cut fancy shapes in wood.

I have teeth that can cut wood into pieces.

I have a handle and am used to put screws into wood. I also help remove screws.

I am useful for planning and measuring a project.

I hold wood steady while it is being worked on.

I am rough and flat. I am used to make wood smooth.

I have bristles and am used to put stain, paint, and shellac on finished wood projects.

Do you know the right name for each of these tools? If not, who could help you learn the names?

Now try matching the pictures to the real thing and practice using the tool. Talk with your leader about which of these tools and materials are safe for you to use yourself. Which are the tools and materials you need an adult to help you with?

You will want to work with soft pieces of wood such as: pine, fir, redwood, cedar.

195

Steps to a Finished Carpentry Project

Planning. Decide what you want to make, and plan what you are going to do. If you are making up your own design, you might want to cut a life-size pattern out of newspaper. If you are using a book as a guide for your project, read over the directions to be sure you understand all the steps.

Collecting Tools and Materials. Collect all the tools and materials you need before you start.

Measuring and Marking. Using your pattern or following a drawing or diagram, measure the places you will need to cut on each piece of wood and mark them with a pencil.

Cutting. Using a saw, cut each piece of wood along the line or lines you have marked.

Putting Pieces Together. Fit the pieces of wood together. There are several ways to join wood together. The easiest ways are:

Glue: Use a strong glue, like white household glue, to join the pieces. Allow pieces to dry thoroughly before moving.

Screws: Screws come in different sizes, with flat heads and round heads. Flat-head screws are used when you don't want the screws to show. Round-head screws are used when you want the screw to show as a decoration. (There are also screws with a crossed slot on top called Phillips screws. You need a special screwdriver for them.)

Screws are put in with a screwdriver. To start the hole for a screw, you can tap a nail into the spot where the screw is to go and pull the nail out. Or you can start a hole by making a small hole with a hand drill.

Nails: Nails come in different sizes. Common nails are used in places where the nail won't show. They have broad, flat heads. Finishing nails and brads have small heads and are used in places where the nail will show.

Sanding. After you have put together your project, you sand it to clean the wood and make it smooth. Sanding is done with sandpaper. (If you wrap the sandpaper around a small block of wood and hold it tightly, you will have a sanding block. This will make sanding easier.) Start sanding with a rough piece of sandpaper. When the wood feels pretty smooth, finish with a finer sandpaper.

Sand with even rubbing strokes in the same direction as the grain lines in the wood. Sanding across the grain will scratch the wood.

Finishing means adding a protective coating to the sanded wood. There are several ways to finish a wood project. Two ways to finish wood are stain and paint.

Stain: Wood stain comes in many shades. It is thin and can be applied to the wood with a rag or a paintbrush. Let the stain dry. If you want a darker color, apply a second coat.

After the stain is thoroughly dry, you can brush on a layer of clear shellac or rub furniture oil into the wood to protect the finish. Shellac gives a shiny look. Furniture oil will give a duller, more natural look.

Wash brushes with shellac on them in alcohol and then in warm, sudsy water.

Paint: Wood that has never been painted or stained before will need to be given at least two coats of paint. The first coat is called the prime coat. The second coat should be an enamel paint, which will dry shiny.

Both flat and enamel paints come oil-based or water-based. Oil-based paints are harder to use and do not wash out of paintbrushes and off hands easily. Water-based paints are easier to use and clean up. They are a good choice for beginners.

Brushes used with water-based paints can be washed with soap and water. Wash brushes used with oil-based paints first in turpentine or paint thinner and then with warm, sudsy water.

Here is a simple way to make a bird feeder. The exact size does not matter, but it should have room for several small birds at a time.

Make a base for the bird feeder by nailing two or three wide boards to narrow crosspieces of wood.

Use smaller boards (about 2 cm thick) for a rim to keep food from scattering. Hold them on top of the base and mark off the lengths you need.

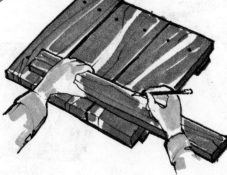

Saw off the lengths
you have marked.

Nail the rim to the base.
Leave space outside it
for birds to perch.

Attach the tray to a pole; use three long nails...

...or place it outside a window, using angle irons and screws
to hold the tray against the house wall.

The World Is Always Changing

Long ago, people had no machines and only very simple tools. Through experimenting, we have made discoveries and have found new ways to help us do our work.

Look around your home. See how many things there are that help you do your work. What rooms are most of them in?

On the next page is a list of some things you might find at home. Which ones can you use? Would you like to learn to use some of the others? Who can help you learn?

- stove
- vacuum cleaner
- iron
- record player
- fan
- sewing machine
- saw
- hand drill

- screwdriver
- mixer
- can opener
- fire extinguisher
- needle threader
- typewriter
- washing machine
- stapler

Talk with other girls in your troop. What can you add to the list of tools and machines that make home life easier?

Here is a disguised list of other things people use. Guess what each one is. Some you will find at home. To see the others, go exploring with your troop in the community.

1. I help pieces of paper stay together. You need to push me in order to get me to work. I make a snapping sound. When I am empty, you must fill me up again.

2. Things pass over me and under me every day. I am strong, and heavy cables make me stronger. Often I am named after famous people or places. People use me to keep dry.

3. My colors blink bright red or green, or sometimes yellow in between. I slow down some, and some I stop. I help your local traffic cop.

4. Letters, numbers, dots, and signs; I print words in clear straight lines. One of my parts will skip a space; another snaps me back in place.

5. I'm real tough. I roar. I eat grass. I spit stones.

6. I make things that look exactly alike (only one or as many as you like). Lighting up is part of my job so I have a fan to keep me cool. You must feed me paper and ink every once in awhile. Just show me what you want, and I'll give you more that look the same.

7. You need a key to get me started. When I'm going I can wipe, honk, roar, stop, or turn around. I can even sometimes play music. I have many different shapes, sizes, and colors. I have lights, wheels, seats, and bumpers. I need water, gasoline, and oil. You need a license to use me.

8. Because my face and insides move, you won't be late for school.

9. When you call me with your finger, I will answer with a ringer. I have letters, numbers, and many voices.

10. I am straight as an arrow with stripes on my side. My stripes are very neat, and I help you keep things that way. I come in different sizes. Sometimes I have only one foot.

Answers:
1. Stapler 2. Bridge 3. Traffic light 4. Typewriter 5. Lawn mower 6. Copier 7. Automobile 8. Clock 9. Telephone 10. Ruler

What is an invention? Machines are one kind of invention. People think of ideas and keep trying until they make them work.

Many things we use everyday come from someone's good ideas turned into an invention. Have you ever thought what it would be like without these things?

Cars: How would you go on a trip if you had no car?
Electricity: How would your food stay cold if you had no refrigerator?
Plumbing: How would your clothes get clean if you had no running water?
Telephones: How would people talk to others who lived far away?

But people didn't always depend on these things.

With your troop, make a chart, pictures, or a mural of inventions you would like to see in the future.

Invention Game

Look around and collect some items like paper clips, paper, foil, a clothespin, straws, bits and pieces of plastic, and styrofoam. Divide the group into teams. Give each team a paper bag containing some of the items you have collected.

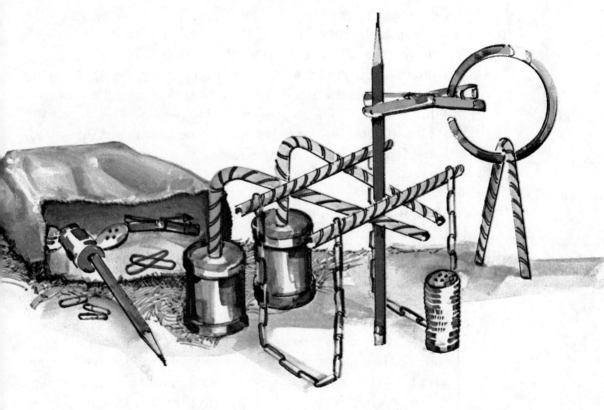

Write out some ideas like:

- Invent a piece of equipment to use in an outdoor playground.
- Invent a machine to take you somewhere.
- Invent something to help you do your homework.

See what your team comes up with—then compare!

Getting Ready for the World of Tomorrow

What do you want to be when you grow up? People keep asking that question. Do you find it hard to answer?

At one time, men were expected to be the workers in factories, offices, and outdoor jobs. "Women's work" was staying at home doing the household chores.

How times have changed! Women now have many choices. You could be an architect, a space explorer, a lawyer, a mechanic, a homemaker, or president of the United States. These are just a few possibilities.

How do you feel when you hear you can be anything you want to be? With so many choices, is it hard to know what you would really like to do?

Here is a game to help you and your troop explore some of the possibilities.

Who Says So?

This game tests different ideas of what is—or isn't—"women's work." You will need a lot of old magazines and scissors and pencils.

The first part is most easily done in groups of about four to five. Each person should have at least one magazine. In your group, go through the magazines and cut out pictures of men and women at work or participating in such things as hobbies, sports, recreation, and home or family activities. As you cut pictures out, sort them into four piles: men, women, men and women together, and a "not sure" pile to use when you aren't sure what the activity is, or whether it's a man or woman doing it. Some pictures may show one person doing something and another person watching. Trim off or X out the watching person before sorting the picture into an activity pile.

After the pictures are cut, go through each pile and write in the name of the activity on each picture. If you find several different pictures of the same kind of activity, keep them all. When you get to the "not sure" pile, try to decide where each picture belongs, or discard it.

Each group now has three piles of pictures: "men's work," "women's work," and "both." That is, you have pictures illustrating what some photographer or artist showed as these kinds of work. What do you think—are they right? Ask yourselves, "Who says so?"

Get small groups together in a larger group to discuss this question. Look at pictures of "men's work" one at a time, and think whether the activity shown is really something that only men can do. Is there any reason why women could not do it? (Remember, not liking to do it isn't the same as not being able to do it.) What, if anything, prevents or discourages women from doing it? If you agree that women as well as men could do the activity, put the picture in the "both" pile.

After going through the "men's work" pictures, do the same thing with the "women's work" pictures. This time consider whether men as well as women could do each activity.

After you finished, did you find that most of the pictures went into the "both" pile? Which pictures did not go into the "both" pile? Why not? Discuss your reasons to see if they were good ones.

What Kind of Job Would You Like?

When she became the first living member of the Women's Hall of Fame, anthropologist Margaret Mead was asked what advice she would offer to girls growing up today. She said, "Try to find out what you can do best that needs to be done—whether it's bringing up children or being an international lawyer."

How do you find out? Explore. Ask some questions.

If you can, arrange to visit someone who works at a job that interests you. Or invite a person to visit your group and talk about her work.

Now, ask yourself some more questions. Would you like to work indoors or outdoors? Do you like to be in quiet or noisy places? Do you like to do the same things over and over again or different things all the time? Do you like to be around a lot of people or a few at a time?

You probably have lots of other questions, and maybe you can't answer them all. Maybe you'll think of some answers and then change your mind. That doesn't matter. Just keep asking; that's how you'll get closer to finding out what you want to be.

Now, you're on your way. You're getting ready for the world of tomorrow!

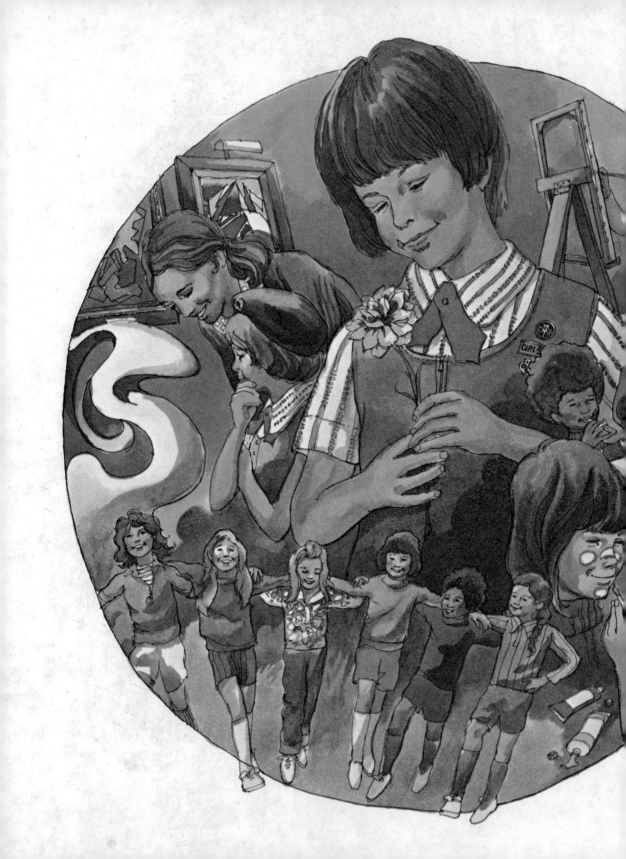

THE WORLD OF THE ARTS

When you think of art, do you imagine a painting in a museum or a statue in the park? These things are part of what we mean by art, but there is much more to art than that.

• Art is seeing.
• Art is feeling.
• Art is learning about ourselves and other people.

Art is also doing. A famous American painter, Robert Henri, said that every human being can be an artist. "It is simply a question of doing things, anything, well."

Art Is Seeing

Sometimes we walk by things every day and never really see their beauty.

Look—

• at your shadow against a wall.

• at a patch of weeds to see how many colors you see.

• at a puddle and the reflections in it.

• at clouds swirling across the sky.

• at the colors of rust on a piece of metal.

• at the design of branches against the snow.

Try this:

• Cut a rectangular hole in an index card. Use the card for your viewer to the world. Hold your viewer up to scenes around your world: out-of-doors • in your school yard • in your home • down the block • out camping. What are the pictures framed in your viewer? Can you paint some? Take a picture with your camera. Do a collage that says something about your world.

• Express the sounds, sights, joys of your world in poetry or movement. Find a piece of music that says what you want to say.

• Listen to music. Look at ballet on TV. Go to an art museum.

The poem on the next page reflects how the Navajo Indians felt about the world they saw around them every day.

Beauty is before me
And beauty behind me,
Above and below me
    hovers the beautiful.
I am surrounded by it.
I am immersed in it.
In my youth I am aware of it,
And in my old age
I shall walk quietly
The beautiful trail.

Art Is Feeling

Art is a way that human beings have always expressed their feelings. Paintings, sculpture, music, dance, poetry, and stories can show happiness or sadness, fear or anger. They all show feelings in different ways. Try to find out how art shows people's feelings by doing some of these things.

Look—

- at pictures in this book. Find five that you think tell something about how people feel. Tell others what you discovered.
- at the windows, pictures, paintings, and building of a church, temple, or synagogue. What feelings do these show? How? Name some ways people of other places and times have shown these feelings through their art.
- at a picture about something sad. Is it beautiful? Does art always have to be beautiful?
- at cartoons. How do they make you laugh?

Listen—

• to the sounds of a train, traffic, boat whistle, birds, insects, or other animals.

• to a hymn or song for a religious service. How do these sounds make you feel?

Think of a new way to say something you feel about your world—about yourself. Try some of these for beginning ideas:

• Create a picture that gives your idea of duty to God.

• Create a picture that tells how you feel about one part of the Girl Scout Promise and Law.

• Make a group of cards with names of different things on them: cookie, boat, train, egg, box, etc. Choose two cards, put them together, and create a picture of the new things they describe.

• Make a mask that shows a feeling; use it for a play or dance.

• Draw your own cartoon.

215

Art Is Learning about Yourself

It is a great joy to be able to do something and do it very well so that you can be proud of it. Sometimes we have to experiment a little to try to find out what we can do best.

Everyone likes different things and can do different things. If you never try, you'll never know what you can do. Some people find that they can play one musical instrument better than another. Some people can sew better than they can paint. You will probably find that you like to do something and are good at it if you try many different things and keep practicing.

Look and try:

• Look at as many art forms as you can find in this book.

• Try to do at least three that you have never tried.

Art Is Learning about Other People

Because art is a language that tells about people's feelings and thoughts, it is a good way of getting to know people.

Can you find out about the people in your own family many years ago? What arts did they practice? Can you find any of the things they made? Is there someone who can teach you the arts they knew? Try to learn at least one art from your family's or country's past.

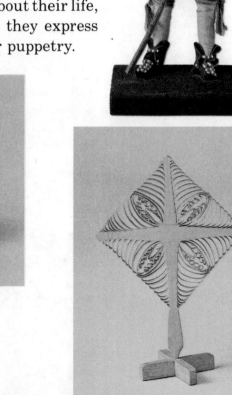

Art can help you to understand people who live in other places than your own. Look in "The World of People" to find arts from other cultures and countries. Have you traveled to different parts of our own country? Perhaps you found that some of the people there had arts that were new to you.

Think and talk about the ways people tell about their life, the things they make by hand, the feelings they express through dances, stories, poems, folk tales, or puppetry.

The Language of Art

Artists use many different ways of saying how they see and feel. Poets use words. Musicians say what they mean in notes, loud or soft, fast or slow; dancers use the movement of their bodies.

Almost all art has some kind of **rhythm.** We can see and hear rhythm, as well as feel it. Our hearts beat in a rhythm; waves lap on the shore in a rhythm; children skip, seesaw, or swing in a rhythm. Rhythm is more than just repeating; it is repeating in a certain way.

Look—

• for repeating designs in fences, lamp posts, bicycle racks.
• at the rhythm made by birds flying.
• at the rhythm of moving wheels.
• at the ripples in a pool of water when a stone is tossed in.

Listen—

• to a poem being read aloud.
• to a ball bouncing.

• to a bird singing.
• to music.

Try this:

- With chalk or crayons, repeat a certain line around a page of paper. Change the size or color of the line. Can you describe the rhythm?
- Make a design repeating a simple shape, such as a square or triangle. Change size, color, or position of the shape to make rhythm.

Repeating something with a certain plan, as you have just done, is often called **pattern.**

Art that you can see, such as painting and sculpture, uses line, shape, texture, color, and space—besides rhythm.

Lines can be squiggly or straight, fat or thin. They can be fuzzy, go around in circles, and look like dust storms. Or they can be very sharp, go straight up and down. Lines are the outside of objects like a mountain or a chair. They also give ideas like quiet, action, joy, tiredness. Lines can also be used to give you an idea of space—to make buildings or trees look far away.

Look—

- for lines in things you see every day.
- at the branches of a tree against the sky in winter.
- for lines of telephone wires.
- for the lines in railroad tracks.
- at the lines in sidewalk cracks.
- at different paintings and works of art to see how artists use lines.
- at different kinds of prints to see how prints depend on lines.

Try this:

- Create a sculpture by gluing sticks or toothpicks together.
- Experiment with pen, magic marker, crayon, chalk, and other items to see what different kinds of lines you can discover.
- Dip a string in paint and drop it on a piece of paper in different places.

Shapes such as circles, squares, ovals, rectangles are also important to artists. Artists put shapes together to create paintings, sculptures, buildings, parks, books, or furniture. Some shapes go together better than others, just as some sounds seem better together than others. Certain shapes seem right for certain things.

Look—

- at the shape of your hand. Can you imagine any better shape to do the jobs it does?
- at the shapes of pots and pans, knives and forks, chopsticks.
- at the shapes of clouds.
- at the shapes of furniture around the room.

Are there some shapes that seem exactly right for their use? Are there some things for which you could think up a better shape?

Try this:
- Look at the front page of a newspaper. Then draw the shapes that the pictures and paragraphs make.

Texture is something you can feel. A feather is soft. Driftwood is smooth. Sandpaper is rough. Many artists try to use more than one texture to make their art more interesting. A potter may combine smooth and rough on the same pot. A weaver may weave grasses, twigs, burrs, shells, and stones into a wall hanging. A photographer might take a picture of a rough wooden building beside a smooth pond.

Look—
- for texture in buildings.
- for paintings that show the texture of satin, velvet, wood, skin, or dry grass.
- at the textures of silk, satin, velvet, wools, burlap.
- at feathers, shells, driftwood, glass.

Feel—
- the smoothness of glass.
- the softness of bread.
- the roughness of tree bark.

Try this:
- Make a rubbing of something with texture by laying paper over it and rubbing with wax crayon.

A very important part of the language of art is **color.** Artists know that color can change the way people feel. Try making up a poem about what colors mean to you.

Color is light. Light coming through drops of water makes a rainbow. See the experiment on page 186. The Impressionists, a group of painters who lived in the 1800s, had a

new way of seeing light. Before that, artists had made grass green, sky blue, and clouds white. But the Impressionist painters tried to use all the many colors we see in morning mist or late afternoon, or on a foggy day.

Look—

- for colors that seem to show these feelings: sadness, happiness, mystery, peace, excitement.
- for color in advertising, posters, packages. What colors do you notice especially? Are there some colors you see more often? Why, do you suppose?
- for colors in nature. How many different greens do you see in one scene?
- for colors in the meals you eat. Do colors make food seem more appetizing? Suppose all the food on the plate was brown, or red. Does it look better to have a variety?
- for color and light together: in a sunset, mist, lights of a city, a garden in the morning, a pool, a puddle after the rain, in a rainbow, through a prism.
- at the paintings of Turner, Monèt, Cassatt, Renoir, Corot, and others.

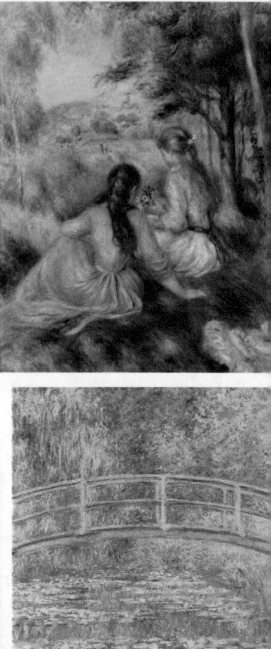

Listen—

- to music for color. These composers wrote good "color" music—Debussy, Bizet, Copland, Moussorgsky.
- to a poem that makes you think of color.

Try this:

- make a color wheel of tissue. Take tissue paper of red, yellow, and blue. Make circles or squares approximately 3 cm across. Cut a cardboard frame to fit the outside edges. Glue tissues lightly in place in center so that they overlap slightly. Glue the edges to the frame. Hold to the light. What color is made when red overlaps yellow? blue? when blue overlaps yellow?
- Make a pinwheel, half red and half green. Spin it. What happens? Make one yellow and violet, or blue and orange.
- Take some pictures with your camera that show mist, steam, sunlight, or shadows.
- Collect many swatches of one color from magazines, pieces of fabric, food wrappers. Mount them on a cardboard and see how many different shades of color you have.

Many things take up **space**. People take up space. Your home takes up space, and even an ant takes up space. Space is an important part of the language of art. Space is very important in buildings and the planning of parks and malls, and in sculpture. It is also important in paintings, because artists want to make you think of space even if you are not in it. Can you do a painting or drawing that would make someone think of space?

Perspective is the way space looks to us as it fades away into the distance. It takes practice to paint space the way our

eyes see it. One way artists show perspective is to paint certain things bigger, so that they will look closer to us. Some artists do not show perspective. Their art makes everything look the same distance from us. To get an idea of art that uses space and art that shows space, do some of the following:

Look—

- at a magazine photograph of buildings showing perspective. Put a tissue paper over it and mark the lines going backward with magic marker.
- at sculptures in parks, downtown, in museums, schools, public buildings, gardens.
- at small pieces of sculpture in clay, wood, stone, metal.
- for pictures of sculpture from other countries. How are they different? How are they the same?
- for sculpture in new materials: concrete, plastic, pink neon lights.

- for a playground, park, village green. Is it a space you like to be in? Would you like a different kind of park?
- at the shape of a stone, a shell.
- at a crumpled piece of paper from all sides.
- for beautiful buildings in your town, some that are old, some that are new.

Try this:
- Fold, cut, bend paper to make it into a sculpture.
- Make a collection of pictures of as many styles of architecture as you can find. Taking a walk will help. Do some drawings of buildings in your town. See "Your Dream Community" on page 142.

The Materials of Art

There is almost no limit to the materials you can use to say something about yourself, your world, and your interests.

Paint, paper, wood, metal, clay, and yarn are materials you may think of for creating art with your hands. But these are not the only possibilities. You can make art of almost anything that has an interesting color, shape, or texture.

There are also arts that use materials you cannot touch: musical sounds, movement, voices, and the written word.

This book suggests a few ways to try out different materials of art. When you discover a kind of art that especially interests you, ask your leader to help you explore it further.

Paint a Color, Paint a Shape, Paint a Sound

Let's start with painting. You might begin by putting everyday shapes together in a pleasing way. Or listen to music while you're painting. New combinations of texture, shape, color, and line may pop into your mind—and into your painting. When you're finished, you might have an abstract painting or a realistic painting.

Abstracts are paintings that do not look like real life. They are just shapes, colors, or designs. The abstract artist may have had a real person, scene, or set of objects in mind, but the way it's painted isn't quite the way it looks to most people.

Paintings that look almost the same as real life are called **realistic.** You've probably seen paintings of people. These are called **portraits. Landscapes** are paintings of scenery. Close-up paintings of dishes of fruit and flowers are called **still lifes.**

Experiment with colors when you paint. Paint a picture of something in your house, but in a different color than it

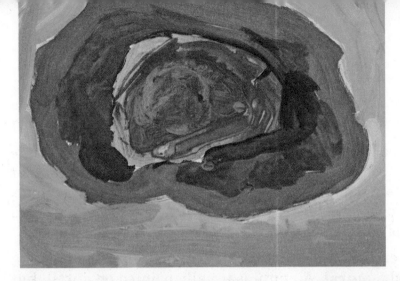

229

really is. Or paint a picture using just the colors you like. Then try one in colors you don't like.

Try a watery color painting. Using a big brush, wet a large piece of paper with water. Sprinkle drops of watercolor paints or food coloring onto the wet paper. See how the colors run together? There are no definite shapes. Does it remind you of something you've seen?

Everyone in your troop can help make one big painting called a **mural.** A mural is usually painted on a wall. But your troop can make a mural on a long piece of paper laid on the floor. Each girl can paint a section. You could paint a long train or a flower garden. What each girl thinks about your troop's last trip to a park, a zoo, or a museum might look good in a mural. You can hang the mural in your meeting place, or make a mural to give to someone else.

Paints you will find most useful are tempera (poster paints) or watercolor. These are easy to use and wash out quickly. Try a variety of experiments: draw a scene, paint a friend's face, draw and paint a simple thing—ball, jar, bottle. Also try felt marker, chalk, crayon, pen, pencil.

The Art of Photography

If you've ever looked through your family's old photographs and found a picture of your mother or father when they were young, you know how much a photograph can tell you. A picture of a girl laughing or a scene from a summer adventure can say something that is hard to put into words. Photographs capture moments that will never happen again.

Photography is a science because it depends on chemicals and machines. It is also an art because it can help you see your world in a new way.

Some girls own their own cameras and enjoy taking pic-

tures. Maybe you do. You can learn how cameras work by making a pinhole camera like the one on page 189.

Taking the Picture

Before you take a photograph, look at your subject carefully. Think about what you are trying to say with your picture. If your subject is some place or something you don't know well, spend a few minutes finding out more about it. Look for interesting designs created by shapes, lines, texture, and light.

Remember these tips:

- Use your camera's viewfinder to see what angle looks best. If it doesn't look good to you, wait until you find the right angle; then take the picture. For instance, you might want to take a picture of a tree by lying down under it and looking up. Or how about photographing your pet at its eye level? Go around and peek through a fence, or climb up on something to get a new angle.

- Try to place the subject a little off center. This is more interesting than putting it right in the middle.

- Make sure no one is walking off the edges of your picture. And see that poles and trees do not look as if they're growing from your subjects' heads.

- Step in close to your subject. Leave out things that only clutter the picture, like electric wires, telephone poles, junk. Most cameras will not focus if you go closer to your subject than four or five feet. If you want a close-up picture of a baby's hands or some buds on a tree, you'll need a camera that can focus on objects that are one to two feet from it. On the other hand, do not step in too close if the area around the subject makes an interesting design and helps you tell more about the subject.

- When you photograph people, try to catch them doing things. It doesn't look natural to have people staring into the camera. But don't have them move too fast, as in running or jumping, because you'll only get a blurred picture.
- Hold the camera very steady and gently squeeze the shutter release button. If the camera moves, the picture will be blurred as if the subject moved. Blurring can also make your photograph more interesting, and you might want to do it on purpose sometimes.

• Take more than one photograph of something that is important to you. You might take it from different angles or at different distances. Professional photographers sometimes take hundreds of pictures to get one perfect picture.

Have your film developed and printed in the way you usually do to have prints or slides made. You can have bigger prints (enlargements) made of your favorite shots. Then you can frame the enlargement.

That Crazy Creation the Collage

A collage is a picture made with just about anything under the sun. Scraps of fabric, buttons, sandpaper, straws, feathers, toothpicks, colored cellophane paper, construction paper, and newspaper are only a few of the things you can glue onto a heavy piece of paper or cardboard to make a collage. You might want to keep collage materials in a box and add new things as you find them.

Try a tissue paper collage. Cut out shapes from different colors of tissue paper. Brush a thin layer of white glue onto a piece of cardboard. Now press down the pieces of tissue you have cut out. Repeat this until the cardboard is covered. Try overlapping the pieces of tissue. What colors do the overlapping pieces make? For a different look, try tearing some of the pieces instead of cutting them. After everything is in place, you can carefully brush a thin coat of glue over the entire design. This crinkles the picture and makes some of the colors run together in an interesting way.

Collect soft and rough and bumpy and smooth things to put into a texture collage. Anything that you think feels interesting can go into a texture collage. A piece of your old corduroy pants, a feather you found at the zoo, or a small pebble from the beach could be put into a collage.

Producing Prints

Prints can be made in many ways. On page 236 you will see examples of different kinds of prints.

In a **wood block print,** wood is carved away. This leaves a design raised above the rest of the wood. The raised design is called a relief. Ink is put on the raised part of the wood and stamped onto a piece of paper.

In a **stencil,** a design is cut into a sheet of paper or specially treated waxy paper. Wherever the paper is cut away, ink will come through. The cut sheet is laid over another piece of paper, and ink is dabbed over it.

In a **transfer print** the design is transferred from one place to another. An example is the leaf print on page 236.

You can make a **relief print** to decorate paper, book covers, stationery, and greeting cards. One of the simplest ways is by carving an eraser or soft wood, like balsa or pine.

Besides a large square eraser or piece of soft wood, you'll need—

- a small knife
- water-soluble printing inks
- a stiff bristle brush or a rubber roller on a handle (called a brayer) and a sheet of glass
- scrap paper
- printing paper
- paper towels for cleaning up

First sketch the design you'd like to print. Keep it simple. Then draw your design onto the eraser or wood.

With the knife, carefully cut away all the parts of the design you do not want to print. Cut about ½ cm deep.

Brush ink over the raised part of the design. If you have a brayer and a sheet of glass, roll ink onto the glass. This makes the ink spread evenly over the brayer. Then roll the inked brayer over the relief design.

To test your design, firmly press the inked side of the eraser or wood onto a piece of scrap paper. If the design is smeared, you may be moving the eraser when you press down. Or your design may not be cut deeply enough. Make several prints until you know the right amount of ink to use. Try printing your design in different positions on the paper and applying different color inks.

When you are satisfied, make your print on good paper. Let your prints dry thoroughly before you use them.

A **cardboard print** is another way to create a design. Instead of cutting away something to make a relief, you will be building up a relief design with cardboard. You'll need—

• heavy cardboard for backing
• scissors
• thin cardboard
• white glue
• waxed paper
• water-soluble printing inks
• stiff bristle brush or brayer
• a wooden spoon
• printing paper
• paper towels for cleaning up

Sketch a simple design you would like to print. Cut the heavy cardboard to the size you want your design to be. Then cut the shapes for your design from thin cardboard. Glue each piece in place on the piece of thick cardboard. Hold each piece down firmly for a few seconds to make sure it sticks.

When all the pieces are glued in place, put a piece of waxed paper and something heavy on top of it to keep the cardboard from curling. Let the entire design dry overnight.

Brush or roll ink over the raised part of the design. Place a piece of printing paper on top of the inked cardboard. Rub

the back of the wooden spoon firmly over the paper. Carefully lift the paper off the cardboard.

You can make a transfer print of a leaf in very much the same way.

Place leaf on pad of newspapers. Roll the inked brayer over the leaf. Pick leaf up carefully by the stem and place it ink side down on paper to be printed. Cover with another piece of paper and rub carefully over leaf with the spoon. Remove paper and then leaf. You can print over and over with the same leaf by inking it again. Be sure to throw away the top piece of newspaper after each time you ink.

Remember to let all prints dry thoroughly before you use them.

Pebbles, Matchsticks, and Beads

A **mosaic** is a picture made from small pieces of colored clay or stone. Many churches, mosques, and public buildings have mosaics on their walls and floors. If you can visit one with your troop or family, you can see how the pieces of the mosaic are put together.

With simple, inexpensive materials you can make a mosaic. You'll need—

- a piece of plywood about 1 cm thick, cut to the size you want your mosaic to be
- small smooth stones, beads, seeds, beans, or used matchsticks
- a strong white glue

Arrange and rearrange your objects on the wood until you see a design you like. The smooth whiteness of navy beans or the interesting stripes on sunflower seed shells will give you ideas for a design. Spread glue on a small section of the

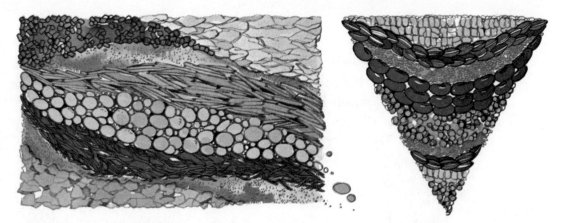

background board and glue part of your design in place. Then work on another small section. Continue this way until your mosaic is complete.

Art in Space

Do you know what statues, mobiles, buildings, and parks have in common? Space. Statues or sculptures use space on tables or ground. Buildings and parks use much larger space. A mobile that dangles in the air uses air space.

Making something that can be seen from all sides is very different from making something flat. You can make a mobile with simple inexpensive materials, even those you collect on a hike—seashells, stones, nuts, pods, beach glass. Mobiles usually hang from a ceiling and the materials are light enough to move in a breeze. Alexander Calder was an artist who made the mobile popular.

Clay, wood, stone, plaster, paper, even snow, sand, and ice are used for sculptures. They are made by modeling, carving, or gluing things together. Changing the shape of a soft material, such as clay, Play-Doh, plasticene, and some kinds of wax, is called modeling.

To model a figure with clay, you'll need: a ball of moist clay, about 12 cm in diameter • a square of linoleum, tile, or plastic to work on • acrylic or poster paints (optional).

If you have not used clay before, push, pull, and play with it awhile. Roll it into coils or small balls. See how it sticks together when it's pushed into a big ball again.

Take a large clay ball and pinch out arms, legs, and a head. You don't need to make a perfect figure. Pinching out pieces from a ball makes a sculpture stronger than adding on pieces. If you want to make a figure, try to think of one that will have a sturdy base. Long, thin pieces of material won't hold up your figure well. A sculpture of someone sitting, lying down, or curled up, will stand by itself.

Once you get a rough shape, put in the details with your fingers or with a small stick, such as a popsicle stick. If you can't finish your figure at one time, put a damp cloth over it to keep the clay moist until you can work on it again.

When the figure looks the way you want it to, put it in a dry place until it is hard. Clay sculptures can also be placed in a kiln, which is a special oven that hardens the clay in a process called firing. Clay can be coated with chemicals. When heated in the kiln, these chemicals will turn into a colorful glaze.

If you can find a kiln to fire your clay pieces, they will last longer. If you can't get them fired and glazed, paint them with acrylic or other paints.

Another way to create sculpture is by carving or chipping away part of the material. This can be done with wood, stone, or even ice. The great Renaissance artist Michelangelo once said that he chipped away the marble until he "found the figure inside." You need a special artist's vision to "see" a figure in a piece of stone, but you will find that some shapes remind you of animals or figures.

An easy way to learn to carve is with a soft material that you can make from plaster of paris and vermiculite. It is soft enough to cut with a kitchen knife, yet looks like stone when you finish. You may need someone to help you make this soft stone carving material. To make it, you'll need—

- plaster of paris
- vermiculite (found in paint and hardware stores)
- a pail to mix in
- rags for cleaning up
- newspapers to work on
- a stick to stir with
- quart-size milk containers cut to a height of 10 to 20 cm
- a small kitchen knife

First, mix the plaster in the pail according to the directions on the package. Throw handfuls of plaster into the water until small mounds form. Stir with the stick. The mixture should be slightly thick at this point.

If you start with ½ pail of water, it should be enough to make several forms for your sculpture.

Add vermiculite, about as much as the dry plaster of paris you used, and stir until well mixed. For harder material, add less vermiculite. Pour the mixture into the cut-down milk containers. Stir once to let out the air bubbles.

Let the mixture set until hard. It usually hardens over-night, but it will set faster outdoors in bright sunlight. When it is hard, peel off the cardboard.

Once the mixture is dry, chip or carve away pieces with a small knife until you get a figure you like. Keep the figure thick and chunky, or thin pieces may break off.

After you have learned to use your jackknife for whittling (see page 379), you can carve a simple figure in soft wood.

Outdoor Sculpture

If you happen to live in an area where it snows, your troop can share the creation of a magnificent snow sculpture. Pile up a big mound of snow, decide what you want to make, and then start at the top and work down.

If you live in an area near the beach, you might be able to use sand to make a sculpture. Try to find damp sand near a shoreline. Bring cups, pails, spoons, sticks, for shaping a super sandcastle. You might even have a sandcastle contest with another troop.

Art to Live With

Architecture and landscape architecture are other ways of using space artistically. Architecture is the design of buildings. Landscape architecture is the design of gardens, parks, and areas around buildings. Architects and landscape architects know how people use different types of space.

Perhaps you and your troop could visit with and talk to an architect. He or she might be able to show you how they sketch the idea and go through the steps for getting a building built.

An architect knows how art relates to the way people live. Architects also consider the whole inside and outside of a building as a work of art. A landscape architect knows that an open field is good for stargazing and baseball and could tell you where to plant bushes and trees to make a cozy and beautiful spot.

You can do something to better understand the art you live in. Take a look at a room in your house. Could a chair, a bed, or a bookcase be moved to create a space you like better?

Think about and plan the space and equipment for a playground or troop meeting place you would like. With cardboard, styrofoam and boxes, glue and paint, build a small version of your ideal playground or troop meeting place.

Think about how architects will design buildings in the future. Build your idea of a space station or a home in the ocean.

You can get the feeling of what architecture is by looking at different buildings. Buildings tell something about people's lives. Look for the old houses in your town. Is there a historic building you could visit? See if you can visit a new building going up. How is it different from the older buildings? Collect pictures, or look in books and magazines or around the town. Then try to draw the different styles you remember. See the section about how your town looked on page 138.

You can also get an idea of the way people live by their homes. See how many different pictures of homes in other places you can find. Can you find one for a desert, for a very wet place, for a cold place, for a warm place? How are they different?

Fun with Fabric and Thread

Much of the fabric around us, in our clothes and our furniture, is made by machine. Years ago, all fabric was made by hand. Wool was cut from sheep, flax for linen was pounded from plant stems, and cotton was pulled from a pod. Then the wool, flax, or cotton was spun into threads. These threads were woven into fabric on a loom.

All this took a lot of time, but people always tried to make the fabric as beautiful as possible. They dyed the fabric bright colors and wove many different patterns on the loom. And they often used stitchery to decorate the finished fabric for pillows, blankets, curtains, and clothing.

Many people still spin and weave in this same way today. Try to find someone who could come to your troop and show you how to spin and weave.

The Ins and Outs of Weaving

Threads that go up and down in a weaving are called the warp. These are usually a little bit heavier than the other threads, which go across and are called the weft. Weaving of some kind is found in almost every country. There are many different kinds of looms and ways to weave. This is only one of many ways to try.

Tapestry Weaving on a Cardboard Loom

In most fabric, the weft threads go straight across and then back again. In a tapestry, some of the weft threads go all the way across, too. But the different color weft threads you use to make your design do not always go all the way across. They are woven back and forth as you need them for your design.

To make a tapestry weaving, you'll need—

- a heavy piece of cardboard 27.5 cm x 35 cm
- a ruler
- a sharp knife or single edge razor blade
- warp thread (strong, firm yarn or cord that doesn't stretch)
- weft thread in several colors (a yarn or cord softer than the warp)
- 2 or 3 blunt yarn needles
- a comb

First, make the cardboard loom. Mark spaces 13 mm apart on the top and bottom of the cardboard. Then, with an adult's help, cut slits at these marks about 13 mm deep.

Now, wind the warp thread around the cardboard through the slits. Begin at the top left corner. Bring the thread down to the left bottom slit, over to the next slit on the bottom, and then back up to the second slit on top. Continue this until the board is covered with warp. The warp should be firm, but not tight enough to make the cardboard bend.

Thread a needle with a plain color weft thread. This will be the background for your design. Go over and under the warp threads from right to left, starting at the lower right corner. When you reach the left edge, turn around and weave the second row. Make two or three more rows like this. Then push the rows down with the comb until they are tight.

You are now ready to start your design. In a tapestry weaving, you can make designs and shapes with different color weft threads. If you want the designs to be close together, bring the different color weft threads around the same warp. If you want an open place in your tapestry, do not overlap the threads.

When you change colors, leave about 5 cm of yarn hang-

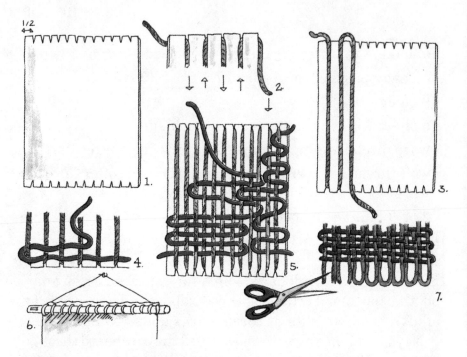

ing loose on the front of your weaving. Start with a new color where the old left off. Again, when you change colors, leave about 5 cm of yarn hanging loose. These loose ends can be woven into your finished tapestry later. Do not pull your weft threads too tight, or the edges will pull in.

When your design is completed, weave four or five rows all the way across, using a plain color weft thread, just as you did to start the tapestry. To finish your tapestry, weave the loose ends into it and take the warp threads off the loom.

Use your tapestry as a table mat or a wall hanging, or frame it like a picture. To hang your tapestry, slip a thin wooden dowel or stick through each loop on the top and the bottom. Tie a cord to the ends of the top dowel and hang it up. For a fringed edge, cut each loop open as you take it off the loom. Then tie the two ends together.

There are many other kinds of weaving. You might want to try weaving a belt on a T-D loom or a loom made with straws. Ask your leader to help you find books about other ways to weave.

246

Stitchery

You can decorate just about any firm fabric with stitchery. Your blue jeans and your jacket might look good with a picture of your pet or a flower stitched on them. You can stitch designs on pillows, wall hangings, and even on a cover for a favorite book. A banner for a church or troop event can be stitched with thick, bright yarn.

Stitchery is an art form used long ago and in many countries. Many years ago, a little girl did a rug in Castleton,

Vermont. It now hangs in the Metropolitan Museum in New York City. Her rug was stitched in the stitches shown here and told about her life and especially her cat. The story of the rug and the blue cat is recorded in a book, *The Blue Cat of Castle Town* by Catherine Coblentz.

On some scrap fabric, try the basic stitches that are explained on the following pages. Someone in your family or in your neighborhood who knows about embroidery, knitting, crocheting, or sewing might be able to help you learn these stitches. Once you know a few simple stitches, making a picture or design with them is easy.

Decide what you want to stitch, and then draw your design in color with crayons or colored pencils on paper. This will give you an idea of what the completed design will look like. Choose your fabric. A tightly woven burlap, linen, cotton, or wool makes a good background. Fabrics that are too thin and flimsy, like organdy or chiffon, or too heavy and stiff, like canvas, are hard to work with.

Choose a needle that has a large enough eye for your yarn. An embroidery hoop, which holds the fabric tight, makes stitching easier, but you can also work without a hoop.

Stem Stitch

The stem stitch is often used to outline shapes. You can sew several rows of stem stitches close together to fill in an outlined shape.

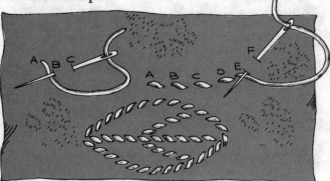

Working from left to right, bring the threaded needle up through the fabric and insert it to the right. Then come out to the left, halfway between where you first came out and last went in. Take another stitch to the right and come out just slightly right of where the last stitch went in. Repeat this. Keep the thread on the same side of the needle at all times.

Satin Stitch

This stitch is good for filling in a shape. This is a simple variation of the satin stitch called the surface satin stitch. Begin at one end of a shape, such as a leaf. Work this one from right to left. Begin at one end of your shape. Bring thread up at bottom, insert at top. Bring thread up again right next to where you went in. Bring thread straight down to bottom again, insert and come up right beside it. If you have spaces between threads, you can turn the fabric around and do the same thing the other way to fill in empty spaces.

Sometimes it is hard to keep even edges on the shape you are filling in. One way to solve the problem is to outline the shape first with a stem stitch.

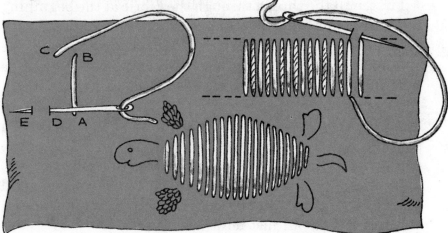

Chain Stitch

The chain stitch is good for outlining figures. You can outline the shape with one row of stitches, or you can make several rows beside the first one in different colors. Or you can make one row inside the other until the whole figure is filled in.

First, pull the thread through the fabric at the beginning of the line you want to cover. Hold the thread down with your thumb, making a loop that goes in the direction of the line you're covering. Then insert the needle into the same hole you just came out of. Pull the thread up but do not pull the loop through. Now come out on the inside of the loop, make another loop overlapping the first, and go back down into the second hole. Come up again on the inside of the second loop, and repeat until the line is covered.

If you pull too hard, the cloth will pucker; if you don't pull enough, the stitches will be loose and untidy. It takes a little practice to find out just how hard to pull.

Discovering Dramatics

Did you ever want to dress up like someone as scary as Bigfoot or as heroic as Florence Nightingale?

After you read stories, do you want to act them out in front of a few friends or a larger audience?

Would you like to write a script for your favorite television program and act it out?

Do you like to tell your friends made-up stories and show off your pet's best tricks?

If you do, then you feel like a lot of other people interested in the art of drama. Drama is telling a story through action. It can be done on a stage, on a lawn, in a basement. Some people even act in parks, on sidewalks, and at shopping malls.

You can act in skits or plays. Or you can put on a puppet, talent, fashion, or magic show. Circuses, carnivals, parades, and pageants are part of drama, too. And you can do any one of these for parents, friends, younger children, or neighbors—at school, at a PTA meeting, at a senior citizens' gathering.

Do it just for fun, as a way to raise money, or as a service to people in your community.

Just Imagine

A fun type of drama to start with is a **skit.** You can improvise in a skit. This means you make up the action and words as you go along. You don't need a stage, a costume, or makeup. All you need is yourself and your imagination. Use whatever you find around to help put on your skit.

To improvise, first think of a situation you'd like to act out. Then think up characters for everyone who'll be in the skit. Now start acting.

You could make up a skit about the Brownie Story on page

49. Decide what characters you'll need, what they'll do, and what they'll say. Then put the skit on for another troop or for the other members of your troop.

Another situation you could act out might be: People are stranded on a train for several hours and they don't know what happened. The conductor is not there to ask and it's dark. They can't get off the train because the doors are locked.

Characters you might come up with are—
- a student who has a test the next day and doesn't have her books
- a small child afraid of the dark
- grandparents on the way to see their newborn grandchild
- someone with a musical instrument
- a clown on vacation from the circus
- a person from another country who doesn't speak English
- a family on their way home from vacation
- someone with a parrot in a cage
- the parrot
- a character of your own that you wish to add

This kind of skit helps you *feel* the way the characters feel, which is a very important part of dramatics.

Paper Bag Dramatics

Anything you pull from a bag full of different objects can give you an idea for an improvised skit. For instance, you might pull a scarf from a bag, tie it to the harness of your imaginary camel, and ride across the desert.

Paper bag dramatics has been a favorite Girl Scout activity for years. Try it at a troop meeting, on a hike, at a camp-out, or with your patrol in someone's backyard.

First collect a number of objects. A cup, a twig, a pencil, a piece of cloth, a straw, a coin will do. Put them into a paper bag. Now divide into groups of two or three girls. A girl from each group reaches into the bag and pulls out an object. Then the group plans and performs a short skit using the object.

Putting on an Act

Plays are usually divided into one or more acts. They tell a complete story. A **playlet** is much shorter and might only tell part of a story in one scene. For that reason, a narrator is sometimes used to fill in the gaps.

You can plan a playlet about almost any story. To get started, look at the story about Juliette Low on page 20. Think about the part of her life you would like to dramatize in a playlet. Decide who the characters will be, what type of costumes they'll wear, how they'll act, and what the background will look like.

Now rehearse the scene. Act out the story and create your own sentences. When you're satisfied, write them down so you will remember them at your next rehearsal. You don't have to say exactly the same words the next time, but it helps to write down something. To explain the parts of the story that are not acted out, a narrator might be a good part to add in this playlet. The narrator could introduce the playlet and tell something about where the story takes place.

You could create a playlet from stories about other famous women in history, too. A dramatization of one episode in the life of Sybil Ludington, Amelia Earhart, Harriet Tubman, or someone special in your town, would make a good playlet.

You can make your playlet more exciting with makeup, simple costumes, and sound effects. Lipstick, rouge, and talcum powder can work wonders, changing you into a fearsome monster, a hilarious clown, or a serious old woman.

You might add a scarf, boots, mittens, jewelry, big sloppy socks, a hat, or an apron to clothes you already have. Paper bags, cardboard boxes, old sheets, yarn, and other odds and ends can change you into different characters.

Sound effects add fun to skits and playlets. A creaking door, a swishing sound, water running, and a scream would be good background for a ghost story. Your voice, musical instruments, and other items found around the house can make many sounds. Practice making sound effects. Shake dry beans or uncooked rice in a can. Knock some pieces of wood or two cookie sheets together. Rattle some aluminum foil. Practice playing a game of guessing what they could be as sound effects. How would you make a sound for a rocket ship, a windy day, or a flock of geese flying overhead?

Wordless Wonders

Another type of drama is **pantomime.** Pantomime is action without words. No sounds, costumes, or objects are used by the actors either. To get the message across to an audience, the actions are exaggerated. A pantomime actor is called a mime.

Pantomime can be part of a play. While a mime is acting, a narrator can be telling a story.

At a troop meeting, one girl can read or narrate a poem while someone else pantomimes the action.

Your whole troop can be mimes in a game. First, ask someone who won't be in the game to write different situations on cards or pieces of paper. Here are some suggestions:

- Walk in shoes that hurt your feet, across an ice-cold stream, in deep wet snow, or on a tightrope.
- Pick up and handle an ice cube, a sticky caramel bun, a baby rabbit, a snake, a butterfly, or a hot baked potato.
- In the middle of a clearing in the woods, you suddenly see a _____. Approach it. Walk around it. Lift it up. Show us what it is by the way you handle it.

• Pretend to land on the moon in a spaceship, and look at a creature coming toward you.
• Toast and eat a marshmallow.
• Bite into a food you've never tasted before.

Put the cards with these situations written on them into a bag or box. Then divide your troop into two teams. A girl from the first team chooses a card and tries to act out the situation silently. The other team tries to guess what the girl from the first group is doing. They have three minutes to guess. Then a girl from the second team picks a card and acts out a situation. The team that guesses the most cards wins.

Plays with Puppets

Put on a play with puppets. A puppet comes alive when you move it and give it a voice. You can act out fairy tales with puppets, scenes from your own life or from books, and even stories from your favorite television show.

Some **puppets fit your fingers.** You can make a mouse puppet for your finger by cutting off a finger of an old glove. Glue on felt ears and a tail. For eyes, glue sequins over paper circles. You can make a house for your mouse from any small box.

Many puppets are made to fit over your hands. They are usually called **hand puppets.** Here are some ideas.

• Make a cat's head by carving a finger-size hole in a styrofoam ball. Glue yarn, felt, or paper onto the ball for the eyes, ears, nose, and mouth. Drape a square of fabric over your hand for the cat's body and put your middle finger into the hole in the ball. Put rubber bands around your thumb and finger tips to form the cat's paws.

• Make an elf from a cutoff sleeve or pant leg. Gather the sleeve or leg at one end and stuff and tie it to form the elf's head. Push a pencil or small dowel into the stuffing to hold the head erect. Cut two holes in the side of the fabric for your fingers. Sew on the elf's face, hair, and clothes.

• Make a puppy by cutting a paper cup in half for a nose and gluing it to the bottom of a paper bag. Add a face made of felt, paper, buttons, or pom-poms.

• Create a spider by gathering and stuffing a circle of fabric into a ball and sewing it to the back of an old glove. Add button eyes and pipe cleaner feelers.

Rod puppets are mounted on thin sticks or rods. A felt flower attached to a stick can grow from inside a cup or a can with a hole punched in the bottom. Felt bees with wings or curly ribbon can fly around your puppet stage.

You can make a rod owl puppet with a styrofoam ball head and a cardboard roll body. Cover the ball with glue, then soak the felt in warm water, stretch it over the ball, and pin it down. Let it dry and remove pins. Cover the cardboard roll with felt, too. Stick a dowel or pencil into the ball and place inside the cardboard roll. Glue felt feathers over the gathered area at the back of the head.

A **marionette** is a puppet that dangles from strings attached to a cross-shaped piece of wood or cardboard called a crosspiece. You can make just about any marionette figure you want from cardboard.

First cut a head, torso, arms, legs, hands, and feet from cardboard. Cut two parts for each arm and each leg. Fasten the parts together with brass paper fasteners. Make the holes large enough for the paper fasteners to move around easily.

Then cut a crosspiece from the cardboard. The crosspiece is also called a crutch or perch; it is used to make the marionette move. Attach the strings to the paper fasteners at the back of the marionette's knees and elbows, keeping the strings long enough to allow for the marionette's movements. Now knot the strings to the crosspiece. Attach a string from the top of the marionette's head to the center of the crosspiece. This will keep the head from bobbing up and down.

Your marionette can be a famous woman or funny clown, depending on how you dress it. Dress your marionette by gluing pieces of fabric or color papers, bits of yarn, stars, buttons, or dots onto it.

Besides putting on a skit, playlet, or puppet show yourself, you can learn about drama by going to the theater. There you'll see why drama has always been great entertainment for people in almost every country. And you'll see the work that goes into producing a full-length play. Sometimes just reading parts of plays helps give you an idea of the art of the theater.

Perhaps plays suitable for your age group are being staged in a school, museum, library, old barn, or theater. Find out with your leader and troop. If your town has a community or children's theater, a tour backstage might be arranged to see props and lighting. You might even see a rehearsal of the play. Drama is one of the many art forms that human beings have used to express their feelings for thousands of years.

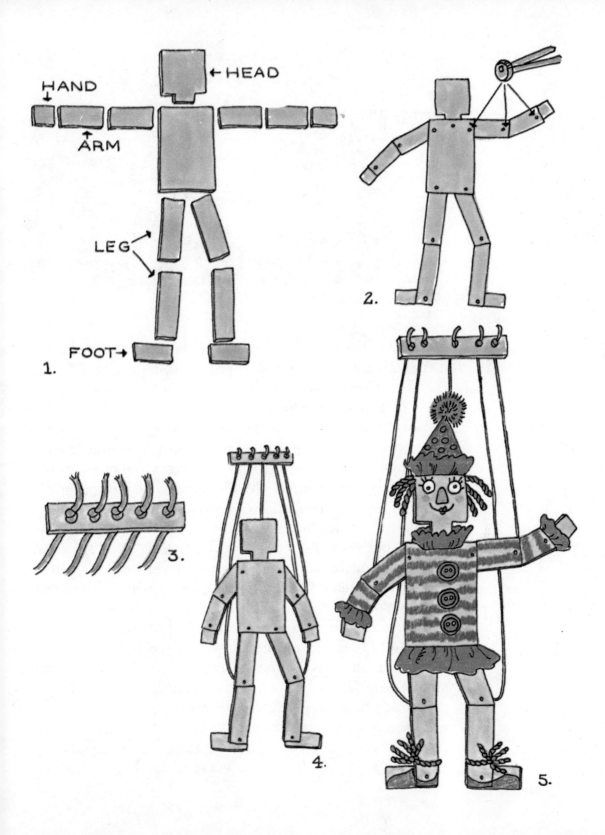

HAND

← HEAD

ARM

LEG

FOOT →

1.

2.

3.

4.

5.

Music

Music, like the other arts, has a language all its own. Since it is an art that we hear, the ingredients of music are things that we hear. Music is patterns of sounds arranged in patterns of time, or rhythm.

Sound is always around us. Close your eyes and sit quietly for a minute. You might hear a radio or television set chattering, people talking, a train rumbling, a foghorn blowing, wind whistling, crickets chirping, someone calling, a bell ringing. You can hear many different sounds.

Music is sound that is pleasing to hear. Music that some people find pleasing, others may not like. Sometimes we don't like music just because we've never heard it before. When you listen a few more times, you might discover that you do like it.

Blow across the top of a soda bottle. Put some water in a glass and tap the glass lightly with a spoon. Listen to the tones it makes. Now try several glasses with different amounts of water. Can you play a tune?

Just as you put together beads in a certain way to make a necklace, different tones are put together in a certain order to create music. Creating music takes special skill and many hours of studying, but everyone can listen to, enjoy, play, and sing some of the music that the artists called composers have created.

Patterns of Sound

Two parts of the language of music are those patterns in music called melody and rhythm. The rhythm of some music that we hear almost makes us want to march in a parade. Others make us feel like dancing, tapping our feet, or clapping our hands. Melody is the tune we like to sing. At times it isn't too easy to hear.

The best way to understand and enjoy music is to play and sing it yourself. Find out how many girls in your troop play musical instruments. Are there enough to form a little music group? Each girl could bring her instrument to the troop once in a while to share her talent. Some girls may have records or tapes that they could bring to a listening party.

All over the world people create and enjoy music. They make music for storytelling, dancing, marching, singing, relaxing, entertaining, celebrating, and praising. Music is used in the theater and in films.

People's language, customs, history, geography—and the instruments they use—affect their music. If you can find records of music of different countries, try a guessing game to see if you can tell what country the music comes from just by the sound.

As you learn more about music, start making a list of the many kinds of music you have heard. Some of the different types of music are: ballads • operas • folk songs • hymns • rock music • choral music • symphony • ballet music • jazz and blues.

Your leader can explain more about these different types of music. When you have heard a few examples, you might plan a musical program of your favorites.

What Do You Hear?

Try to find and identify different musical instruments on records or from live music.

How do old instruments like the harpsichord or clavichord, dulcimer, lute, and fife sound compared to newer instruments?

Castanets, the bouzouki, the glockenspiel, the balalaika, the sitar, drums like the dun dun or the gudu gudu are instruments from other countries that have distinct sounds. Can you find out what country they are from?

Try to identify instruments used in orchestras and bands. Listen for instruments that are hit, such as drums, gongs, cymbals, or tambourines. They are called percussion instruments. The ones that are blown are called woodwinds and brasses. Flutes and clarinets are woodwinds. Trumpets, trombones, and tubas are brasses. String instruments, such as violins, violas, cellos, guitars, and harps, are plucked or played with a bow.

Someone at your school or in your neighborhood who understands music can help you learn to recognize these different instruments by their sound.

Make Your Own

You can make some simple instruments with ordinary, inexpensive things. Use them to accompany your singing and dancing for plays and choral readings.

Beating Rhythms

You can make rhythm instruments to hit together out of dowels, which are round sticks of wood. For rhythm sticks, saw a 12 mm dowel into two 30 cm long pieces. To make claves, which are used with calypso and Spanish music, you need shorter and fatter sticks. Cut two 20 cm long pieces from 2.5 cm dowels. Sandpaper the sticks and round the ends. Play the rhythm sticks by hitting them together in the air. Claves are played by holding one stick firmly in the palm of your hand and hitting it with the other.

Shaking Rhythms

A good instrument to use with Latin American tunes is a tin can shaker that is very much like American Indian rattles. To make one, first find two tin cans the same size. Remove the contents, but don't entirely remove the covers, because they must be taped back on. Clean the cans inside and out, and scrape off the labels under hot water. Into one can put paper clips, nails, or tiny pebbles. Into the other put rice, dry cereal, or sand. Reseal the cans by taping the lids back on tightly. Then tape them together with adhesive tape. Paint a design on the cans if you wish. Play the cans by shaking or tapping them lightly.

263

Tapping Rhythms

Simple castanets can be made with cardboard and bottle caps. Cut a 15 cm long, 5 cm wide piece of heavy cardboard. Ask your leader or other adult to help drill or punch a tiny hole through the center of each bottle cap. Then make a hole 2.5 cm from each end of the cardboard. Place the bottle caps flat sides down over the holes in the cardboard. Push a string through the holes in the bottle caps and the cardboard. You may need a needle for this. Tie and knot the strings tightly to hold the bottle caps firmly on the cardboard. To play the castanets, center the cardboard in the palm of your hand and bring fingers and thumb together, so the two caps strike one another. You are now ready to tap out a Spanish dance. Paint some designs or glue bits of foil on your castanets to make them more colorful.

Beat It

You can make drums from many different kinds of containers including cereal boxes, coffee cans, or potato chip cans. They don't have to be round.

Make a simple drum with a coffee can. First remove both ends of the can. Cut two pieces of brown wrapping paper about 5 cm larger than the ends of the can. Stretch the paper tightly across the ends, and secure in place with string or strong rubber bands. You can decorate the outside by painting it with signs or covering it with decorated paper.

For a drum that lasts longer, try to find some pieces of thick rubber and leather shoelaces. Cut holes in two circles of rubber. Lace tightly to stretch drumheads as tight as possible.

Strike It

Here is an instrument that you might want to ask an adult to help you make. It is a three-note marimba, which is a type of xylophone. Three pieces of wood, each a different length and a different note, will be attached to a clothesline and played with a mallet. You'll need—

- a piece of wood approximately 90 cm long sawed into three pieces, all 2.5 cm deep and 5 cm wide
- 77 cm of clothesline
- a 30 cm long piece of 6 mm dowel and a large wooden bead for a mallet
- a saw
- small nails just over 2.5 cm long
- a ruler
- white casein type glue
- a pencil

Saw one piece of wood approximately 30 cm. Hold it loosely and tap with your mallet. It should sound like the C note on a piano or pitchpipe. If it's too low, sand off a little.

Saw the second piece of wood to a little more than 29 cm. Tap as before. This should sound like D.

Saw the third piece 28 cm. This should sound like E.

Arrange the pieces of wood in order C, D, and E. You can make a whole scale by cutting smaller and smaller pieces of wood to make higher notes.

Put a mark on each piece of wood about 10 cm in from each end. This is your guide for placing the clothesline. Lay the clothesline on these marks. Go up one side first. Nail the clothesline to the wood with small nails. Leave a loop at the top, then come down the other side, nailing the clothesline to the wood.

Your three-note marimba is now ready to be played. You can tap out simple melodies with one or two mallets. To play, hang it on a hook, hold it in your hand, or lay it on a table.

Can you figure out why the different lengths of wood create different sounds? What else can you make this way? How about different lengths of metal pipe? See page 181 for an experiment on sound.

Some girls in your troop may play instruments such as the flute, recorder, drums, piano, or guitar. Use these or your homemade instruments or inexpensive instruments like a tonette, a flutophone, or an Autoharp, to accompany your troop singing, or put together your own combo.

Music to Sing

Did you know you carry one musical instrument all the time? It is your voice and you can take it anywhere. Girl Scouts sing together at troop meetings, on hikes, and at campfires. One of the highlights girls always report at a big Girl Scout gathering is the singing. They often sing in parts. There are different ways of singing in parts. Everyone may sing the same song, but with small groups starting at different times. Sometimes the singers start at the same time, but some sing at higher and some at lower levels.

When you are learning to sing in parts, you should start with simple songs and work up to more difficult songs.

A good song to start with is "Bingo," an old folk song that has been sung by children for many years. The troop sings it all together.

"Bingo" can be an action song. Ask a girl who has been to Girl Scout camp to show you the actions that go with the song.

Bingo

Mar-y had a lit-tle dog and Bin-go was his name, Sir.

B - I - N - G - O   B - I - N - G - O

B - I - N - G - O   Bin-go was his name, Sir.

Allelujah
Two-part Round

Go on to a round, something a little more difficult. In a round, voices follow each other around and around singing the same melody. There are two-, three-, four-, or even 16-part rounds. Rounds are a first step in learning harmony. To get the idea, start with a two-part round. "Allelujah" is an old round that is often sung as a grace.

Now try a three-part round with "Music Shall Live." You can play a guitar with it. Begin each part where the numbers are. The letters show which chords to play.

Music Shall Live
Three-part Round

Try this two-part song. It's an easy version of music in a famous opera called "The Magic Flute."

Sweet Music Enchanting

from "The Magic Flute"

English version by
J.E.T.

W.A. MOZART
(1756–1791)

Sweet_ mu - sic en - chant - ing falls_ soft on the ear: La ra la, la la, la, ra, la, la, la, la, ra, la! It_ ban - ish - es trou - ble, our cares dis - ap - pear. La ra la, la, la, la ra la ra, la, la ra la! It_ la!

After you've sung several two-part songs, you'll begin to hear the harmony. Try this old Girl Scout favorite—"Each Campfire Lights Anew." Try to make up some harmony of your own. The song expresses the love of camping and joy of friends together that Girl Scouts share.

Each Campfire Lights Anew

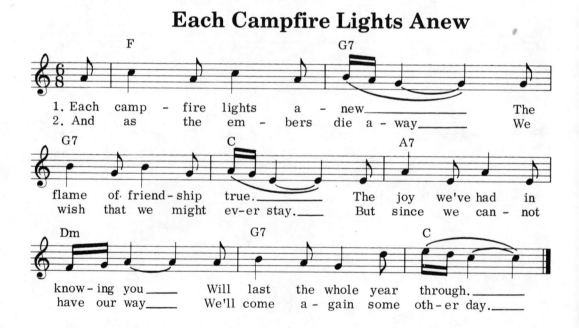

1. Each camp - fire lights a - new_____ The flame of· friend - ship true._____ The joy we've had in know - ing you_____ Will last the whole year through._____

2. And as the em - bers die a - way_____ We wish that we might ev - er stay.____ But since we can - not have our way_____ We'll come a - gain some oth - er day.____

"Early One Morning" is a 300-year-old song that can be sung just as melody alone. You can also add the higher melody (the descant) and an alto.

Turn to pages 33 and 37 in "Girl Scouting Is..." and page 149 in "The World of People" for more songs to try.

Early One Morning

Not too fast

Old English

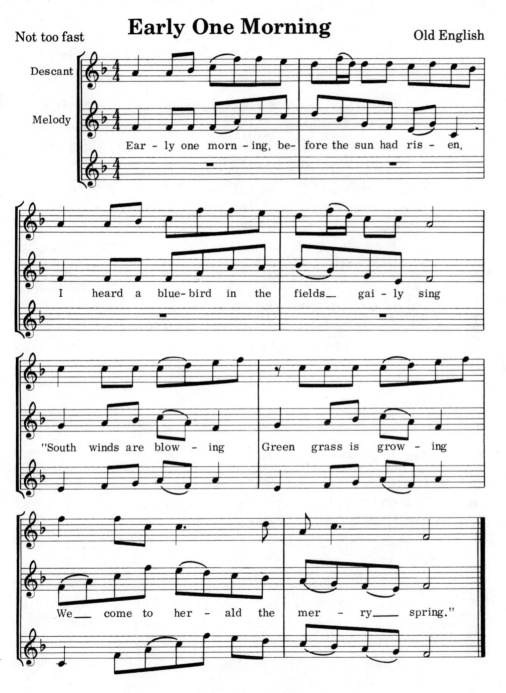

Descant

Melody

Ear - ly one morn - ing, be- fore the sun had ris - en,

I heard a blue-bird in the fields__ gai - ly sing

"South winds are blow - ing Green grass is grow - ing

We__ come to her - ald the mer - ry__ spring."

2. One autumn afternoon, just as the sun was setting,
   I heard a bluebird on a tree pipe a song
   "Farewell! We're going, Cold winds are blowing.
   But we'll be back when the days grow long."

Dance Awhile

Glide back and forth like a panther in a cage. Leap into the air like a grasshopper. Twirl around and around like a top.

Movements like these have been put together for thousands of years to create dances that tell about people's feelings. Space and human bodies are the ingredients for dance. You can think of dance as a pattern in space.

From ancient pictures we know that nature inspired the first dances. People imitated the running of animals, the falling of rain, and the rippling action of wind. But these pictures cannot tell us exactly what the dance movements looked like or what the music sounded like. Only where there was a school or religious group that kept the dances alive do we know exactly how a dance was done. We now use films and tapes to record the movements of a dance and the music played with it. There is also a way of writing down a dance.

The Dances People Do

In almost every country, there are traditional dances called folk dances that people do for special holidays and events and just for fun. Folk dances change slowly over the years. In Asia, for example, some dances are still done the same way as they were 2,000 years ago.

Now people are becoming interested in saving folk dances. Often there are annual festivals in communities where you can see and hear lovely folk dances and songs of many different peoples and countries. Try to go to a festival with your troop. Ask someone to teach your troop some of these different dances.

Most folk dances of the United States and Europe are danced by groups of people in squares (square dances), in circles (round dances), or in two rows facing each other

(longways sets). "Bow Belinda" is an example of an American folk dance that is a longways set. For a lively time, sing the tune and clap your hands as you dance.

Try the dance in "The World of People," page 162. Today's popular dances say as much about the twentieth century as folk dances do about past times. What dances do you like?

You or your friends might be learning ballet, tap, modern, oriental, or musical theater dances at school or at a dance studio. These are done mostly for stage presentations.

Bow Belinda

American

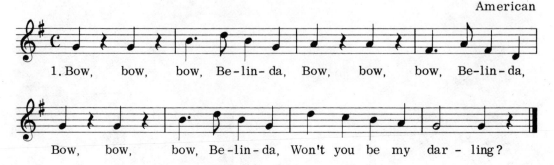

1. Bow, bow, bow, Be-lin-da, Bow, bow, bow, Be-lin-da,

Bow, bow, bow, Be-lin-da, Won't you be my dar-ling?

2. Right hand up, O Belinda, etc.
3. Left hand up, O Belinda, etc.
4. Both hands up, O Belinda, etc.
5. Shake that big foot, shy all 'round her, etc.
6. Promenade all, O Belinda, etc.

Formation:
Longways sets of about six couples, men on left, women on right. Partners face, and there should be five or six feet between the lines.

Figure 1:
Top man and bottom woman advance to center, bow, step back to place; top woman and bottom man do the same.

Figure 2:
Top man and bottom woman advance, join right hands, turn in place and retire; top woman and bottom man do the same.

Figure 3:
As above with left hand.

Figure 4:
As above with both hands.

Figure 5:
Same couples, with arms crossed on chest, advance to center, pass right shoulders and go around each other clockwise, back to back.

Figure 6:
With hands crossed in skating position, all skip and cast off to the left, headed by top couple who make an arch at the bottom under which other dancers pass; the second couple will now be at the top.

Repeat till all have been at the top.

Learning More

There are a lot of things you can do to understand dance better. You can learn more by attending a ballet or modern dance performance. It's also fun to know the stories of ballets such as "Swan Lake," "Giselle," and "The Nutcracker." Try to find out about such dancers as Isadora Duncan, Martha Graham, Margot Fonteyn, Judith Jamison. Discover what they and other dancers have done. Invite a dancer to talk to your troop and to demonstrate different dances. Also, girls in your troop who take dance lessons might put on a talent show.

You can even create a dance yourself. First, listen to several different kinds of dance music. What motions do they make you think of? Decide on a favorite piece of music, and think of different motions to go with the different sounds. Try to dance them yourself, or try being a choreographer. A choreographer is a person who thinks of different movements and arranges them into a whole dance. When the dance is worked out in space, it can be written down for other dancers to do.

The Wonderful World of Words

Because you use them all the time, you may forget that words belong in the world of art, too. In books, poems, and plays writers use words to tell others about things they've seen, emotions they've felt, and ideas they've thought.

The Joy of Books

Someone once said that books are like friends—and they truly are! Just think—books can take you places you've never been; introduce you to people you've never met; tell you about things you never heard of; and give you hours of fun, enjoyment, excitement, or just quiet entertainment.

There are all kinds of books for everyone to enjoy—mysteries, adventure stories, animal stories, poetry, historical stories, stories of famous people, how-to books, cookbooks, picture books—something for every age and interest. About 500 years ago, books were so rare and special that only kings and nobles had them. Before the printing press was made, every book was written, illustrated, and put together by hand. Books are still precious, but now machines can print and bind books so that more people can afford them.

It is nice to have books of your own, but if you don't, there are libraries where you can read and borrow books. Learning how to use a library is important so that you can find the books you want. Most libraries are set up the same way. If you move from Kansas to Florida, the library will still have cards to tell you the names of books and who wrote them and a number to tell you where a book is located. Sometimes the library is far away and books come once in a while to different towns in a bookmobile or traveling van.

You could start your own troop lending library. Have a book roundup. See if you can round up (collect) from friends,

family, neighbors, other girls in the troop, books that people will lend or give to the troop. Make a list of books and cards for checking in and out, and set up your library in a troop meeting room, or at school, or in someone's home. After several girls have read a book, you can have a book discussion or act out skits for other girls. What was it about? Who were the main characters? What did you like about it?

Here's another way to share books. Each girl makes a list of her favorite stories to share with other troop members. Then girls can make a list of books they would like to read. You might take turns reading aloud some of these favorite stories at troop meetings.

Write It Down

You don't just have to read or listen to other people's words. You can try writing yourself. Here are some ideas:

- Write a news article about an activity your troop did and send it to the editor of the Girl Scout council newsletter or bulletin.
- Write a piece for the local newspaper or school newspaper about something important to your school or community. It could be the problem of litter, an old building that your troop feels is worth saving, or a story about a person important to the community.
- Together with a few girls from your troop and another troop, publish a neighborhood troops' newspaper.
- Create a book about your neighborhood. Write about people, places of interest, trees, flowers, or anything you think is interesting. Include writings by different girls, drawings, and photographs. Finish it off with a decorative cover. The book might be lent to someone who is confined to home or given to a new family moving to the neighborhood.
- Write a booklet about yourself, your family, your friends, your home, your pets, and your favorite things. Include photographs and drawings and items, such as a pressed leaf or a ticket stub, that remind you of something special.
- Put together a book of poems written by members of your troop.

Pen a Poem

Poems can give a special meaning to everyday experiences. To write a poem, first think of an incident, object, or person you would like to tell others about. Then try to find words that create sharp pictures in your mind to explain your idea. Write them down in an order you think fits what you're trying to say.

Like music, poetry has rhythm. Reading poetry aloud helps you feel the rhythm or beat better. Many poems rhyme. This means that the words at the end of different lines sound alike. Cat and hat rhyme.

Read these poems to find out how rhythm and rhyme work and to get an idea of how to write a poem yourself.

Cat

The black cat yawns,
Opens her jaws,
Stretches her legs,
And shows her claws.
Then she gets up
And stands on four
Long stiff legs
And yawns some more.
—DOROTHY BARUCH

Only My Opinion

Is a caterpillar ticklish?
Well, it's always my belief
That he giggles, as he wiggles
Across a hairy leaf.
—MONICA SHANNON

A limerick is a poem that tells a silly story. All limericks have the same pattern of rhyme and rhythm. Read this one aloud.

Limerick

There was an old lady whose chin
Resembled the point of pin;
So she had it made sharp, and purchased a harp,
And played several tunes with her chin.

—EDWARD LEAR

Words can be used in unusual ways. Listen to these poems with made-up words. They don't always make sense, but the poems still have a catchy sound.

Jabberwocky

'Twas brillig and the slithy toves
Did gyre and gimble in the wabe;
All mimsy were the borogoves,
And the mome raths outgrabe.

—LEWIS CARROLL

If I Ran The Zoo

A zoo should have bugs
So I'll capture a thwerll
Whose legs are snarled up in a terrible snerl
And then I'll go out and I'll capture some chuggs,
Some keen-shooter, mean-shooter, bean-shooter bugs.

—DR. SEUSS

In Japan, short poems called haikus have been written for thousands of years. They often describe something in nature.

Lilies

I thought I saw white clouds, but no!—
Bending across the fence,
White lilies in a row!

—SHIKO

"Where Go The Boats" is a longer poem about nature. Notice how these lines have the smooth, flowing movement of a quiet river. It is a good poem to read aloud at a ceremony. In "The World of People," page 156, there is a ceremony from Thailand using paper boats. This might be a good song or poem to use with that ceremony. You will find the music for it in the *Girl Scout Pocket Songbook*.

Where Go The Boats

Dark brown is the river
Golden is the sand
It flows along forever,
With trees on either hand.

Green leaves a-floating,
Castles of the foam,
Boats of mine a-boating—
Where will all come home?

On goes the river
And out past the mill,
Away down the valley,
Away down the hill.

Away down the river
A hundred miles or more
Other little children
Shall bring my boats ashore.
—ROBERT LOUIS STEVENSON

You might want to set aside some time during your troop meeting or a ceremony for reading poems you or other people have written. You could also create a book of poems written by members of your troop.

A Book You Can Make

If you were to visit a library that had old and rare books, you would see the most beautiful works of art. Some books had leather covers with gold and other metals pressed into them. Others had embroidered or painted covers. Some books even had real jewels in their covers. And the pages, which had colorful drawings in the capital letters and margins, were as beautiful as their covers. Beautiful books are still being made.

You can make your own booklet and decorate it. Try this one first.

Fold in half two or three sheets of paper the same size. Cut decorated paper slightly heavier, or plain colored paper, the same size. Fold in half for the cover. Staple these together or sew as shown.

Next try a little more advanced booklet.

For a 12.5 cm × 17.5 cm booklet, you'll need—
- 2 pieces of 17.5 cm × 30 cm color construction paper
- 2 pieces of 12.5 cm × 17.5 cm cardboard
- 2 pieces of 12.5 cm × 30 cm color construction paper
- 1 piece of 12.5 cm × 17.5 cm color construction paper
- 4 or 8 pieces of 17 cm × 24.5 cm white bond paper
- 1 piece of 17.5 cm × 22.5 cm color construction paper
- stapler

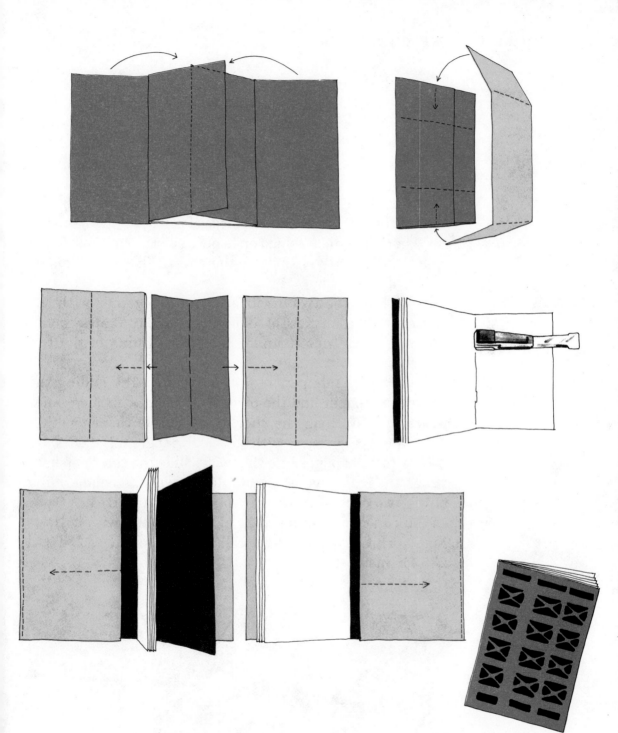

First make the covers. Place the 12.5 cm × 17.5 cm pieces of cardboard in the center of the 17.5 cm × 30 cm pieces of color paper with the 17.5 cm sides of both going in the same direction. Fold in the ends of the paper 6.5 cm around the cardboard. The side where the fold meets is the inside of the cover.

Now make a liner for the inside of the covers. On the short ends of the 12.5 cm × 30 cm pieces of color paper, fold in 6.5 cm. Then tuck these folded ends between the cardboard and paper at the shorter ends of the cover. This is the inside lining of the cover.

Next, bind the two cardboard covers together with the 12.5 cm × 17.5 cm piece of color paper. Fold the paper in half the long way. Tuck it under the inside lining of the two covers.

Make the inside papers for your booklet by folding the white bond paper and the piece of 17.5 cm × 22.5 cm color paper in half along the short side. Staple them together twice along the crease with the color paper on the outside.

Now put the pages into the book. Slide the color paper, to which the inside pages are stapled, under the inside lining of the two covers where the binding was inserted.

You can decorate the cover of your booklet with a drawing, a print, or a torn-paper collage. Look at pages 234 and 235 for instructions.

Arts and You

All the arts help you see your world in a new way. And they help you tell others about yourself. Arts are something you can do and enjoy your whole life. As you grow older, you'll probably learn more ways to paint, to make a sculpture, to weave, to act, to sing, to dance, to write. Once you have tried doing some art form, you can appreciate the arts of others so much more. You may not become an artist yourself. But, no matter what your age, the arts will help you see the world in fresh and wonderful ways.

THE WORLD OF THE OUT-OF-DOORS

Step outside and look around. There is a whole world to explore. Games to play, secrets to uncover, experiments to do, skills to learn, songs to sing, sounds to hear, trails to find, and a surprise around every bend.

Come.
  Fly a kite,
    Tie a knot,
      Catch a spider web,
        Count the stars,
          Listen to a worm,
            Follow a drop of water,
              Cook a tasty stew,
                Design a woozel,
                  And see your world in a new way.

Start Wherever You Are

I meant to do my work today.
But a brown bird sang in the apple tree,
And a butterfly flitted across the field,
And all the leaves were calling me.
And the wind went sighing over the land,
Tossing grasses to and fro,
And a rainbow held out its shining hand—
So what could I do but laugh and go.

—RICHARD LE GALLIENNE

Where will you go? What will you do to discover the world of
the out-of-doors? Do you live in the city? Look on your own
city block, outside your door, in a vacant lot, in a zoo. Look
up and down and all around.

Do you live in the country? Look in the fields and the

woods. Explore an orchard, a pasture, a fencerow, or a barnyard.

Do you live in a suburb? Look in your own backyard, down your street, or around the corner.

Does your troop have a favorite outdoor spot: a meadow, tiny creek, sandy beach, or a park? Visit it at different times of the year. Visit it in the rain, when snow is on the ground, when the wind is cold, when the sun is hot, or at sunset. Snoop, search, sniff, taste, explore, ask questions, and wonder, or just sit quietly, and let things happen.

What has changed since last you were there? What did you discover this time that you never noticed before?

How wide-awake are your eyes and ears? How much can you discover by touch and smell? Here are some games to play and things to do the next time you go out.

Bees and Butterflies. The next time your troop is anyplace where there are a lot of flowers, pretend that all of you are bees and butterflies. Zigzag from one flower to another. Look at a blossom from the insect point of view. Stick your finger down into the blossom to find the pollen. How would you get to it if you were an insect?

Feel the pollen and smell it. Be careful that you don't run into a real bee!

That's My Leaf. Each girl takes a leaf from the same kind of tree and looks at it carefully for one minute. Then put all the leaves in a pile and stir them up together. Can you find your one-of-a-kind leaf? What makes it special—different from all the other leaves? Press the leaf carefully. Send pressed leaves to one-of-a-kind friends, and tell them how they are like the leaves.

Listening Post. Find a spot just for you within sight of your leader and listen carefully for two minutes. Then come together and tell each other what you heard. How many sounds did you hear? Could you tune out sounds from the world of people?

Stake a Claim. You and a partner play this game by taking a piece of rope about one meter long and tying the ends together with a square knot. Drop the rope down on the ground anywhere you like. Together look carefully at everything inside your circle. How many different things can you discover?

Animal Home Hike. On your next hike, look for animal homes and discover the different ways they are built. Perhaps you will see a spider web, an insect gall, or a bird nest. You might even find the front door to some animal's underground home.

Is There a Dragon in Your Backyard?

How well do you describe what you see? Long ago, explorers came back from faraway lands and wrote stories of wonderful and strange plants or animals they saw. Later people read

these reports and drew pictures of the things described. On the opposite page is a picture of what an artist thought an explorer saw and what the explorer thought he was describing.

Can you describe the things you see in such a way people can draw a picture of them or find what you were describing? Or will they go looking for dragons in your backyard? Test your ability by describing something you saw today to a friend, and see if she can draw a picture of it.

How do you feel about the animals in the picture? What kind of words do you use when you describe them to others?

The words you use often depend upon what you know and feel about the animals. If a kitten scratched your nose, you will remember her swift paws, sharp claws, and how your nose hurt. Will the person who thinks about a kitten as a ball of fur and purr know what you are talking about when you describe her?

Look at these pictures again. Did you really describe them, or did you tell how you feel about them? What could you do to find out more about them?

Eco-Notes

You have probably heard the word ecology many times. Perhaps you have used it yourself. Do you know its real meaning?

Ecology is the study of the relation between living things and their own piece of the natural world. If someone cuts down the bushes where a bird is used to eating berries, the ecology of that bird's world goes wrong. If the bird flies away and your garden is ruined by harmful insects which the bird would have eaten, then your world is not what it should be. All living things depend on one another.

When you have learned to be a keen observer of nature, you can start keeping a record of what you have seen. Get a notebook and pencil to use only for your eco-notes. You might also want a small magnifying glass to examine details of a flower or to look a bug in the eye, and a ruler to measure insects and interesting holes. (You can use the ruler to poke under leaves, too.) It is a good idea to have a bag to keep your tools and treasures of outdoor exploring together.

You might start your eco-notes by just recording where you went and what you saw. Then you can start adding details, such as the weather on each trip, a list of different birds you saw, the time of sunrise and sunset, information about pollution and what it does to living things.

Sometimes you will want to put down your feelings about these things. Could you write a poem about something beautiful you saw outdoors today?

Your Environment

Environment means the living space that surrounds you and all things that share it with you. The sun's heat and energy, the smoke, dust, pollen carried on the air, water, and soil are all part of your environment. So are the plants and animals that live around you.

Your environment also includes things that you need but can't see or touch, especially the love and warmth of home, family, and friends.

Whether you live on a farm, in a big city apartment, a house in the suburbs, or a mobile home, you depend on your environment for everything you need to live. You also give something back to your environment.

Plants and animals also take something from and give something to the environment. Plants get energy from the sun and use it to manufacture food from air, water, and minerals. The green coloring in their leaves turns this into a kind of sugar, which the plants use to grow and to make roots, leaves, flowers, and seeds.

Some animals eat green plants and not other animals. This kind of animal is called a **herbivore** (her-be-vor). It lives on the sugar stored in plants.

Animals that eat other animals are called **carnivores** (kahr-ne-vors), which means "meat eaters." A hawk is a carnivore. Can you find other carnivores in the picture?

Many animals eat both plants and animals. They are called **omnivores** (om-ne-vors), or "everything eaters." Unless you are a vegetarian, you are an omnivore. How many omnivores do you see in the picture?

This is a picture of a **food chain,** showing how energy from the sun flows from plants through animals. The energy goes through more than three links in the food chain. It always begins with green plants, and the last animal in the chain is the one not eaten. Can you follow the food chain above?

Often more than one kind of animal needs the same plant or animal for food. Then the food chain becomes a **food web.** Here is a food web you might find when you are at camp.

Materials in nature are used and reused. At the end of the food chain, the tissues of dead plants and animals are broken down by tiny living things known as decomposers. Some decomposers are bacteria and fungi. When this happens, carbon dioxide is returned to the air and water and minerals are returned to the soil.

A forest can maintain itself without human help, if nothing is taken from it by humans. A vegetable garden cannot just go on living, because when you harvest the green plants you take minerals away from the soil. A gardener has to replace them by putting minerals (fertilizer) in the ground.

Eco-Action

Girl Scouts have a special name for learning about our environment and taking care of it. The name is Eco-Action.

You can see many ways that eco-action relates to two parts of the Girl Scout Law: "to use resources wisely" and "to protect and improve the world around me." Now, what can you do about it?

Visit a nearby pond, beach, or vacant lot and see how people have been hurting the environment by the things they do. Are there things your Girl Scout troop might do to make this place better for people, plants, and animals? Could you, as a Girl Scout, get other people to help?

People are the only animals that can think, plan, and make choices. For hundreds of years, however, people have been planning without thinking and have made choices that hurt the environment.

For example, poisons used to kill insects and weeds have gotten into the food chain and endangered animals farther along the chain. Some of these endangered species will soon be gone forever unless people start making choices that will save them. Learn about some of the choices, such as getting rid of insects by breaking their food chain rather than poisoning them. Help to inform other people in your community.

Find out what people who care are doing to protect the environment. A good place to start is with your own Girl Scout council. What kind of eco-action is going on in camps that the council owns? Ask what kind of an outdoor good turn you can do the next time you are at camp.

Have you ever seen a sign, **Lou Henry Hoover Memorial?** This sign means that Girl Scouts are watching over a place to make sure that no one disturbs the plants and animals in their natural habitat. Lou Henry Hoover was the wife of President Herbert Hoover. She was also elected president of Girl Scouts of the U.S.A. Mrs. Hoover loved the out-of-doors, knew a great deal about outdoor things, and shared her knowledge and love with thousands of Girl Scouts. She was a great camper, and that is why so many memorials to her are in Girl Scout camps.

Be a Habitat Detective

The place that is best suited to an animal's living habits is called its **habitat.** Even in the largest city, you can find animal habitats if you have the patience to keep searching. (Remember, furry things are not the only animals. Birds, worms, fish, and insects are animals, too.)

Most wild animals are timid and have learned to hide from people. Some of them only come out at night. But if you look closely, you will find clues that can lead you to where they live. In the country, you might be lucky enough to see a trail that animals follow to water. In the city, what kind of signs will you look for? Learn to recognize animal tracks (footprints), starting with the tracks of your pets. How do a dog's track and a cat's track differ?

Other animals put their hind legs ahead of their front legs and bound along. You can tell from the tracks how far such an animal jumps each time. Some animals walk on both heels and toes, just as people do. Can you find a track of a heel-and-toe walker?

You can **make casts of animal tracks** with plaster of paris. Place a ring of cardboard about 4 cm high around the track. Pour plaster of paris, mixed with water according to directions, into the ring. Let it get hard. When you remove the cake of plaster, the shape of the animal track will be raised on top of it.

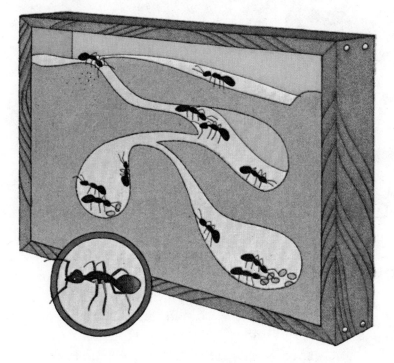

Animals Where You Live

When you track a small animal to its home nearby, or when one comes to your home, you might be able to watch it for a while if you will keep very still.

Sometimes you need to make a temporary home for something very small, so that you can watch it close up without hurting it. Find out how to make a bug trap, a cricket cage, or an ant farm. After you have learned how the creature acts, always take it back to where you found it.

Make friends with an earthworm. **To make a worm hotel,** you need a quart jar with a metal lid, some wet sand, and some damp earth. Put a layer of sand in the bottom of the jar, and cover it with a layer of earth. Keep on adding a layer of sand and a layer of earth until the jar is filled to about 4 cm of the top. Punch holes in the jar lid, and go on a worm hunt.

Tiny piles of dug-up earth on the ground (they are called worm castings) will show you where a worm tunnel is. Go back at night, or after a heavy rain, and catch two worms when they come out of the tunnel. If you pull on a worm before it is completely out of the ground, you might break it. But here's the wonderful thing: worms can grow back parts they have lost. That is called regeneration. If you should break a worm, put the broken piece in your worm house and it will probably go on living.

Put the lid on the jar and keep it in a dimly lighted place where you can watch the worms tunnel through the earth. They work only in the dark. Feed them tiny bits of carrot scrapings, lettuce, cabbage, or hamburger until you are ready to take them back to their home.

A worm is a special kind of animal. Have you really looked at an earthworm or other kinds of worms?

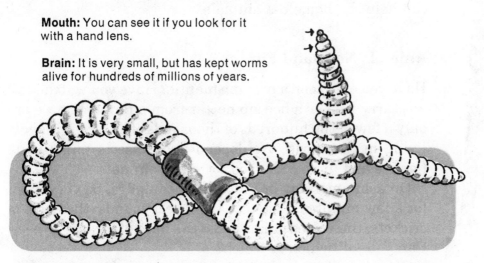

Mouth: You can see it if you look for it with a hand lens.

Brain: It is very small, but has kept worms alive for hundreds of millions of years.

Food Storage and Gizzard: Under segments 15-19.

Intestines: From gizzard to the worm's end.

Feet or Setae: There are two pair on every segment; you can feel them by gently rubbing the underside of a worm.

Ask what pets the girls in your troop have, and you will probably find that there are many different ones. Some people like hamsters; others like cats, dogs, birds, fish, or turtles. And some people treat farm animals, such as cows, horses, sheep, and chickens, as pets.

All pets need kindness and care. They depend on you for food and water. They need exercise and clean places to rest. How do you take care of your pet?

If you ever visited the ASPCA, the Humane Society, or an animal shelter in your town, you probably saw animals there that weren't wanted any longer. When you kept on asking for a pet, were you ready to take the responsibility that goes with it?

Visit the animal shelter together, to see what you can learn about taking better care of your own pet or how you can help the homeless animals.

Animals Near and Far

Have you ever seen a praying mantis? Have you watched an ant carry food or a bee sip nectar from a flower? These are only a few of the hundreds of thousands of different **insects** living in the world. We depend upon insects to pollinate flowers and to provide food for other animals.

On a summer day or around the campfire, be very quiet for a few minutes. Listen to the insect sounds: the chirp of crickets, the voices of katydids, the hum of locusts or bees. Can you tell which is which?

Snakes are soft and wiggly, as worms are, but they are a different kind of animal known as **reptiles.** Some reptiles are not soft outside. They have shells or tough, heavy skins to protect them. Turtles, crocodiles, and alligators are reptiles. So were dinosaurs, before they died out. All reptiles are cold-blooded. Their temperature is the same as the air around them.

There are only a few poisonous snakes. You should learn to recognize and avoid them if they live in your part of the country. Most snakes are harmless to people and pets. By eating mice and insects, they actually do us a favor. Snakes cannot hear. They know a person or animal is coming when they feel vibrations on the ground. A snake sheds its skin as it grows. If you should find a snakeskin someday, notice the part that came off over the eyes.

Frogs, toads, and salamanders are **amphibians,** living partly in the water, partly on land. Amphibian means "living in two places."

Toads and salamanders live more on land than in water. You may find a toad out looking for food in a garden or in a wood. Toads and frogs look a great deal alike, but the toad's skin looks nubbly. Look for salamanders after a rain, in damp, woody places.

Frogs like both land and water. Listen for them on spring or summer evenings. Spring peepers or tree frogs make a high-pitched peep. Bullfrogs make a low croak. Toads sing, too. To make a noise, a frog or toad fills his throat with air until it swells like a balloon. The air goes back and forth over his vocal cords, and out comes music.

Try making your own peeps and croaks in "Frog Round" from the *Girl Scout Pocket Songbook.*

You probably wouldn't say "hello" to an insect or snake, but you might to a chipmunk. Maybe that is because chipmunks and most other little, furry things are **mammals**—as we are. Mammals are warm-blooded and have fur or hair. The mothers make their own milk to feed their babies. A bird, fish, reptile, amphibian, or insect is an animal, but not a mammal.

Look at the pictures of mammals on this page. Do some of them surprise you?

Bird Watching

Birds get around so much that you can see them almost anywhere. If you have never paid much attention to them, you have been missing something. They are beautiful to watch, and you can learn many things by observing them.

Different birds have different habits. They even like different things to eat. Watch the ones around your house and notice where they nest, what they use for building nests, and what they use for food. You will begin to understand how they fit into the food chain and their importance to the environment.

A good way to have birds to watch is to put a bird feeder where you will be able to see it.

Watch the feeder to see which birds eat only seeds and which will only eat food scraps. Then you can provide a cafeteria menu to attract many different birds.

Keep a list of birds, where you saw them, and what they were doing. If you see one you do not recognize, make a note of these points:

• What size is it? bigger than a pigeon? smaller than a sparrow? the same size as a robin?

• What is the shape of its bill, crest, feet, wings, tail?

• What color is it? What are its markings?

• What sound does it make?

• Where was it? on the ground? in a tree? on the water?

Then you can look in a bird book and find out the stranger's name.

At nesting time, you might help birds by putting out scraps of yarn and other building materials for them. Later on, you may see a piece of your yarn in a nest overhead.

Birds like to keep clean, but it is not always easy for them to find a bathtub. Make one for them, and keep it full of water.

People in the Audubon Society and other bird clubs are glad to help new bird watchers. Look for these organizations in your telephone directory.

Treasures Underfoot

Do you come home from a hike with your pockets full of stones? Do you want to know what makes certain rocks sparkle or how the fossil of a tiny shell got into a piece of sandstone?

307

If you do, some people would say you have rocks in your head. Others will call you a rock hound. That means a person who has a special eye for rocks and minerals, and wants to learn all about them.

Rocks are made up of minerals. Minerals come from the earth, and there will never be any more of them in the world than we have now. People, plants, and animals need many different minerals just to keep alive. You can see why we should be concerned about understanding minerals and using them wisely.

Salt is a mineral that we use every day. It comes in small crystals.

Here is a way to see how salt crystals are formed.

You will need a cup of warm water, four tablespoons of salt, and a pie pan. Stir the salt into the water, and pour the salty water into the pan. Set the pan in a safe, warm place. In a few days, as the water evaporates, you will find a ring of salt crystals around the edge of the pan. Look at them through a magnifying glass. Are they all the same shape? Are they the same shape as other kinds of crystal you have seen?

You may have seen a box of sea salt on the shelf of a supermarket. It was made by evaporating sea water, just as your water evaporated from the pan and left salt.

The next time you go to a museum or walk by a jewelry store window look at the interesting crystals on display. When you find rocks on your hikes, look at them with a magnifying glass. Do any contain tiny crystals?

Plan a prospectors' hike with your troop. A schoolbag, a miser's bag made from a bandana (see page 348), or the sack from your lunch will be handy for your rocks. Never go rock hunting alone, and be sure to follow the outdoor safety rules on page 323.

Take eco-notebooks and felt-tipped pens on the hike. With the pen, mark a number on each rock you find. Then write down the number in your observer's notebook, along with the place where you found the rock and what you already know about it. When you get home, ask a rock hound to visit a troop meeting and tell you more about the rocks you found.

On your hike you may discover some colored rocks. Scratch their rough edges across a piece of paper. If any of them should leave a colored mark, you can use it to make paint the way the American Indians did long ago.

Here are things you can make with minerals and rocks.

What about Weather?

Long before we had satellites to help us forecast the weather, farmers and sailors had ways of guessing what the weather would be. They watched the sky and felt the wind. They made up rhymes like this one to help them remember:

Red sky at night, sailors' delight.
Red sky at morning, sailors take warning.

Have you heard other weather rhymes, or read them in books?

Weather is made by the air around us. We feel warm or cold according to the air temperature. When the air moves quickly, we say the day is windy.

Wind velocity means how fast the air is moving. The higher the velocity, the stronger the wind is. Use this scale of wind velocity to decide whether it is windy enough to fly a kite or too windy to build a fire.

Air soaks up water like a great sponge. Drops of water gather around tiny drops of dust in the air and form a cloud. The drops fall to the earth as rain, sleet, snow, or hail. Did you know the particle of dust is still there in the center of every raindrop?

Here are some clues for predicting weather.

If the WIND is blowing from	and the CLOUDS are	then the WEATHER is apt to be
W or NW to N	Cirrus	Good
NE or E to S	Cirrus	Rainy or snowy in a day or two if the wind is steady.
NE or E to S	Cumulus	Fair—but if these clouds build up, they may bring a storm.
NE or E to S	Cumulonimbus	Rainy soon, thunderstorm.
NE to S	Stratus	Rainy or snowy in fifteen or twenty hours, usually a steady rain.
Westerly	Stratus	Overcast sky or light drizzle.

You can learn the different kinds of clouds by making a cloud chart with cotton pasted on paper.

- Stratus clouds will look like solid cotton strips.
- Cirrus clouds look like thin wisps of cotton.
- Cumulus clouds will look like puffs of cotton.
- Cumulus-nimbus clouds will look like big cauliflowers with wisps of cirrus feathers coming off the top.

311

Beaufort Scale of Wind Velocity

	Speed	Description	Observe
O	0-1 mph. 0-1 knot	calm	no wind at all...smoke rises vertically...sailing craft becalmed...sea is like mirror.
1	1-3 mph. 1-3 knots	light air	smoke drifts slowly...wind vanes do not move...ripples on the water.
2	4-7 mph. 4-6 knots	slight breeze	feel wind on face...leaves rustle...small wavelets... sailing craft sail close hauled.
3	8-12 mph. 7-10 knots	gentle breeze	leaves, twigs, loose paper move constantly...a light flag waves... good kite flying weather...very small waves with crests appear.
4	13-18 mph. 11-16 knots	moderate breeze	dust, snow, papers blow about... small branches move...ideal sailing.
5	19-24 mph. 17-21 knots	fresh breeze	care needs to be taken with all fires...small trees or shrubs sway...moderate-sized waves... dust devils stirred up.
6	25-31 mph. 22-27 knots	strong breeze	build fires only in fireplaces or charcoal grills...large branches sway...wires whistle...difficult to use umbrella...small craft off water.
7	32-38 mph. 28-33 knots	moderate gale	use only alternate fuels, no open fires...whole trees in motion... inconvenience in walking... waves beginning to build.

8	39-46 mph. 34-40 knots	fresh gale	twigs break off trees...storm warnings hoisted...garbage cans overturned...difficult to walk against the wind.
9	47-54 mph. 41-47 knots	strong gale	damage to roofs, chimneys, tv antennae...branches break... larger sailing craft use minimum sail...high waves.
10	55-63 mph. 48-55 knots	whole gale	trees snap and are blown down ...considerable damage to build-ings...huge waves with over-hanging crests...visibility reduced.
11	64-72 mph. 56-63 knots	storm	widespread damage to homes and property...extremely high waves ...sea covered with long patches of foam...visibility reduced.
12	73-82 mph. 64-71 knots	hurricane	destruction of nearly all property ...air filled with foam and spray ...almost no visibility.

At camp, you may want to set up a weather station and fly weather flags to tell people what to expect.

Neighborhood Trees

The next time you go outside, stop and say "thank you" to a tree.

Why? Trees make the street cooler. Their leaves filter and purify the air. Trees cut down on noise and serve as a windbreak. They provide homes and food for many animals, and pleasure for all of us.

Just for fun, look at the trees in your neighborhood and see how different they are. Do their branches bend to the earth, point to the sky, or spread out like a fan? Is their bark rough, smooth, or peeling? black, white, gray, or greenish? Are the leaves pointed, rounded, or needlelike? sawtoothed, or smooth-edged?

Can you find—
• a tree with a tall, straight trunk like a flagpole?
• a tree that has been injured?
• a tree that has food for birds? for insects? for people?
• a tree that has a home for birds? for mammals?
• a tree that has flowers? seeds? buds?

You can even learn something about a tree that is no longer there, if its stump is left. A rubbing of the top of the stump will show you how old the tree was when it was cut down. Take a piece of paper large enough to cover the stump, and fasten it in place with thumbtacks. Take a crayon and run across the paper in one direction, not back and forth. Prints of the tree rings will show on the paper. Trees form a new ring each year; by counting the rings, you can tell how old the tree was. The rings are widest when the growing conditions were best. Wide rings could show years that were rainy or years when the tree has few other plants near it.

You can take a tree census. Make a map of your neighborhood and locate each tree on it. How many are there? Which is the oldest tree? the biggest? the tallest?

What could be done if you find a whole area without trees? Is there something your troop can do? Who could help you?

Adopt a tree that you specially like. Find out who lives in it, who visits it, who gets food from it. See how many others like it there are in the neighborhood. Write a poem or song about your tree. Draw pictures of it in every season of the year. Make bark rubbings and leaf prints from it.

Pots and Plots in Lots of Spots

Anyone who wants to grow things can be a gardener. You can garden in whatever space you have, from an eggshell filled with earth to a large vacant lot. Just give your plants the simple things they need to grow, and wait. Nature will do the rest.

What is it that a plant needs? The plant will tell you. Try different environments for two plants of the same kind and about the same size:

- Place the two plants side by side. Water one and don't water the other. What happens to the one without water?

- Put one plant on a windowsill where it will get lots of light and the other in a spot where it will get very little light. What happens? Look at the leaves of the plant on the windowsill. Which way are they facing?

- Transplant one plant in sandy soil and the other in dark brown garden soil or store-bought potting soil. Watch them for a while to see if there is a difference in the way they grow.

You will find that growing things need water, air, space to grow, minerals, sunlight, and warmth. Different kinds of plants need different amounts of space for their roots.

Here are some ideas for starting a windowsill garden that won't cost you a penny.

Grow a garden in a dish. Cut off the top 5 cm of a carrot or any other root vegetable. Then cut away the greens from the top. Put the piece of vegetable in a dish of water, up to but not covering the top, and watch for sprouts. This will take a while, and you will have to keep adding water as it evaporates.

Or let the vegetable be its own pot. Cut off the top 5 cm of a carrot or any other root vegetable, and hollow out the insides. Fill with water and hang in the window. Watch what happens!

Recycle seeds and pits from the fruits and vegetables you

eat. Don't expect every one of them to sprout, but keep trying and be patient. Some will grow!

An avocado pit makes a handsome tree that will grow for years and years. Save the pit from a ripe avocado and let it dry a day or so. Peel off the brown skin. Stick toothpicks in the pit and balance it point end up in a glass of water. In three or four weeks a root will appear. After the root has started to grow, the top of the pit will sprout green leaves. Plant your avocado pit in a pot that is 15 cm across. You will want to be sure that one third of the pit is above the soil level of the pot. An avocado needs lots of water and sunlight.

The seeds from one green pepper will make enough plants to share with several friends. Plant by covering them with a thin layer of soil. Thin out and transplant seedlings when they start to grow. A green pepper plant needs a very large flower pot or a tub.

Pumpkin, watermelon, or squash seeds also need a lot of room. They do better out-of-doors, but you might try planting some in a large pot or a plastic garbage bag full of soil. Be sure to provide drainage so that water won't stay too long around the roots of your plant.

What else could you recycle for your garden?

Did you ever see a potato start to sprout in a kitchen storage bin? The part of the potato plant that we eat comes from the plant's underground root system. Its eyes are stem and leaf buds. Start your own potato plant by cutting a potato in sections, with an eye in each section. Plant each section in a pot of earth. The chunk of potato has enough stored food to nourish the sprout until green leaves appear.

Try a mystery pot. Fill a large flower pot with soil from the out-of-doors. Do not plant anything in it. Put the pot in a sunny window and water it for a few weeks. Do any plants start to grow in it? How do you suppose the seeds got there?

Or how about a mystery lot? Toss a handful of seeds over the fence of an ugly vacant lot or building site. See what happens.

For the outdoor adventurer with elbow room—Ask yourself:

• What kind of garden do I want? flowers? vegetables? both?
• What grows well where I live?
• How much space is needed for the things I want to grow?
• How much space do I have in my garden?

You can learn many of the answers by reading directions on the back of seed packages, seed catalogs, or the garden section of your newspaper.

Ask gardeners in your neighborhood to help you.

Worlds Beyond Ours

Have you ever tried to count the stars? You could never count them all, but on a clear night you can count the stars in one constellation. A **constellation** is a group of stars you see close together in the sky. If you put make-believe lines between them they seem to make a picture.

Get a book at the library that shows the constellations, and read the stories that were told long ago about these groups of stars. Or tear out monthly sky maps from your newspaper.

Look for constellations in the sky. The Big Dipper is a good one to start with because the handle and edges of the dipper point to other constellations. The North Star is in the Little Dipper. When you face the North Star, it is easy to tell directions.

Have you ever heard the saying, "constant as a star"? Stars are always found in the same relationship to each other. They are constant in other ways, too. They rise and set about four minutes earlier every day.

You can check the accuracy of your clock by a star if you have a west window, a clear view of a rooftop, and a straight pin. Here is how. Stick the pin into the rail or windowsill so

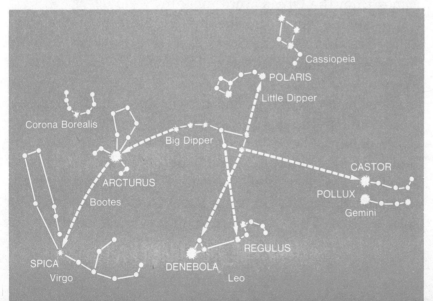

Sun

45 cm
75 cm
1.20 m
1.66 m

5.85 m

10.80 m

44.55 m

21.60 m

33.90 m

44.55 m

it is upright. Leave the pin in position. Pick any bright star just above the rooftop and sight it with the pinhead. Watch the star set below the rooftop. Mark the hour, minute, and second it drops out of sight. The next night be at the window early enough to find the same star and sight it again as it sets below the rooftop. Check the time, and subtract this time from the first reading. If you find the star set 3 minutes and 56 seconds earlier, *your clock is on time*. If not, reset your clock. Stars are dependable!

We live in a galaxy made up of billions of stars. The galaxy looks something like a giant pinwheel. Its rim is what we call the Milky Way.

The big star that we call the sun is the center of our solar system. Around it travel nine planets and their moons. Now there are also space satellites and space junk that people have launched into orbit around the earth.

The **planets** go around the sun at different speeds and in different orbits. The Earth, our world, is one of them. We are much closer to the other planets than we are to the stars. Planets glow with light reflected from the sun, instead of twinkling as the far-off stars do. Because of their orbits, they seem to wander about the sky. The name "planet" comes from the Greek word meaning "wanderer."

You can see four of the planets easily without a telescope. They are Jupiter, Mars, Venus, and Saturn. Use the monthly star maps in the newspaper to help you locate these sky wanderers.

Some night at camp, find a clear spot about 90 meters square and set up a solar system to show the distances between planets. Here is what to do. Have girls with flashlights represent the sun and each of the nine planets. The sun stands in the middle of the field. Using the chart on this page, the planets pace out from the sun to their places in the solar system. The planets, reading down from the top, are

Mercury, Venus, Earth, Mars, Jupiter, Saturn, Uranus, Neptune, and Pluto.

When everyone is in position, turn on the flashlights and start orbiting. Everyone orbits counterclockwise around the sun.

Lonely out in space? Check in a book on stars and have girls be satellites for the planets and go into orbit around them. (Jupiter has 12 satellites. How many does Earth have?) The rest of the troop can be spaceships. To reach a planet, each person will have to plot her own orbit so it intercepts that planet's orbit at the right time. Good luck!

Perhaps some day you will be an astronaut journeying into space on a real rocket ship. Or you may be an astronomer or computer programmer helping to discover the mysteries of stars millions of light-years away. Or would you rather design a telescope to discover new galaxies or star swarms in space?

For now, let's go stargazing!

> Stars over snow,
> And in the west a planet
> Swinging below a star—
> Look for a lovely thing and you will find it.
> It is not far—
> It never will be far.
>
> —SARA TEASDALE

Going Farther from Home

Going places is one of the best parts of Girl Scouting. You can go on hikes, on camping trips, or on trips by car, bus, train, plane, ship, bicycle, or subway to explore the world around you.

Before you go on any trip, your troop will have to make plans so everyone knows what to do, what to bring, and who needs to know about it. In your troop meeting, talk about:

- How will you travel? Can you go by one kind of transportation and return by another? How much will it cost? Will you travel in uniform? What else should you take? Will you take sack lunches or eat in a restaurant?

- How long will the trip take? What time must you leave? What time will you return home? How much time do you need for visiting and exploring? Do you need to make reservations or ask permission to come?

- Will rain change your plans? Should you make a plan to use in case of rain?

A walk around the block can be full of surprises. Here are some things to do when walking in town:

- See how many shapes and colors you can find in trees and buildings. Even streets and sidewalks have patterns of light and dark, lumpy and smooth.

- Look up for birds. Look down for animal tracks.

- Listen for the different sounds of the city, and notice what makes each sound. Which ones are pleasant? Which ones hurt your ears?

- Watch for signs of changing seasons.

- Pay attention to pollution. Can you see where people are trying to do something about it? What could you do to make your community cleaner?

Be Prepared!

Do you know your telephone number at home? On any trip away from the troop place, have a plan for getting in touch with parents in case of trouble. Each girl, as well as the leader, should know exactly what the plan is. In a troop meeting, talk about:

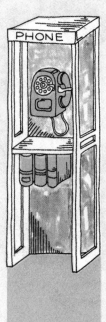

- how to use a pay telephone.
- a safe place for you to carry money for this purpose.
- whom you could call for help if parents were not at home.

Safety rules are especially important when you are walking in a group:

- Always walk in single file or in twos.
- Stop at street crossings and wait until the whole group catches up before starting across. If other people want to pass, step to one side.
- Where there is no sidewalk, keep to the side facing traffic. Stay together. Step off the road for oncoming cars.
- Obey the instructions on signs at the roadside and in public places.
- If you must walk along a road after dark, wear something light-colored so drivers can see you. Mark the right sleeve with reflector tape. Carry a flashlight.
- If you are caught in a thunderstorm in the country, stay away from tall trees; they attract lightning. Get under cover of low-lying bushes or the shelter of a rock ledge.
- Never ask for or take rides from strangers.
- Think about safety when you are traveling by car or bus, too. Keep your head and hands inside the windows. Stay in your seat. Don't bother the driver.

If you are going somewhere by car, bus, or train, keep a sharp lookout for sights you have not seen before. Are there signs pointing to places you might like to visit someday? Start a list of them in your observer's notebook.

Good Outdoor Manners

While you are enjoying the out-of-doors, remember to be considerate of other people and of living things in nature.

- Walk around planted fields, never through them. Don't go onto private property unless you have the owner's permission. Leave gates as you find them.

- Pick up after yourself and others as you travel, so the place will be ready for the next visitors.

- Leave no trace of your trip in the campsite or picnic area, in the bus or train, or on the street.

Have a Good Trip

After you come back from a trip, tell others what you saw and did. Tell them what you think they would enjoy and what you would do differently another time. Thank everyone who helped with your trip.

Where will you go the next time you plan a trip?

Trail Markers

Being able to follow a trail is one of the oldest skills in the world. American Indians and the pioneers of this country used simple trail signs and familiar landmarks to find their way. Boat pilots look for channel markers and harbor lights. Highway signs are like trail markers for people who drive cars.

There are special trail signs for hikers. Girl Scouts have used them for many, many years.

Before you go hiking, try laying a trail at your troop meeting place for other girls to follow. To make the trail signs, you can use rocks, grass, yarn or cloth strips, bricks, twigs, or anything you find handy. The signs should be shaped exactly like those in the pictures on the next page. Make them big enough to be seen easily, and don't place them too far apart.

If your trail is not to be used again, take away the signs so that they will not confuse other hikers. Be sure you don't take away any sign until the last girl has passed it and found the next one.

You can also lay a trail with notes. One note might say, "Go left three blocks down Main Street to Sherman Boulevard. Look for a message under a brick by the mailbox." The note under the brick will tell where to go next.

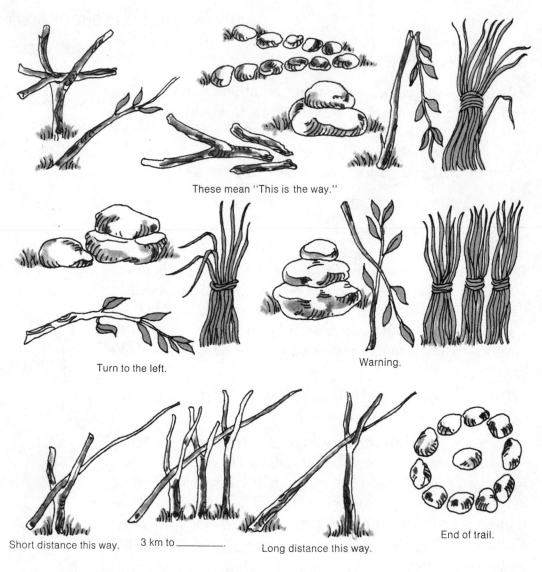

These mean "This is the way."

Turn to the left.

Warning.

Short distance this way.   3 km to _____.   Long distance this way.

End of trail.

Compass Directions

Instead of saying go left or right or straight ahead, you can use compass directions to lay a trail.

A compass needle is a small magnet. It points to the magnetic north of the earth. When you know which direction north is, you can find all of the other directions.

The letters on a compass are N for north, E for east, S for south, and W for west. To find which way is north from where you are standing, hold the compass flat until its needle comes to rest. Then turn the compass until the letter N is under the tip of its needle.

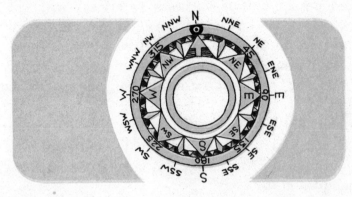

There are numbers on a compass, too. They represent the 360 degrees of a circle. The sign for degree is °. East is the same as 90° on the compass face. West is 270°. What would 180° be?

The Girl Scout pocketbook called *Compass and Maps* will show you how to use a compass. Learn how to use one and lay a compass trail for someone to follow.

Directions in the Sky

Sometimes when you are out-of-doors, you will not have a compass with you. Then you can use the sun or stars to find directions.

In the morning, the sun is in the east. If you stand with your left shoulder toward the sun, you will be facing south.

In the afternoon, the sun is in the west. If you stand with your left shoulder toward the sun, you will be facing north.

Whenever you are facing north, the east is to your right, west is to your left, and south is behind you.

Mapping the Directions

Still another way of showing people how to get somewhere is to draw a rough **sketch map.** In town, you can show the streets a person will use or cross, where she will turn, and things to look for—like a grocery store, a vacant lot, or a stoplight. In the country, you would use roads, fences, and natural landmarks, such as a big, dead tree or a high hill. If you know how long it takes to walk from one spot to another, put that in.

You may not have room on your map to write the name of everything. Signs like the ones shown here are a shorter way of giving this information. You can make up others as you need them.

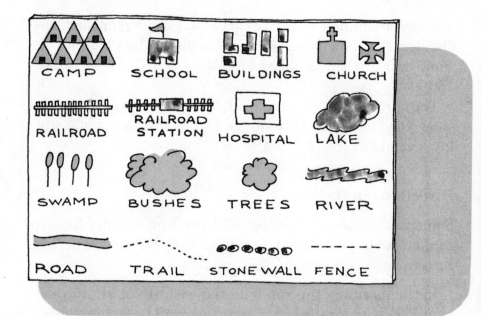

But how will people know what the signs mean? Put a list of signs and an explanation of each one in a corner of the map. This is called a **legend.** Look at a road map or a map in a book, and see what other things are included in the legend.

State road. Edgecomb .3 mi→

Jackson's orchard

poison ivy

raspberry patch

to Lookout Hill and weather station

culvert

redwinged blackbirds nest

brook

"Polliwog Pond"

farmhouse
stone wall
trees
bushes
footpath
swamp

by Jane Gilson

After you have practiced making rough sketch maps, try making a **map with compass directions,** distances drawn to scale, legend, date made, and your name as map maker. You can read about how to do it in the Girl Scout pocketbook, *Compass and Maps.*

Your pace is a good way of measuring distances. Mark off the length of one hectometer (100 meters) on a level of ground. Pace it ten times, starting each time with your toe at one end of measure. Count the number of steps you use; is it about the same each time? When you have decided what is a natural pace for you, divide 100 meters by the number of steps you usually take. That will give you the length of one step or pace, and you can use this measure for any distance on the ground.

Now mark off the longer distance of a kilometer. Practice timing yourself to see how long it takes you to walk the kilometer comfortably over level ground. This will give you a way of judging distances by the time it takes you to walk

them, and also a guide for telling other girls how long it will probably take to walk from one place to another.

You can measure the distance across a vacant lot, or even a river, without crossing it. Stand facing the river, and hold one hand above your eyes like a hat brim. Tip your head until the outer edge of your hand touches the opposite shore. Keep your head and hand in the same position and make a quarter turn. Locate an object on your side of the river that the edge of your hand now touches. Mark the place where you have been standing, and then pace to the object. The measurement of that distance will be about equal to the distance across the river.

Signaling

People send messages to each other all the time. You signal someone when you wave, smile, or frown, or when you use the Girl Scout sign. The flag on the back of your bicycle is a way to signal to people in cars that there is a bicycle ahead of them.

Morse code is an international system for signaling messages by dots and dashes. When you learn Morse code, you can send messages by sound, light, flag, or a combination of all three.

INTERNATIONAL MORSE CODE

A ·−	G −−·	N −·	U ··−
B −···	H ····	O −−−	V ···−
C −·−·	I ··	P ·−−·	W ·−−
D −··	J ·−−−	Q −−·−	X −··−
E ·	K −·−	R ·−·	Y −·−−
F ··−·	L ·−··	S ···	Z −−··
	M −−	T −	

In the daytime you can use a flag or bandana to send messages.

When it is dark, you can signal with a flashlight or whistle. Here's how:

	Flashlight	**Sound**
Dot	Short flash	Short blast
Dash	Long flash	Long blast
End of Letter	Short darkness (count 1)	Short silence (count 1)
End of Word	Long darkness (count 1-2-3)	Long silence (count 1-2-3)

DOT   DASH   END OF LETTER

END OF WORD   END OF SENTENCE   END OF MESSAGE

Signal all dots and dashes for one letter without stopping. (A stop means the end of a letter.)

To get attention, send four A's (·−·−·−) without stopping. When someone wants you to repeat a word, she signals: IMI (··−−··). When she gets your message, she signals: T (−). To erase a mistake, signal: eight E's (········). Then signal the word correctly. To show that your message is completed, signal AR (·−·−·).

Start learning Morse code by memorizing these letters, E (·), I (··), S (···), H (····), T (−), M(−−), O (−−−). Baden-Powell learned E, I, S, H, the four letters made up of dots, by remembering the sentence: "*E*nemy *I*s *S*ecretly *H*iding." He learned T, M, O, the dash letters by remembering: "*T*ake *M*orse *O*rders." See how many words you can make up by using these seven letters. Practice until you know all seven by heart. Then learn all the letters in your name.

−−/·−/·−·/·/// ··−/·−−−/ / ·−//−−/−−·/·−/−−/·///···−/···/··/·−/−−−//
−−/−−−/ ·−·/···/·///−·−·/−−−/−··/·//

Wide Games

A wide game is a trail. It has a story or theme, and everything done along the trail is part of the story.

You can play a wide game at camp, in the city, in your troop meeting place, or on the block where you live. You must follow the trail prepared for you and carry out all of the activities. A wide game can be as simple as a game in your troop meeting place or knot tying. The story might be about a beautiful princess held captive by a wicked old witch. In order to help her escape, you have to perform a variety of tasks, using different knots or a combination of knots.

Or a wide game might be an all-day exploration of your city using compass directions, maps, and trail signs. You might use public transportation to visit museums, civic buildings, and other places of interest, testing your Girl Scout skills of observing, listening, sketching, mapmaking, following directions. What kind of a story would you write for such a wide game?

Plan a wide game for your next outdoor day or camping trip, telling a story about an imaginary creature who is looking for the perfect habitat.

Let's Go Camping

Let us go camping together
Let us go camping together
A canvas roof and a cookfire bright
Let us go camping together.

—MARIE GAUDETTE

If you ask Girl Scouts what is so special about camping, you will get many answers. One will tell you about the friends she made at camp, another will tell about the fun she had sleeping in a tent. Others will tell you about watching some baby animals who shared the campsite. Still others will tell you about a long woodland trail, hiking, going swimming and boating, about campfire ceremonies or cooking smells.

Camping is a combination of many things found throughout this book: singing, dramatics, hand arts, photography, hiking, outdoor cooking, and stargazing, to mention just a few. But you do these things with a difference, because camping is living in the out-of-doors, not just visiting it.

Think of what you've learned to do for yourself, and for other members of the family, so that you can live comfortably at home. Many of the outdoor things you have already done with your troop will help you to be a good camper. Now you need to learn the ways of living at camp.

Girl Scout campers learn the **eight outdoor skills:**

- Know and practice good outdoor manners in town and in the country.
- Know how to dress for the outdoors in your locality, in relation to expected weather.
- Know how to tie, use, and release a square knot and a clove hitch.
- Know how to handle and care for a knife.
- Know how to make, use, and put out a fire for outdoor cooking.
- Know how to cook something for yourself, something for the patrol or troop.
- Know simple first aid for cuts, insect bites, skinned knees.
- Know how to protect the natural world.

335

Girl Scouts do three kinds of camping. When you go to **day camp,** you spend the day there and go home at night. A **resident camp** is a place where you go to stay for a week or more at a time, living in tents or cabins with girls your own age. At both day and resident camp, you will find many girls of different ages camping together. Each group of campers has its own leaders, usually called counselors, who help the girls plan what to do and find out how to do it. Each group sends someone to the camp council to help plan special programs, ceremonies, and campfires that everyone attends.

Troop camping is camping together with your own troop. It may be for overnight, for a weekend, a week, or as long as you want. You can go at any season of the year. Your troop might sleep in tents, in cabins, or under the stars.

Ask your troop leader or an older Girl Scout to tell you about your Girl Scout council's day and resident camps, and how you can go to them.

Troop Camping

When you go troop camping, you can plan to hike, tie knots, learn to build fires, and cook over them. You can earn badges while learning about the stars, the weather, and how to find your way with a compass or map. You can plan campfires, ceremonies, wide games, and parties. You can do things that take time—like weaving a belt, painting a picture, or making a new friend—because you will have time to do it. As you become experienced campers, you can follow wilderness trails, camp comfortably when the snow is deep, take part in big encampments with lots of girls from all over the United States.

Sound like fun? Read about going camping in this book. Ask your leader when your troop can go troop camping.

WHAT I WANT TO DO AT CAMP	MOST OF ALL	IF THERE IS TIME	NOT AT ALL
nature wa			

How to Plan a Troop Camping Trip

What do you want to do when you get to camp? In your troop
meeting, talk about why you want to go camping. You will
find everyone has ideas, more than can be done on any one
camping trip. How will you plan so everyone has fun?

Start by writing down everyone's ideas on a large sheet of
paper. Then, let everyone check what—

• she wants to do most of all.

• she might want to do if there is time.

• she does not want to do at all.

337

When everyone has finished the list, it might look like this:

PLANNING CHART			
What I want to do at camp	Most of All	If There Is Time	Not at All
Sleep in a cabin	‖‖ ‖‖ ‖	‖‖	//
Sleep in a tent	‖‖	‖‖	‖‖ ‖‖
Go on a hike	‖‖ ‖‖ ‖‖	//	///
Learn to lash	‖‖ ‖‖	‖‖ ‖‖	
Cook over a fire	‖‖ ///	‖‖ ///	////
Go fishing	////	///	‖‖ ‖‖ ///
Learn trail signs	‖‖ ////	‖‖ ‖‖	/
Learn new songs	‖‖ ‖‖ ///	‖‖ /	/
Find out about the stars	‖‖ /	////	‖‖ ‖‖
Do crafts	‖‖ ////	///	‖‖ ///
Discover what animals live at camp	‖‖ ///	////	‖‖ ///
Have a campfire	‖‖ ‖‖ ‖‖ ‖‖		
Have fun learning to use compass	‖‖ /	‖‖ ///	‖‖ /
Play games	‖‖ ‖‖	‖‖ ‖‖	

Could you plan a weekend camping trip so all campers in this troop get to do a lot of things they want to do very much, and not many things they don't want to do?

Nearly everyone in this troop wants to have a campfire, hike, lash, learn songs, and play games. These should be no problem. Since most girls checked "sleep in a cabin" and many girls checked that they didn't want to "sleep in a tent," it seems wise to plan to stay in a cabin this time.

What about the few girls who want to do special activities and the ones not interested in some items on the list? Could the troop break into interest groups some of the time so that everyone has a chance to do the things she enjoys? Could a girl who is not interested in cooking swap her cooking kapers with a girl who is? Could those who wanted to sleep in a tent learn how to put one up so that they will be ready for tent camping the next time?

What do you and the girls in your troop want to do when you go camping? List your ideas so you and your troop will know how to make the kind of plans everyone will enjoy.

More to Think About

After the troop decides why you want to go and what you want to do, the next step is to decide the best time to go. Will you go in the summertime, in the fall, in the spring, or during the winter? Will you go for a weekend, for two or three days during a vacation, or for a whole week?

Where can you go? Does the council have a place for troop camping, or will you go to a nearby park or someone's backyard? Does someone have to reserve a camping site for your use? Are there cabins, tents, or other shelters at the site? If not, where will you sleep?

Your leader will help you find the right camping place for you, and she will probably make the reservation. She will know or find out what equipment is there for your use.

How will the troop get to the camping site? Can the camping site be reached by public transportation (bus or train)? Will the troop rent a bus? Or will parents and friends provide the transportation? When the transportation has been decided, you can set the times for leaving and returning home. You will also know how to pack clothing, equipment, and food so you can handle it.

How much will the camping trip cost? Add together the campsite fee and the cost of transportation and food. Is there anything else you will have to spend? Then decide whether the money comes out of the troop treasury or whether each girl will pay her share of the cost.

Once you know where you are going and how much it will cost, you can tell your parents about the camping trip and get their written permission to go.

Do you need to practice making a bedroll, tying knots, or cooking on a vagabond stove? Are you going to make some of your own camping equipment? Be sure to allow time for these things, too, at troop meetings before you go.

What Happens When You Get There

Now you know where you're going, when you're going, and what you want to do on your troop camping trip. What about all those things that seem to happen so easily at home, like deciding what to eat, cooking, and cleaning up? You have to plan for camp living. Allow plenty of time at troop meetings to decide what to eat at every meal, who will buy the food, what you will use for dishes, and who is responsible for pots and pans.

Make a schedule of camp chores that have to be done. Then you will know how much time you have for outdoor things the troop wants to do. Don't plan every hour of the day. Leave some time for each girl to do whatever she wants, whether it is washing socks, watching a spider spin a web, weaving a basket, flying a kite, listening to a bird's song, or just doing nothing at all.

Plan to arrive at the campsite in time to get settled before dark. It's a good idea to have everyone bring her own supper for the first night, instead of planning to cook a big meal. As you plan each camping day, remember that when a meal takes a lot of preparation, you have less time for other things.

As you talk about this in troop meetings, make a list of—
• what you need to know before you go troop camping.
• what you must decide before you go troop camping.
• what you need to do and prepare before you go.

Kaper Charts

It is very important to know not only what jobs must be done at camp, but also who will do them. Camp is more fun when everyone knows what is expected of her. Divide up jobs like cooking, getting water, cleaning the latrine, building the fire, setting the table, and keeping the campsite clean so that everyone takes turns and does her share.

Girl Scouts call the list of jobs and who does them a **kaper chart**. Each job is a kaper. Here are some ideas for different kinds of kaper charts.

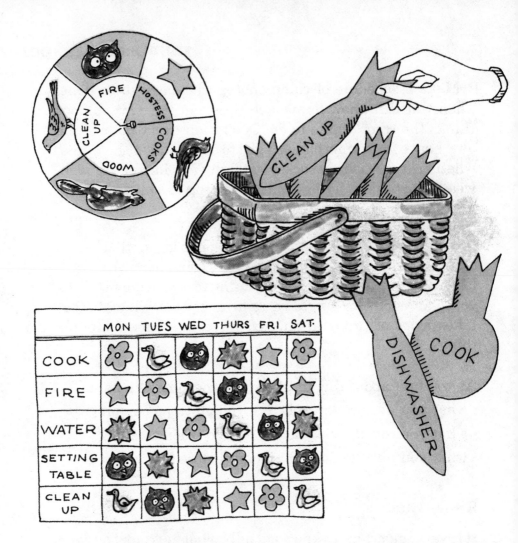

	MON	TUES	WED	THURS	FRI	SAT.
COOK						
FIRE						
WATER						
SETTING TABLE						
CLEAN UP						

A kaper chart is not just for fun. It lets each girl help decide how the jobs are divided, and it is a record of what has been decided. At camp, anyone can look at the chart and know when she will be the fire builder, cook, or clean-up person.

Two special reminders:

- Exciting activities for everyone should not be scheduled too soon after a meal. You want to be sure the clean-up people will not miss them.
- Be sure to make a final clean-up chart.

Protecting the Natural World

As a Girl Scout, when you make plans for outdoor adventures you will want to be sure you do nothing to harm the world around you.

Before you start planning your camping trip, talk about what happens to any place when many people use it. What would it do to the campsite if—

- every girl collected ten acorns for a craft project?
- the wood gatherers took all of the old logs for firewood?
- the troop picked all of the wildflowers in bloom?
- you dumped dishwater and grease into a nearby stream or pond?
- everyone cut a stick for a toasting fork from the same bush or campsite?

It is not only what you take away that can hurt a campsite. How about what you leave?

As you plan meals, think of ways you might cut down on trash. Could you buy food and drinks for the first day in #10 cans, and use the empty cans for craft projects at camp? Could you save space in packing, as well as disposal, by putting supplies from boxes and cans into plastic bags? If some recipes call for aluminum foil, can you think of other ways to cook the same things? (Any aluminum foil you toss away is still like aluminum foil 30 years from now.)

When you reach your campsite, take a good look around to discover what plants and animals live there. What can you do to protect their habitat?

Some things you might not know are:
- If you throw chewing gum on the ground, a bird, a turtle, or some small animal might die from swallowing it.

• The flip tops and plastic holders of soft drink cans injure small creatures. People have also been hurt by swallowing flip tops. Don't put them into cans before you drink. Pack them out when you leave.

Be careful of fire. Know how to put out a fire before you light one. Know and observe fire regulations for the place and the time of year you have chosen for camping. Know where to get help, and how to get out of camp safely, in case of fire.

Paper products and small amounts of garbage can be burned in your clean-up fire. Pack out and take home all other garbage and trash.

If you think it would be kind to scatter leftover bread and other food for small animals to eat, think again. What additional creatures would be attracted by a temporary food supply? When the camping season is over, what will happen to animals that become dependent on handouts?

Save water and keep it clean. Turn off faucets so they won't drip. Use soap, not detergent, for washing. Place drains and tooth brushing pits away from plant life and water supply. Chlorine, toothpaste, grease, and detergent hurt plants as well as small animals.

Prevent soil erosion by keeping to paths that you find on the site and not raking fallen leaves away from paths and camping areas.

Be careful not to pitch tents near some animal's food supply or over its path to water.

Noise affects all living things. Show consideration for the wild creatures, and for other campers too, by keeping your voice at a normal level.

When you go home, leave the campsite as clean as you found it, or as clean as you wish it had been left for you.

What to Take

Most campers take far more to camp than they need. Since you must carry everything you take when the troop goes camping, think before you pack.

First of all, think about the weather. Hot weather calls for one kind of clothing, cold weather another. No matter what the weather or time of year, clothing should be lightweight, sturdy, and comfortable.

Think about your feet. You will depend upon them for foot power. Wear shoes that are comfortable and give your ankles good support. Wool socks absorb perspiration better than cotton or synthetic ones and protect your feet from blisters. If you can't wear wool next to your skin, try wearing wool socks on top of thin cotton ones.

Two or three lightweight sweaters, worn over one another, protect you from the cold and let you take one off when it gets warmer. A ski cap in winter or brimmed hat in summer protects your head from sun, wind, and weather. A ski cap will also keep your head warm at night. Jeans or slacks protect your legs from sunburn, insect bites, and scratches. Wool slacks are needed for chilly evenings or colder weather.

Cotton underwear is usually worn by campers in all but cold weather. Flannelette pajamas or nightgowns are more practical than lightweight ones. If the weather turns cold, pajama bottoms are a good substitute for long underwear when worn under jeans.

In wet or snowy weather, a raincoat or poncho and boots will protect you from the wind and rain. If you don't have a poncho, make one out of an old shower curtain. (See page 121).

What else will you need to take to be comfortable and keep clean? Make a list of everything you plan to take on your next camp-out. After you have made a list, look at it again. Can you cross anything off?

How different will the list be when you pack to go to resident camp for two weeks? winter camp-out?

Take the list to camp. This will help you when you pack up to go home.

Equipment You Will Need

Start collecting and making your own equipment before you go camping. Then you will be ready for hikes and trips with your troop or your family. You will need for yourself—

- a jacknife and sharpening stone
- a piece of rope about 2 meters long
- a bandana
- a canteen
- a sit-upon (see page 120)
- a flashlight
- a cooking kit—plate, cup, fork, spoon, small frying pan, kettle, and a bag to keep it all in
- a ground cloth and bedroll or sleeping bag
- a sack or knapsack to carry and store your equipment

Your troop will need—
- a grill to hold pots over the fire
- a first aid kit
- a water bucket to use as a fire bucket
- a frying pan, nest of kettles, or large kettle
- can opener, big serving spoon, pancake turner
- pot holders or work gloves
- tin snips

- hand axe
- waterproof matches
- pack basket, tote bag, or tote box to keep everything in

You can make these for your camping trip—
- a nest of kettles from tin cans
- a portable shower
- toasting forks from wire coat hangers
- stuff or tote bags from old dungarees
- a storage box and worktable
- dunking bags from dishcloths
- a container to scald cutlery from a tall juice can
- a canvas or denim bulletin board
- a miser's bag from a bandana
- a hiker's hip pack from cloth scraps

All these from plastic bottles

Caution: Never recycle bleach bottles for use as containers of drinking water, washing water, or food.

Bandana Tricks

Here is what you can do with a large bandana:

- Carry your hike lunch.
- Bring home your trail treasures.
- Wear it as a pixie cap.
- Wear it as a neckerchief.
- Use it as a cowboy mask on dusty road.
- Make a hand puppet.
- Use it as a sit-upon.
- Use it as an apron.
- Use it as a pot lifter.
- Use it as an emergency bandage.
- Make a signal flag or trail marker.

Can you think of other ways to use a bandana? In some lands, children carry their things to school in a bandana. Japanese children call a bandana a furoshiki.

349

The Bedroll or Sleeping Bag

The blanket bedroll is easy to make and is good for overnights and sleep-outs away from the campsite. It is handy when you head for your site in a car or bus, but hard to carry on longer trips or when backpacking. Inexpensive lightweight sleeping bags are practical and take much less room. Most come with their own "stuff bag." Try out your sleeping bag or bedroll before you go camping to be sure that it is warm enough.

This is how to make a bedroll with three blankets:

1. Place ground cloth flat on ground. It should be 30 cm longer than blanket. Place first blanket down center of ground cloth.
2. Place second blanket down center of first blanket.

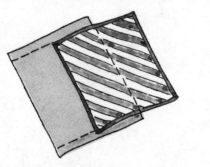

3. Place third blanket on top of first, covering half of the second blanket.
4. Take sheet and fold it in half. Place on third blanket with open edges down center of the blanket.

5. Fold uncovered part of third blanket over the sheet. Then fold the half of the second blanket over it. Then fold the half of the first blanket over that.

6. You can roll some of your clothes and equipment in a bedroll. Lay them on top of the blanket. Now fold the half of the ground cloth over the blanket.

7. Tuck in ends and roll from bottom to top.

8. Tie with two half hitches.

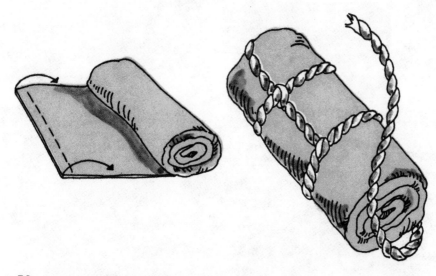

If you are cold at night, put extra bedding, tarp, plastic, or even newspaper under you. Can you guess why?

How to Carry Your Own Equipment

Can you carry it easily? Can you carry it a long distance up the path to your campsite? Ask yourself these questions when you pack for camp.

There are many ways to carry things. You can put them in a suitcase, you can put them in a duffel bag, or you can carry them in a backpack.

There are many good backpacks available in all sizes and styles. Experienced campers are always ready to tell you about the different kinds.

The lightweight knapsack or rucksack is a good pack. Pick one that fits your back. Will it hold all the equipment you need to take?

A pack frame will hold a sleeping bag, a pack bag, and lots more.

You can make a handy pack from an old sack and a rope. Use small stones in the corners of the pack to keep the rope from slipping. You can even make a pack from a pair of old jeans.

Practice packing your backpack, suitcase, or bedroll, using every centimeter of space. Try not to mix everything up. Arrange things so that you will be able to find what you want without unpacking everything. This is easier if you put each item or group of items in its own plastic bag. Fit these plastic bags into their proper place in your pack.

The Camping Place

The campsite is your home while you are living there. If you are going to use the camp for only a few hours, you will probably just put all your things neatly in one place.

If you are staying longer, or coming back for several days in a row, you will want to have a place to keep your equipment, a place to cook, and a place to eat. If you stay all night, of course, you need a place to sleep.

The Roof over Your Head

If you spend the night in a cabin, you will have a place for each troop member to sleep and to keep her things. There will be places to keep your food, perhaps even a stove and refrigerator to use.

If you live in tents, you live in a special way and do things differently from the way you do them at home. Probably you will share a tent with some friends; you may have three of them sleeping in a tent with you. With so many of you in such a small space, you need to keep your things in order.

Tips on Tenting

Tent ropes are there to hold up your tent and nothing else. If you hang things on them, you will have a sagging tent. Put up a clothesline (see page 358) for towels and wet clothes.

Never pin anything to the canvas. Pins make holes in the canvas, which let the rain in. Lash a hook to the tent pole (see page 358) for your jacket or poncho.

Sunlight reflected in a mirror can make enough heat to burn tent canvas or start a fire. Protect your camp by putting your mirror under cover.

Don't touch the tent canvas when it rains. Touching it breaks the air bubbles in the cloth and lets the rain through. When it rains, loosen the slide or taut-line hitch on the tent rope, because wet rope shrinks. When your tent is dry again or whenever the tent rope sags, tighten the rope so your tent is firm.

If your tent has a fly or extra roof, keep an air space between the fly and the tent roof. This is added protection when it rains and keeps you cooler when it is hot.

When it is hot, roll up the tent sides so the breezes will blow through the tent. Ask someone to show you how to roll the canvas to the inside so it won't catch the rain, and tie it so you can put down the sides again without going out of the tent.

Today most tents are made of fire-retardant material, but no tent is fireproof. Never place a candle, lantern, or open flame in your tent. If you are pitching your tent, place it far enough from the campfire or cooking fire so that the wind cannot blow a spark onto the canvas.

Most Girl Scouts look forward to pitching and striking their own tents and learning how to take care of themselves and their possessions in all sorts of weather.

Practice pitching a tent in a park or in someone's backyard before you go on the camping trip. Then you know how to do it, what the tent looks like when it is up, and how much room there is in it. If you will be carrying it any distance, try carrying it around the block. Important, too, is learning how to fold the tent the right way for storage. The Girl Scout pocketbook, *Tents and Simple Shelters*, will show you how. Be sure you know how many pieces (poles, canvas, ropes, and pegs) you started out with.

355

Your Outdoor Kitchen

When you go camping, or even to someone's backyard for a cookout, you need—

- a shady and dry place to store food.
- a safe place to build a fire.
- a place to prepare food.
- a place to eat.
- a place to wash dishes.
- a place to store garbage until you take it home.

Look at the kitchen site on page 355.

- How many different ways does the troop store its food?
- What kinds of food do you suppose they keep in each storage place?
- What other way could the troop have set up for food preparation?
- What do you think the troop is having for dinner?
- Where else could the troop have put a dishwashing place?
- What tips would you give on how to take care of garbage?
- Where would you place the fire safety equipment, the kaper chart, towel rack, or other equipment? (See page 358.)

Tips for Comfortable Camp Living

- Make a clothesline by tightly twisting two cords together, and you won't need to take clothespins with you.
- Lash a hook to your tent pole.
- Keep your shoes dry and off the ground.
- Store nonperishable foods in a bag hung by a rope from a sturdy tree branch. The #10 tin can will keep squirrels from reaching the food.

FIRE

FIRE

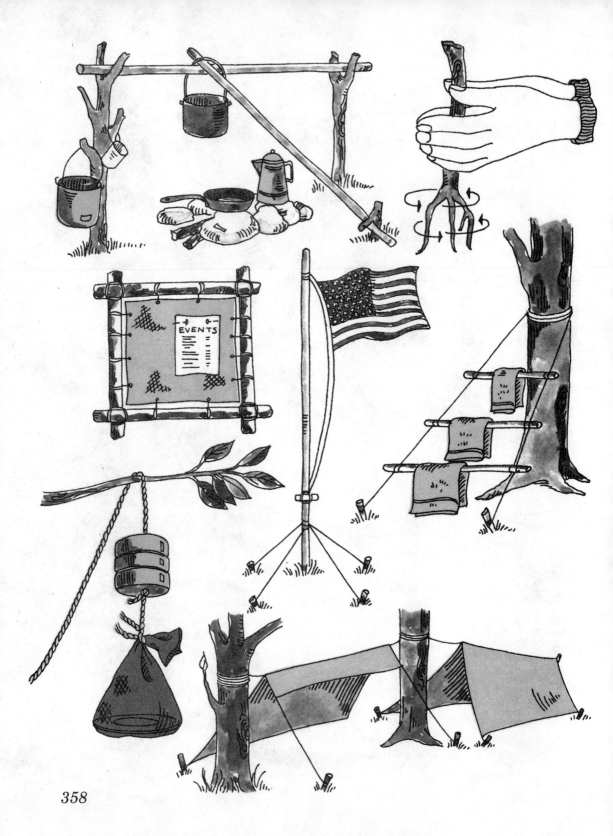

- A handy bush can become a pot rack.
- A tripod washstand of dowels.
- A cooking crane.
- A rack for towels or laundry.
- An oriole cache is a cooling system made from two #10 tin cans and some cheesecloth. Join the two cans with spreaders made from coat hanger wire. Fill the top can with water and put food in the lower can. Wrap both cans with cheesecloth, stuffing the top edge of the cheesecloth into the water can. Hang the cache in a shady place.
- Whittle an egg beater from a branch. Twirl it with your hands.
- Make a special rack for your fire safety equipment.
- Lash a flagpole and bulletin board.
- Rig a cover for your woodpile or other supplies.
- Use your poncho for a sleeping shelter.

Fires

Before you can cook outdoors, you must have a fire. Your fire may be very small, just big enough to cook a pancake, or large enough to cook food for your whole troop.

In places where you cannot have a wood fire, Girl Scouts cook on vagabond stoves with Buddy burners, or on charcoal stoves with charcoal briquets.

Any kind of fire is a responsibility. You must get permission to build a fire. You must have an adult around when you are using one. You need to know how to put out the fire properly.

Buddy Burner

A Buddy burner is a fuel and can be used with a vagabond stove. It is also good emergency fuel to have on hand if your stove at home does not work. The smoke from a Buddy burner is very black; do not use it inside a room. Be sure to use it out-of-doors. **Make a Buddy burner** by recycling a tuna fish or pet food can, a strip of corrugated cardboard a little narrower than the depth of the can, and melted paraffin or candle ends. Roll cardboard into a coil that fits loosely in the can. Or you can fill a tin can loosely with sawdust, instead of cardboard, and pour in the paraffin. Ask an adult to melt the paraffin and pour it carefully over the cardboard almost to the top of the can.

Paraffin should always be melted in a tin can set in a pot of water on the stove. Use low heat. Melt small amounts at a time. The vapor given off by the melting paraffin might start to burn; have a lid from a larger tin can on hand to smother any fire.

Vagabond Stove

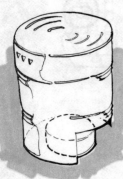

Make a vagabond stove from a #10 tin can. You will need a pair of tin snips, gloves, a punch opener to make the stove, and a roll-type can opener to make a smooth edge on the can when you take off the can lid.

The open end of the tin can will be the bottom of your stove. Wearing gloves, take tin snips and cut a door about 7.5 cm square from the open end. Using the punch opener, pierce three or four holes at the top of the can on the side opposite the door. These are your air holes and serve as a chimney.

To use the Buddy burner and vagabond stove, find a level

spot for your stove, so that the food you cook will not slide off the top. Light the top of the Buddy burner with a match. Using gloves, place the vagabond stove over the Buddy burner.

A Buddy burner gets very hot. Make a damper from the lid of the Buddy burner tin and a piece of coat hanger. When your fire gets too hot, cover part of the burner with the damper. Practice until you can tell how much heat you need for cooking.

The first time you use your stove, wipe the finish off the tin can lid after the stove has heated up. Hold stove with a pot holder, and wipe it with a paper towel.

You can cook on the lid of your vagabond stove, or you can use a small frying pan, or heat a kettle of water on it. You can even bake a small cake on your stove top. Place the cake pan can (tuna fish can is a good size) on top of two small twigs. Make an oven by upending an empty #2½ can over the cake. It will take about 20 minutes to bake a cake. When you are through cooking, put out the fire by covering the Buddy burner completely with its damper to smother the flame. The paraffin will be hot and liquid; so leave the damper in place, and do not pick up the Buddy burner until the fire is out and the paraffin cool and hard. You can also put out the fire by turning the vagabond stove upside down on top of the Buddy burner and leaving it there until the paraffin is cool and hardened. One Buddy burner will last through several cookouts.

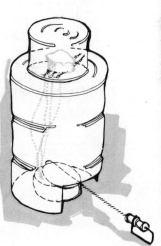

After you have cleaned off the top of your vagabond stove and the cooking tins, store them and your Buddy burner inside the stove. If you put a coat hanger wire handle on the stove, you can carry it with ease.

Charcoal Fires

Charcoal briquets are good fuel to use in place of wood. Charcoal fire burns a long time and needs little refueling. In some places, this is the only kind of fire permitted. Start the fire at least one-half hour before you are ready to cook. It takes that long for the coals to get hot enough to use. Do not use liquid starters or chemicals to start charcoal. They are dangerous. Use plenty of tinder or crumpled newspaper, or a fire starter such as those on page 365.

Charcoal Cooking

Charcoal, like other fuels, needs air to burn. If you are using a ready-made charcoal stove in a park or your backyard, it has been designed for air flow. If you are making your own charcoal stove, you have to think about getting air to the charcoal.

Make your own charcoal stove from a #10 tin can, three pieces of sturdy wire screen, and a piece of coat hanger wire.

Remove top of can with roll-type can opener. With punch opener, punch a row of air holes around top and bottom edge of can. This time the open end of your can will be the stove top. Push wire screen halfway down into can to make a grate. This holds charcoal near the top for cooking and keeps air under charcoal. To keep screen from slipping, curl second piece of screen into a coil, and put between grate screen and bottom of stove. Make a stove top out of the third piece of wire screen. This supports your hamburgers or your pot.

Set the stove on cleared ground, rock, bricks or a driveway, and put a fire starter (directions, page 365) on the grate. When fire starter is burning, carefully add four or five charcoal briquets. Allow briquets 30 minutes to reach the "ember stage" for cooking.

You can improvise a larger charcoal stove for troop use

with two grills and eight flat stones, bricks, or cinder blocks. Here's how. When you are finished cooking, soak each piece of charcoal in water. If you are not sure it is out, and you are leaving the campsite, put the wet charcoal in a tin can with a tight cover and take it with you. When the charcoal dries, it can be reused.

Wood Fires

There are five steps to building a wood fire. They are:

1. Make a safe and suitable place.
2. Have a supply of tinder, kindling, and fuel.
3. Build a foundation fire.
4. Build it into the kind of fire you need.
5. Put out the fire as soon as you are through with it.

When building any fire, be sure to choose a safe and suitable place:

- Choose a spot with no overhanging tree limbs.
- Choose a spot away from the trails or traffic patterns.
- Use a ready-made fireplace OR clear the ground of leaves and make a fire circle OR improvise a raised fireplace—using a wheelbarrow, large can, or sandbox—in areas where danger is great.
- Make a fireplace the right size to hold your grill, kettle, or frying pan. Make it out of logs or bricks or flat stones. Be sure not to pick slate, shale, or schist stones, because these rocks break and sometimes explode when they get very hot.
- Always have a large bucket of water, sand, or dirt and a shovel near, ready to put out the fire before you light the first match.

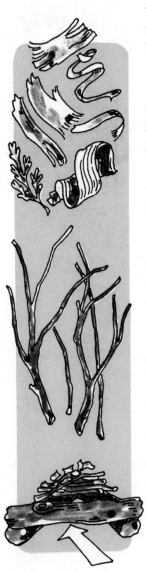

A wood fire needs three different kinds of fire material: tinder, kindling, and fuel. The match lights the tinder, the tinder lights the kindling, and the kindling starts the fuel burning.

Tinder is small, no thicker than matches. It burns as soon as it is touched with a match. Tinder is dry wood. It snaps and breaks but does not bend. Use small twigs, wood shavings, or dried weeds for tinder.

Kindling is dry wood, thin as a pencil up to as thick as your thumb. Kindling should snap rather than bend.

Fuel is the larger wood that keeps your fire going. Fuel might be charcoal briquets or dry, seasoned wood. Many Girl Scouts choose to use tinder and kindling to start the fire, and then switch to charcoal briquets for cooking—to save wood.

Stack your wood in three separate piles: tinder, kindling, fuel. Build your woodpile far enough from the fire that no sparks can fly into it no matter how often the wind shifts. If you are a fire builder in the morning, take a handful of dry tinder to bed with you the night before to keep it dry.

A **foundation fire** is made of tinder and kindling, and its job is to make enough heat to get the fuel burning. When it is burning, you can make it into the kind of fire you need. You will need about four handfuls of tinder and four handfuls of kindling. Use three pieces of kindling to make a small triangle or rack. Carefully lay pieces of tinder on the triangle or rack. This way there is air underneath the tinder and there is space for your match. Why air? Because in order to burn, a fire needs three elements: fuel, heat, and air.

Fire always burns upward. When lighting your tinder, you must light it from the bottom. Kneel near the fire and strike the match close to the wood. Dip the match down so the flame catches on the wind, and cup your hand around the match. Hold the match beneath the tinder until the flame burns up through the tinder. Then carefully place additional tinder and kindling onto the fire. Place each piece of kindling on separately so you do not smother the flame. Sometimes you must blow at the base of the fire to give it more air.

Place the wood so that there is a small amount of air around each piece. Place the pieces close enough so one piece of burning wood will light those next to it. When the kindling is burning, begin adding fuel. Your fuel may be wood or charcoal. Use just enough fuel for cooking needs.

Can you build a fire so that you can cook something for yourself and for your troop?

Waterproof Matches

Waterproof your matches by dipping them into thin nail polish. Dip them one at a time or in small bunches. Keep matches in a small tin box along with a strip of sandpaper to strike them on.

Fire Starters

Fire starters are handy to make ahead and have ready for the times it rains, or if you have a campsite without much tinder. Fire starters are sticks of used candles, a twist of paper napkin or newspaper, or strips of cut-up milk cartons. Ask some adult to help you make these egg fire starters ahead of time so that you will be ready for your next cookout.

- Fill cardboard egg cartons half full of sawdust or wood shavings.

- Pour melted paraffin or candle ends over sawdust until each space is full.
- When cool, break apart each "egg" or store the whole carton. Place one "egg" in the kindling and light a match.

Cooking Fires

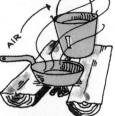

These wood fires are all started with a foundation fire. When your fire is going, add fuel, and build the fire into the kind you need.

Teepee Fire: A quick, hot fire. Use it under a kettle to boil water or make a stew.

Hunter's Fire: Concentrates heat on your pots. (Holds pots of different size safely.)

Trench Fire: Similar to hunter's fire—conserves fuel and heat.

Criss-Cross Fire: Produces coals or a long-burning campfire.

Which kind of fire would you use to heat water for clean-up, for an all-camp campfire, to bake biscuits or a pie, to cook breakfast, to make a pot of soup, to toast a slice of bread?

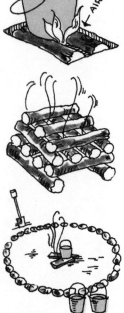

Try not to use more wood on the fire than you need. A Girl Scout uses as little wood as she can because it is one of our natural resources and should be conserved. As soon as you are through using your fire:

- Let fire die down as much as possible.
- Use shovel to break up and spread out coals. Place big lumps in water bucket to soak.
- Stir coals, sprinkle them with water—and then stir them again. Repeat until there are no live coals or gray ash anywhere in your fire bowl.
- When you can hold your hand on the spot where the fire was while you count to 25 and not feel any warmth, your fire is out.

Hints for Hungry Campers

After you learn to make a fire, you can boil a kettle of water and fix something hot, like soup or cocoa, to eat with your meal.

There are many menu tricks you can perform with a kettle of boiling water. Remember, before the fire is lit, fill a pot with water and test to see if the grill is steady and sturdy enough to hold the pot—and to see if you can lift the pot when it is full.

Set the pot of water on a grill over a hot fire. Cover the pot to keep ashes from blowing into it. When the water boils, you are ready to make:

Soup—by adding dried soup mixes or bouillon cubes.

Cocoa—by adding instant cocoa mix, the kind you use with water, not milk.

Rice—using instant rice.

Tea or instant coffee—for your troop leaders.

Make pot washing easier. Before you fill the pot with water, soap the outside of the pot only, by rubbing it with bar soap or spreading it with a thin layer of liquid soap. Then the carbon black from the flames will come off easily at clean-up time.

Place a green stick across your pot when you are making soup, cocoa, or spaghetti. This will keep the contents from boiling over.

One-pot meals are easy to make and clean up after. Here is a favorite Girl Scout one-pot meal. Look for others in cookbooks.

Campfire Stew

2 pounds hamburger
1 onion, peeled and cut in small squares
1 tablespoon fat
2 10¾ ounce cans condensed vegetable soup
salt and pepper to taste

Add salt and pepper to hamburger, and separate hamburger into little pieces, or make little balls of it.

Put fat in bottom of kettle. Fry hamburger and onion until the onion is light brown and hamburger is well browned all over. Pour off excess fat.

Add vegetable soup and enough water to prevent sticking. Cover and cook slowly until meat is cooked through. Serve hot.

Did it taste good? The next time you cook out, try another meal in a pot.

Cooking up a Storm

When you camp out and cook out, you will want to try a lot of different recipes and learn how to make nourishing meals in many different ways. Try some of your favorite recipes from home or see how you can adapt recipes from other cookbooks to outdoor living.

Your own Girl Scout camp cookbook, *Cooking Out-Of-Doors,* is full of recipes to try. The recipes are grouped according to: fireless foods, kettle and skillet meals, toasting, broiling and planking, baking, ember cooking, gimmick and gadget cooking.

Start a troop recipe book including such important information as preparation time, type of fire used, and time needed for cooking.

What kind of a fire will you need to cook it?

Trail Meals

On outdoor days, picnics, hikes, or when you go day camping, you probably need to bring lunch with you.

When you go on an overnight camping trip, take a sack supper for your first meal. You will be less rushed setting up camp.

When packing your lunch: Pick foods that travel well, nothing soggy, squashy, squishy, or sticky.

Include something juicy, something munchy, something crunchy, something sweet.

Something hot, something cold in a vacuum bottle is nice to take.

Pack heavy items at the bottom and light items, which might bruise or crush, at the top of your bag. Stand sandwiches on end so they won't get soggy. Don't forget a napkin. Put your name on your lunch bag.

What will you pack in your lunch bag? Read more about food habits on page 116.

Did you know that you could pack a tasty, nutritious meal in one sandwich bag? This way you can keep your lunch handy in your pocket or tuck it in the hike bag you wear on your belt. The secret to a good pocket lunch is selecting foods that are highly nutritious and take up very little space. For example: A one-ounce cube of cheese or a hard-boiled egg and a slice of summer sausage 1.3 cm thick, plus six whole wheat or rye crackers, are as nutritious as two sandwiches. To this add five dried prunes, or eight dried apricot halves or dates and two pieces of hard fruit-flavored candy. Fill the gaps in the sack with raisins and nuts for nibbling along the way. What other foods can you combine into tasty pocket lunches?

Gorp is a name for nibbles to take on a long hike. Everyone has her own recipe for gorp. One recipe you can try is: Mix together two cups each of candy-coated chocolate, salted peanuts, raisins, chopped dried apricots, and four cups of bite-sized shredded wheat or rice cereal. Allow one cup of the mixture for each person. Carry a sack of gorp with you on your next hike.

What other healthy, hearty trail foods can you find in your grocery store?

Planning Meals

When you plan the menu for a cookout or camping trip, each girl should have a chance to suggest her favorite foods.

Remember that your body needs different kinds of foods, not just desserts. Your body is like an engine, and food is the fuel that makes it go. The right foods are found in the basic four food groups. Plan each day's menu to include some food from each of the four groups. (See page 115.)

In planning a meal, ask yourself:

What foods are in season and what is the weather like? If you are cooking outdoors in hot weather, how will you keep your meat and milk and butter from spoiling?

Will you have different tastes and colors in your menu? Have you something crisp, something soft, something wet, something dry, something sweet, something new?

Will religious observances affect the menu?

Do you have enough money to buy what you want? If not, can you substitute foods that cost less?

How long does your recipe take to prepare and cook? Can you fix part of your meal ahead of time?

What other plans do you have for the day? What would happen to your other plans if you planned a lunch that took three hours to prepare?

If you plan to take foods on a trip, are you fixing foods that carry well and need little equipment?

Write down the menus and how many people you are going to feed. Then list what you need to buy and how much. Next list equipment you need for cooking and eating. From this make lists for shoppers, girls in charge of equipment, and cooks.

Knots to Know

Did you know that there are over 8,295 different knots and hitches, each designed for a very special purpose? You don't have to be able to tie them all. But because you will use knots and hitches in so many things you do as a Girl Scout, you will want to start by learning the most useful ones.

1. To put a knot in the end of a rope, you need to be able to tie an **overhand knot.**

2. To tie a package or join two cords of the same thickness, you need to be able to tie a **square knot.**

3. To fasten the end of a rope after it has been looped over a post, around a bedroll, or around a flagpole, you need to be able to make a **half hitch.**

4. To loop a rope or cord around a ring, you need to be able to make a **lark's head.**

5. To fasten one end of a rope around a tree or post, you need to be able to tie a **clove hitch.**

6. To shorten the rope without cutting it, you need to be able to make a **sheepshank.**

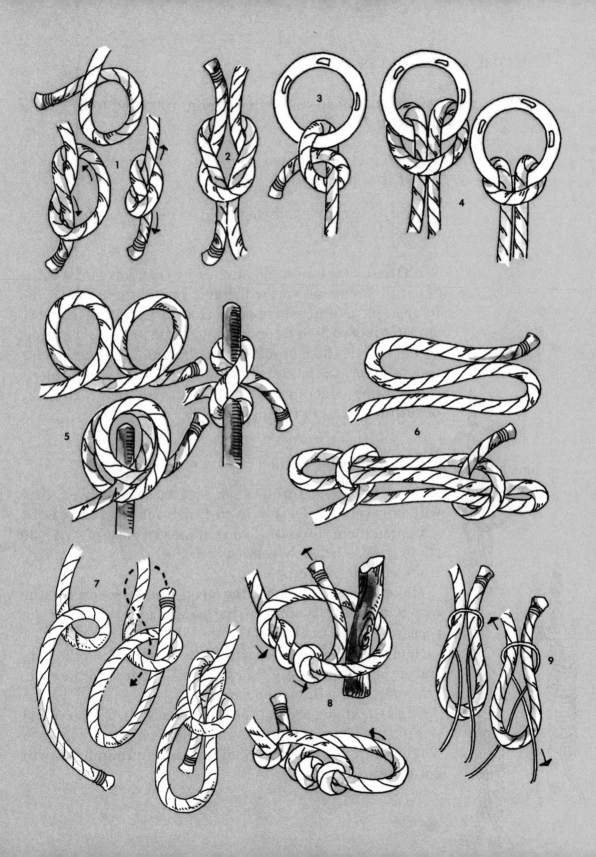

7. To make a loop that will not slip, you need to be able to make a **bowline.**

8. To make a loop that will slide, you need to be able to make a **taut line hitch.**

9. To tie a big rope to a little rope, you need to be able to tie a **sheet bend.**

With these nine knots and hitches, you can solve most of the "knotty" problems you will have. Learn these knots and hitches and practice them every chance you get. Bring a 180 cm length of rope to troop meetings, and practice the knots so you can tie them blindfolded or behind your back. Make up a relay or wide game using the knots, or try some projects in macramé. Macramé is using knots artistically to make beautiful and useful things.

Whipping Rope Ends

If the ends of your rope are not secured in some way, they will unravel. The best way to finish off rope ends is by whipping them. To do this, you will need a piece of string 30 cm long. Use brightly colored string so that you can keep track of your own rope easily.

Make a loop at one end of the string and lay loop along the rope with the ends of the string hanging off the end of the rope.

Hold the string in place with your thumb. Wind the long end of the string tightly over the loop and around the rope. The short end will be left hanging.

Wind the string around the rope for at least 2½ cm. Wind tightly but do not overlap. Tuck the end you have been winding through the loop. Hold it with your thumb so it will not loosen.

Take the short end of the string and pull slowly. The loop will disappear under the winding. Pull until the loop is halfway under the winding. Trim the ends to make a neat whipping.

Hanking a Rope

Hanking is one way to keep your knot-tying rope or clothesline neat. A hank of rope can be slipped over your belt, or be hung on your pack or stored away.

Take a rope 2 meters long, and make two or three loops about 15 cm in one end of the rope. Wrap the long end of the rope evenly around the loops starting at A and working toward B. When you get to B, stick the end of the rope you have been wrapping through one of the loops.

Gently pull on the loop on side A to see which loop will tighten the loop on side B you have used to anchor your rope.

Putting Two and Two Together

Lashing is a way to join sticks and poles together. You can make equipment for camp using pieces of string, cord or binder's twine, poles and sticks. Before you start lashing, be sure you can tie a clove hitch, a half hitch, and a square knot.

Practice lashing before you go to camp. Lashed articles are fun to make, and when you don't need them any longer, they are easy to take apart. Don't count on using dead wood from the campsite. Plan to bring your own poles, broomsticks, bamboo, or dowels.

Before you leave camp, take apart any lashing you have done, and take home the wood you brought, to use another time.

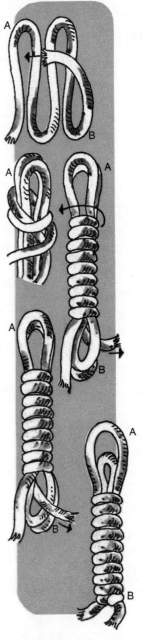

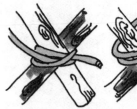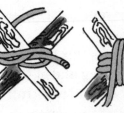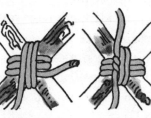

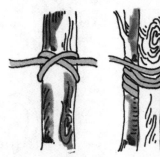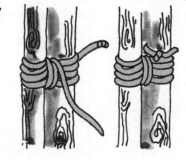

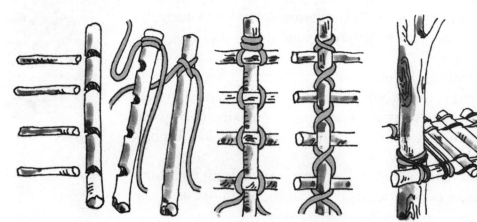

Square Lashing

Place two sticks across each other. Tie a clove hitch around the upright stick.

Bring the long end of your cord firmly over the second stick, around the upright stick, and down and over the second stick—four times as in the picture. Then tighten by winding the cord very tightly between the sticks so that the cord you have already wound is pulled even tighter. This is called "frapping." Join both ends of the cord in a square knot and cut the cord ends short. Tuck ends into center of lashing.

When you have learned square lashing, you will be able to join sticks and poles together in other ways. Look at the pictures on this page. See if you can bind two sticks together in an X shape. Sheer lash two or three sticks together, side-by-side, or continuous lash tabletop or shelf. See the pocketbook of campcraft skills, *Knots and Lashing,* for more instructions.

The Camper's Friend— The Jackknife

A jackknife is a camper's friend. You will use it again and again for whittling a toggle, cutting a rope, scraping a carrot, or trimming a branch. It deserves the best care. It is a tool, not a toy.

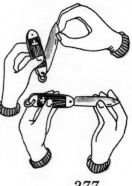

Opening the jackknife. Put your thumbnail in the slot of the blade. Keep your finger away from the cutting edge. Pull the blade out all the way.

Using the jackknife. Hold the handle with your whole

hand like this. Always cut away from you. Keep at least an arm's length away from anyone else.

Whittling a point. Shape the stick by cutting off little chips of wood, one at a time. Do not try to cut off big pieces. Cut slowly so your knife will not slip.

Cleaning the jackknife. Keep your knife clean and dry. Hold the cleaning cloth at the back of the blade, away from the cutting edge. Wipe carefully across the whole blade. Oil the hinge with machine oil. Never clean the blade by rubbing it in dirt or sand. This dulls the blade and makes the knife hard to open and close.

Closing the jackknife. Hold the handle of the jackknife in one hand with the sharp cutting side of the knife upward. With the fingers of your other hand, push the blade. The knife will close halfway. Then push the blade again. The knife will snap shut. Always be sure your fingers are away from the cutting edge.

Sharpening the jackknife. A sharp knife is safer and more useful than a dull one. Learn how to keep your jackknife sharp with a sharpening stone (called a carborundum stone).

Hold the stone in one hand and the open jackknife in the other. Keep your fingers below the top edge of the sharpening stone. Lay the flat side of the knife blade on the flat surface of the stone. Keep the knife blade flat. Move the blade over the sharpening stone in a circle. Turn the blade over and sharpen the other side.

Passing the jackknife. If you are using a jackknife, close it before you pass it. If you are using other knives such as paring knives, grasp the blade along the dull edge and pass the handle to the other person. In this way you have control of the sharp edge of the knife.

Keep your knife in your pocket when you are not using it, or make a lanyard or sennit of macramé and hang your knife from your belt.

Don't be an initial carver! It is not good outdoor manners to mark up anything with a knife.

You will use other tools when you are in camp. Using any sharp-edged tool is a responsibility. You are responsible for your own safety and that of others. Learn how to use tools safely, how to take care of them, and how to keep them in good condition.

This is what you need to know about any tool before you use it—
• what it does.
• how to clean it, hold it, sharpen it.
• how to handle it safely.
• what to do with it when it is not in use.

Whittling

Use your knife for more than cutting twigs or pieces of rope. Try your hand at whittling, and before you know it you will be whittling every scrap of lumber, piece of driftwood, or wood chip you can lay your hands on.

Always sharpen your jackknife before you start. Look on page 378 to review how to sharpen a knife. To make a cut, brace wood and knife with thumb and cut a V, taking a chip. To round an end, cut at an angle as you turn the stick. To decorate a project, mark a design with a pencil or tip of your knife, make a "stopper cut" straight into the wood, and then cut away small bits up to the cut.

Smooth your project with your knife. Then use medium sandpaper, rubbing with the grain or length of the stick. Finish with very fine sandpaper. Do not use your knife on the article after sandpapering if you can help it. Fine particles of sandpaper caught in the wood can damage your knife blade.

When you have finished smoothing your article, rub it with paste wax, let dry, then polish with a soft cloth to bring out color in the wood. Wax shoe polish will stain and polish at the same time.

If you have whittled a pin and need a clasp, cut a slot in the center of the back of the pin. Fill the slot with plastic wood. Push the back of a safety pin into the plastic wood. Let it dry for at least two hours before wearing it.

A toggle is a handy thing to make. You can use it as a button, a fastener, to "stop" a rope, or as a hanger. Cut a toggle from a 7.5 cm straight stick. Round off both ends. Mark the center of the toggle and make a V cut carefully all around the stick, being sure not to cut it in two. Sand and polish your toggle. Fasten a cord in the notch with a lark's head knot and hang it from your belt until you find a place to use it. Make a set of toggles in all sizes.

A hiking stick is a project you start whenever you find just the right stick. First peel the stick and round the ends. Next carve your "signature" around the stick near the top. The signature tells everyone that this is your own stick. Your signature could be triangular cuts, or rings of different widths cut around the stick. When everyone in the troop has voted on a troop signature, place this signature just below your personal one.

Now comes the fun. Each time you do something special in the out-of-doors, add a symbol to your stick. Then, when you are showing younger girls how to whittle, you can tell them about these outdoor experiences as you share a skill.

Sing Me Your Song, O

Whenever Girl Scouts gather, you will hear the sound of music. Girl Scouts sing around the campfire, at kapers, as they hike along the trail, when they give thanks to God before meals, during colors and Scouts' Own, and just for the joy of singing.

The Girl Scout songbooks are full of songs that Girl Scouts sing everywhere. Take a "hike" through a songbook and list songs that you already know and ones that might be fun to learn. Learn songs to use when you are hiking, working, or exploring the out-of-doors. Learn a different grace for every meal and find songs that tell stories, express deep feelings, or can be acted out around the campfire.

Campfires and Wood Smoke

The close of a camp day can be a special time. When you are camping with a small group, you may want a little fire, just large enough to heat a pot of cocoa to drink as you sit around, laugh, talk, tell stories, or sing. Or you might gather instead at some special place along the river, on a hillside, in a forest clearing, or even under your kitchen tarp to talk, sing favorite songs, or put on dramatic skits and stunts.

There will be times when you will want to plan a very special campfire—perhaps on the last night of camp to celebrate some event or to entertain or honor people who helped you get ready for this camping trip.

The group planning the campfire will collect ideas from everyone and organize the activities. They will see to it that there are people to build and light the fire, serve the treats, lead songs, take part in the program, do the clean-up, and see that everyone knows what she should be doing.

What will you do? Campfires are times for singing songs and putting on plays or skits—for listening to legends, to stories about the stars or about the history of the area. You may want to include a special opening, a closing, a fire-lighting ceremony, or make a ceremony of burning wishes you have made in the campfire. Will your wish be to come back to camp again?

Snacks are always a welcome part of any campfire event. Popcorn, somemores, marshmallows, or apples to toast over the fire, chestnuts to roast in the fireplace, fruit, hot cocoa are favorite campfire treats. Think about this so that the treat fits into the plans and the kind of campfire built, and will not detract from any ceremonial closing.

How Did It Go?

No camping trip is over until all of the pots are scoured, bills paid, equipment checked and returned, and the experience evaluated by all.

It is not enough to say, "we had an awful good time," or "let's not go again." Talk about the camping trip. How was it good or not so good? Which activities did the troop like best?

What did you like best about the campsite? Do you want to go back to the same place next time?

How did you have to adjust or change your plans? Did you learn how to cook something new in the out-of-doors or how to build a fire to fit the pot? What would you like to cook next time? How did the things you did help you discover something new? Did you make friends with someone you hardly knew? Did you learn more about yourself? Did you allow enough time in troop meeting to plan for the camping trip? What will you do differently the next time?

Most important of all, when will you go camping again?

And as the embers die away—
We wish that we may ever stay.
But since we cannot have our way—
We'll come again some other day.

Index